For Mary Jo —

I'm so glad we have connected ____ not only in the pool, but with Peace Corps connections. A wonderful friendship to keep up FOREVER!

Enjoy —

Jane

To Africa
With Spatula

A Peace Corps Mom in Malawi
1965 - 1967

by
Jane Baker Lotter

Copyright © 2002, 2003 Jane Baker Lotter

Second Edition

International Standard Book Number: 0-9715173-0-4

Publication design, typography, page layout production, and project coordination by Jeanne Pietrzak, Graphic Gold, Davis, California.

Cover design by Robin Walton.

Cover collage of Africa by Jane Baker Lotter.

Cartoons by Phil Durand.

Photographs by Will and Jane Lotter.

Editors:
    Jane Baker Lotter
    Patricia Powers Allen

Published by Lotter Press
P.O. Box 73234
Davis, CA 95617-3234

www.ggweb.com/books/lotter
www.lotterfamily.com/books
e-mail: bookinfo@lotterfamily.com

Manufactured in the United States of America.

10 9 8 7 6 5 4 3 2

Dedication

To my husband and very best friend, Will, whose humanitarian soul and spirit of adventure got us into all of this (thank goodness). His love, encouragement and guidance sustain us always. Our life together has never been boring!

To our sons, Don, Mike, Scott, and Rick – for being such good sports and helpers (our own "Junior Peace Corps") through those early years in Africa. And now in these later years, for their positive feedback and support during the writing of this book. May our grandchildren enjoy reading about their dads.

To Patricia Powers Allen (Pat), my tireless co-editor, other best friend and wonderful neighbor for fifty years.

* * *

Special Remarks

"Jane Lotter, writing of her experiences in the late 1960s as the wife of a Peace Corps country director and mother of four young sons, has produced an important piece of history. The history of the Peace Corps is incomplete without the story of the families who participated as in-country staff. They, too, are Peace Corps heroes.

Jane's 1965-1967 letters home from Malawi are a compelling record of the critical role that staff and their families played in the success of the Peace Corps. The 162,000 Peace Corps Volunteers who have served over the 40-year history of the Peace Corps were able to do their work because families like the Lotters also served, sacrificed, supported and made possible the success of the Peace Corps."

John Garamendi
Peace Corps Volunteer Ethiopia 1966-68
Former Deputy Secretary of the United States Department of the
    Interior

Patricia Garamendi
Peace Corps Volunteer Ethiopia 1966-68
Former Associate Director, United States Peace Corps

Table of Contents

The Letters

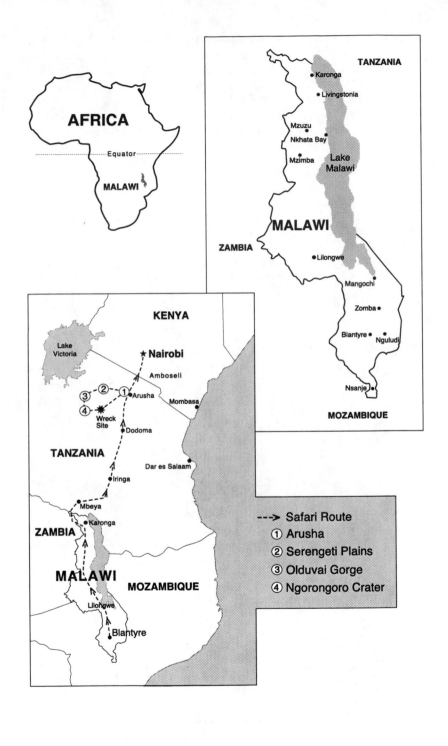

We're Going *WHERE?*

One summer day the phone rang. "Congratulations! You're going to Malawi."

"We're going *WHERE?*"

It was late August of 1964. For weeks we had been waiting for THE phone call from Sargent Shriver, the Peace Corps Director, telling us where Will would be assigned as a Peace Corps staff member.

But where in the world was Malawi?

Until June of 1964, my life had been of the normal, average sort. From that time on, it was neither normal nor average. We lived in Davis, California, a pleasant university town. My husband Will had been a faculty member for twelve years at the University of California at Davis, where he coached a succession of sports, including football, baseball, and track, and in addition taught physical education classes. We had a pleasant home and four pleasant (usually) boys between the ages of three and twelve. Just an average, pleasant family, albeit a little heavy on the masculine side.

Then, one fateful day, Will happened to have lunch on campus with a professor who was directing a Peace Corps training program at UC Davis for volunteers headed to India. In those early days of Peace Corps the training was often held on campuses in the U.S., whereas now all the training is held in the host countries. Will was voluntarily helping with the physical training portion, and they were joined at lunch by a representative from the Peace Corps Washington office.

During that lunch, Will uttered the words that would change our lives. He said, "I think the Peace Corps is the best thing this country has going. If I didn't have a wife and four kids I'd be in it in a minute."

The Peace Corps representative looked at him and said, "You know, Will, the Peace Corps is looking for people like you for staff positions. We need people who have had experience working with young people, and with older people as well, to run the programs and supervise the volunteers. We're glad to take the families of our staff appointees. I think you would be a fine candidate for a staff position."

Will had never ridden his bicycle home from campus as fast as on that day. He burst in the door yelling, "How would you like to go into the Peace Corps?" at the same time trying, unsuccessfully, to appear sane and reasonable while dropping this bombshell.

After I picked myself up off the floor, took Will's temperature and heard the full text of the lunch conversation, I heard myself saying giddily, "Let's go for it!"

Just two months later Will was in Washington, DC, where he went through seventeen interviews in three days. He came home brimming with stories of all the interesting Peace Corps people he'd met. The final and most exciting interview for Will was with Sargent Shriver, who was then the director of the whole Peace Corps program. He found Shriver to be a friendly and fascinating person.

The Washington interviews were just the beginning of the process. There were physicals for all of us, as well as countless FBI checks. Then the next big hurdle was having to get permission for an almost unheard-of two-year leave from the University. And last, but not least, was The Home Interview.

I will never forget it. After scouring the house and the boys from top to bottom, role-playing how to pretend to be polite and well-behaved, we hoped we were ready. Our interviewer arrived. He was probably a very nice man, and we must have shared some pleasant small talk, but I don't remember that. I do remember this man in his tweed jacket, sitting on our hand-me-down sofa with his arms folded, puffing on his pipe and intently peering into my face with one eyebrow raised. He asked penetrating questions and waited for lofty philosophical answers from me. Will was already "in" and now it all depended on me.

"Well, Jane." Puff, puff. Stare. Clear through my head. Eyebrow cocked. Silence. Puff, puff. "What do you do?"

(Oh my God — what do I *do*? How do I answer?? I wash? I iron? I clean? I vacuum? I cook? I do dishes, windows, and even toilets? I root at Little League games and UCD football games? I'm a perpetual Den Mother? Had he failed to *notice* that I had four little boys?)

I could not think of a single lofty or witty thing to say, let alone a word of more than two syllables. I think I mentioned that I make a pretty mean spaghetti, which may have been the longest word I used. I must add that in the sixties in our area, unlike the way it is today, hardly any mothers worked outside the home. Today his question would not have been unusual. Honestly, if the truth must be known, I have no clue to this day as to what I said.

And then. Puff, puff. Penetrating squint. The eyebrow again. Silence. Puff, puff. "Jane. Do you realize that your boys will probably not have a solid bowel movement for two years?"

Now I have to admit that when under stress I am occasionally afflicted with fits of giggles at terribly inappropriate times. I looked across at Will, who was giving me his stern, "Oh no, you wouldn't dare!" look. For once in my life I was able to fight down the dreaded eruption and reply, inanely, "Oh, is that so?"

In spite of this last test, the whole family was actually accepted into the Peace Corps.

Up to that time, the extent of my worldly travels had been just two trips out of California. The first was a dreadful family trip one summer in the old 1936 Dodge all the hot way to Missouri to visit Grandma Baker when I was eleven years old. All I remember about that trip other than being miserably hot, was teaching my younger sister, Nan, to blow spectacular bubble gum bubbles for half the trip and then for the other half trying to get them out of her hair and eyebrows; Dad stopping the car more than once to spank all of us alongside the highway; one of my little brothers making a huge puddle, actually a lake, in the middle of the only (and last) nice dining room we went to.

My other trip was to a three-day conference of university women campus leaders in Minneapolis when I was a senior at the University of California at Berkeley. My very first flight ever, to an interesting and important conference, and the airline lost my luggage! I had to wear the same clothes for three days, so all I remember about that whole trip was my mortification at having to show up in my gray sweater and skirt every day of the conference.

Those were my total travel experiences.

Will's travels were somewhat broader. He was a naval aviation cadet in World War II where he fought the Battles of Cottonwood, Arizona; Corpus Christi, Texas; Norman, Oklahoma; and Sanford, Florida; winning his fighter pilot wings just as the war ended. Neither of us could exactly claim the title of "seasoned traveler."

We were both born and raised in the San Francisco Bay area, Will in Alameda and I in Berkeley. We met on a blind date for coffee between classes at Cal Berkeley in 1946. Will brought along his beautiful collie, Star. As a child, I had devoured all the Terhune books on Lassie and Laddie, and had always wanted a collie of my own. I immediately fell in love with Star. Everyone who knows me well has heard my claim that I married Will Lotter for his dog. Star lived to a ripe old dog's age and was with us for our first three kids.

After graduation from Cal in 1949, Will taught for three years at San Ramon High School in Danville, California, then a small high school of one hundred eighty students, where he coached every sport, taught English, and served as Dean of Boys. In 1952 he was hired at UC Davis as a physical education faculty member and coach of many sports. We bought a home near the campus and set about raising our growing family.

Twelve years and four sons later, when the Peace Corps offer came up, we surprised a lot of people. We were so happily settled in Davis, people couldn't imagine that we would voluntarily leave for two years. But we were young and healthy and just couldn't pass up the opportunity. Retiring from football in 1963 after nine years as head coach, in 1964 Will was serving as the first Director of Recreation and Intramurals at UC Davis. Many people wondered why in the world we would leave all this. The truth is that Will had "itchy feet," and I guess I must have had some sense of adventure too. This Peace Corps offer came at just the right time.

Looking back now, more than thirty-five years later, Will and I agree that we've never been more together about a decision affecting our lives and the lives of our four boys. This is not to say that there were no doubts and worries about possible illness and other potential mishaps, but it didn't dim our enthusiasm for this great venture. We'd passed all the tests, and now we simply had to wait for an assignment.

Then the phone call and those words: "Congratulations! You're going to Malawi."

"We're going *WHERE*?"

During most of his seventeen interviews, Will had been given the idea that we would be going to Nepal, where a backpacking type like Will was needed. We were entertaining romantic images of snow-capped mountains, climbing Mount Everest — well, not really climbing it, but trekking around it. We had all learned to say "namaste," which is "hello" in Nepalese. Now this! Where in the world was Malawi, anyway? And why were we being sent *there*? A year later we had our answers.

Two of Will's seventeen interviews in Washington, DC had been in the Peace Corps Africa regional office, one of them with the Director, Bob Poole, and this, we learned much later, was the key reason for being assigned to Malawi. Will had been so set on going to Nepal that he hardly listened to Bob's talking about Africa and about Malawi, where Bob had been the first Peace Corps Director. That part of their conversation seemed so irrelevant to Will that he didn't even mention it to me.

Instead, he'd told me how he and Bob struck up a great and immediate friendship, Bob having played football at Yale at the same time that Will played at Cal. Bob had played in the East-West game and Will in the Rose Bowl the same year. A small sore point was Will's telling Bob that he was on the Cal baseball team which won the national baseball championship in 1947 by beating Yale. But they were still friends. A year later, when we were all staying with the Pooles in Nairobi, where Bob was then Peace Corps Director for Kenya, Bob confessed that Sargent Shriver had "owed him one" and so Bob had requested Will for Malawi. Mystery solved.

The reactions of our friends and families were mixed, to put it mildly, when we told them we were going to Africa with the Peace Corps. From, "You're what? Going to darkest Africa with all those little boys?" (accompanied by looks that clearly said, "those Lotters are crazy") — to, "Wow! How exciting"— or — "You're leaving your comfortable home to go live in a mud hut with a thatched roof for two years?" In spite of their reservations, they gave us several great send-off parties.

The centerpiece on the dinner table at my parents' house when all my family was assembled to say goodbye was, uh, interesting. In those days and when I was growing up it was not uncommon to see cartoons about Africa in which there was a large black cooking pot containing white people, the pot being surrounded by black people (cannibals by implication). Luckily, we don't see these cartoons anymore. So guess what the centerpiece was? It was a little round three-legged black clay pot with six tiny people in it! I inherited that pot when my folks died and I still laugh every time I arrange flowers in it. (You had to know my mom.)

When packing some household items to ship to Malawi, little did I know the value my spatula and pancake griddle would acquire. Many people have symbols which represent themselves, like a certain cute animal or a religious icon. I think one of mine now is definitely a spatula. You will come to see why.

We survived all the necessary shots, tried to convince Star's successor, Sparky, that we would be back, that he would like the family that would be renting our house, and we were off. We were excited and eager — anticipated future unsolid bowel movements notwithstanding. At least I wouldn't have to be a den mother for a whole two years.

About the Letters

If I were asked to name the most wonderful gift I've ever received, the hands-down winner would be the lovingly assembled copies of all my letters from Africa. I had not kept carbon copies of any of my letters. Out there we had no access to Xerox machines, and I'd never even seen a computer.

My Sunset Court neighbor and best friend, Pat Allen, saved two-and-a-half years' worth of my letters, typed up copies of the handwritten ones, and then had them all copied on legal-sized paper — a hundred twenty-three pages of single-spaced, wall-to-wall typing, one inch thick. After we came home, Pat surreptitiously enlisted the aid of our son, Scott, to help her organize and collate the letters. I still marvel that this ten-year-old kid didn't let the cat out of the bag. They put them together in spiral-bound form, and gave them to me for my birthday in 1967, the year we came home. It was a total surprise. What a gift!

In Malawi I had typed each letter on a clunky old portable manual typewriter, with two carbon copies — one for my family, one for Will's family, and one for Sunset Court, the neighborhood in Davis where we've lived since 1952. It never occurred to me to make a copy to keep for ourselves. Sunset Court (the Center of the Universe!) is a cul-de-sac where nine families have all raised our kids together since the early fifties. So the third copy of my epistles, addressed "Dear Court," was just as much for "family" as were the other two.

Pat was the Guardian of the Letters. She had the foresight to know that these letters would be a diary of our African odyssey and that if we didn't have something with the immediacy of the letters, perhaps after a while it would all seem like a dream — especially for our four sons. My letters were never intended for a publisher's eye. They were simply letters home to family.

Over the years, however, many friends have read this collection of letters and commented that I should see about getting them published. Flattered as I was, I knew that they would have to be pared down and cleaned up — but I didn't have a clue as to how to go about doing this.

Then, in 1992, we had a visit from our good friend Ted Sneed, one of our former Peace Corps Volunteers with whom we've remained close over all these years. Ted took my letters home to read. Later he called with this offer: "Jane, I'd like to put your letters on the computer and help you edit them for publication." I was overwhelmed. Here was the perfect person — someone who knew Peace Corps, knew Malawi, and most of all, knew our whole family well. Dear Ted. I'm not sure he realized the extent of the project he was taking on, but being between jobs, he insisted that he had the time to do it.

Ted waded and weeded through the sea of rambling letters and then typed them all into his computer. What a job. In the process, he eliminated many private family references, neighborhood jokes, and other items that would not be of interest to a general audience. The resulting manuscript was greatly reduced in bulk. Another priceless gift. In 1993, Ted's contribution inspired me to begin my first serious and, as it turned out, quite prolonged efforts toward the writing of this book. Having to learn to use a computer was no small part of the task.

In reading over my letters more than thirty years after the fact, I found that there were some gaps, as well as things that needed explanation or comment from me. Working from memory and from additional cards and letters we later found in our parents' homes, I have filled in a few of the gaps or omissions and have incorporated them into the letters. Other changes I have made from the original letters are for more intelligible reading, such as some clearer wording, grammatical corrections, and expansions of stories that had been too abbreviated for full enjoyment. I have put my current-day comments or additions in italics and brackets. Still, the letters are pretty much as I wrote them at that time.

In Africa in those days there were terms in everyday use that I now find offensive and which I have changed. For instance, it was common to refer to a "houseboy" or "garden boy." The people who worked in our home were adults, not boys. So I have changed those designations to "housekeeper," or "household help," and "gardener." In addition, we referred to many of the PCVs (Peace Corps Volunteers) as "boys" or "girls" (i.e., the "boys" up at Mzuzu, or the "girls" at Mzimba). I have also corrected those references to acknowledge the fact that all of the Volunteers were adults.

Make no mistake — our experiences as a salaried Peace Corps Staff family were entirely different from those of the Peace Corps Volunteers. We had a nice house (no mud hut with thatched roof) and a car. We did not have to walk or ride bicycles everywhere. We did not live as the village people lived. For the Peace Corps Volunteers, who usually lived much like their Malawi counterparts, I have the utmost respect and admiration.

[This is the Christmas letter we sent from Washington, DC before we went to Malawi. It went out to many people with whom we correspond only at Christmas and who had no idea we were doing this.]

New Year's Greetings From Washington, DC!

December 1964

This letter is a combination Christmas, New Year's, and Lotter Bulletin. For our friends who haven't heard, Will has taken a two-year leave from the University of California at Davis, where he has been teaching and coaching for twelve years, to take a staff position as Deputy Director of the Peace Corps in Malawi, Africa.

As Deputy Director, Will will be working with and supervising the two hundred sixty or so Peace Corps Volunteers in Malawi, and working with the host country government on implementing the various Peace Corps projects. There are three primary projects: education, with some one hundred ninety Peace Corps Volunteer teachers in secondary schools and in teacher-training schools; agricultural cooperatives, with twenty-five Volunteers; and a public health and tuberculosis control project with forty Volunteers. The last project is the only one of its kind, and if successful will have great impact on future Peace Corps programs. There are also two lawyers helping set up a new judicial system.

Our boys are: Don, twelve; Mike, eleven; Scott, seven; and Rick, three-and-a-half. We flew from San Francisco to Washington, DC on December 6, 1964. Just boarding a huge airplane was already an adventure for our excited crew. All the frantic preparations — packing, getting the house (complete with dog) ready to rent, and shipping our things — were already worth all the effort. We checked into a hotel near the Peace Corps and even this was an adventure, we dare say for the management as well.

The very next morning, Will's intensive training began, Jane also getting in on a week of it. We heard fifteen or twenty Heads of Divisions speak on a wide variety of subjects such as Peace Corps policy, management, political history of Malawi, Volunteer selection and training, medical and psychiatric aspects, etc., etc. There is so much to learn our heads are spinning.

Will spends every day poring over the Malawi files and talking to as many people as possible about every aspect of the job to come. He has four-hour lessons every day in Chinyanja, the national language. His teacher is a Malawian named Samson Mbvundula (pronounced "mm-voon-doola"), who is very friendly, smiles all the time, has beautiful white teeth, a handsome black face, and incredible patience.

A word the boys have just learned and especially love is "galimoto" which means "car." "Gali" means dog, and "moto" means fire; and together they mean "car." Samson, Will's teacher, thinks this is probably what the first car looked like to Malawians. A smoking dog! Also the boys have learned their first sentence in Chinyanja, "Moni bambo"— (Good morning, sir). Jane gets by with "Me Jane."

A little about Malawi: it is a small, beautiful country, formerly called Nyasaland. It was part of the Federation of Rhodesias: Northern and Southern Rhodesia and Nyasaland, all British Colonies. Nyasaland became independent in July of 1964 and changed its name to Malawi. It is often referred to as the "Switzerland of Africa," with a variety of physical and climatic conditions from mountains of ten thousand feet to valleys and lowlands. It is only five hundred twenty miles long and fifty to a hundred miles wide. It lies along Lake Malawi (formerly Lake Nyasa), which is three hundred fifty miles long. A fresh water lake, it is said to be two thousand feet deep — one of the deepest lakes in the world. Malawi is bordered by Tanzania (formerly Tanganyika), Mozambique (formerly Portuguese East Africa), and Zambia (formerly Northern Rhodesia). How can they ever keep maps up-to-date these days??

Malawi is a highly populated country with almost three million people; it is an impoverished, developing country, determined, however, to help itself, with a top priority placed on the education of its youth. In the past two years the Peace Corps has been able to increase the number of secondary students by 84% and the number of secondary schools by 37%.

Our home in Malawi will be in Blantyre, the commercial center of the country. Blantyre, which was David Livingstone's favorite spot in Malawi (then Nyasaland), was named after his birthplace in Scotland. It has an elevation of 3600 feet and a temperate climate. The boys are disappointed that we are going to live in a regular house in the city rather than a grass hut in the jungle, but we hope they will adjust. The schools are reported to be excellent, and the kids were delighted to hear they will probably learn to play soccer and rugby. Within minutes of the city are mountains to climb and excellent fishing. We just saw some slides of Malawi and it looks beautiful.

Our itinerary is as follows: we leave Washington, DC for

London on January 16, a Saturday morning and Scott's birthday. I wonder how you could beat a plane trip to London for an eighth birthday? We stay that night and all day Sunday and will squeeze in all the sightseeing possible. Sunday night we fly to Rome, but with a stop of only an hour; then on that night down the east side of Africa to Nairobi, Kenya, arriving on Monday morning. We get to stay there until Tuesday morning and are thrilled. This is where the Nairobi National Park, one of the largest big game preserves in the world, is located. The Park is only fifteen minutes from the airport. Tuesday morning we fly to Mombasa and Dar Es Salaam in Tanzania, and from there to Blantyre. We can hardly believe this is us we're talking about.

After our initial three days in the hotel in Washington, DC (have you ever tried to keep four excited little boys quiet in a hotel room?) we were lucky to find an apartment of sorts in Arlington, Virginia, just across the Potomac River from Washington, DC, and only a twenty-minute bus ride to the Peace Corps building.

[Here, I am skipping over the six weeks in Washington, DC and all the sightseeing adventures we had, to a brief description of our "apartment of sorts" from a letter I wrote on the last days we were there]:

"We won't shed a tear leaving this old house. I just hope it holds together until we get out. Doorknobs fall off in our hands, all the lights are burning out, the thirty-gallon water heater is for all three floors and we have another family with three children upstairs. The kitchen floor slopes so much to one side that the other day Donnie spilled a whole half gallon of milk (!#%$&'*) and it all rushed to one side of the kitchen and then — you'll never believe it — it *all* disappeared through a crack under the baseboard. Magic! Marvelous! We looked in the next room, ran downstairs and peered up at all the ceilings for milk — none. This is a feature I'm going to try to get in Davis. Having just seen the movie *Mary Poppins,* the kids call it our Mary Poppins trick.

Aside from that, I will be glad to leave this one-and-a-half bedroom — did you get that? — one-and-a-half bedrooms for six people, $185 per month haunted house. Grand Central Station haunted house. People roam through at all hours because all of our doors (bedroom, bathroom, living room and kitchen) open onto the same landing that all the other renters have to use. Startling sometimes."

We are having a great and busy time and are looking forward to many more new experiences. The Peace Corps is doing an inspiring job and we feel so lucky to be a part of it. We've met so many wonderful people, all of whom go out of their way to make the boys feel a part of it all too by calling them "our new Volunteers." They really will be a part of it, as we hope that the Volunteers in Malawi will feel that our home is their "home away from home."

One last item: Will had a letter from Gordon Nelson, the Peace Corps staff man he will replace in Malawi. It seems they are assuming we will take Gordon's house, as he said, "I'm afraid my travel orders won't come through by February 1, so you will have to stay in the Ryalls Hotel or the Peace Corps Field Center longer." And the Nelsons live right next door to Dr. Hastings Kamuzu Banda, the Prime Minister of Malawi! However, Peace Corps Washington says we can choose whichever we want.

How to sever American-Malawi relations fast — move all those noisy Lotters next door to the Prime Minister.

"Tsalani bwino" (stay well), and we'll see you in two years!

Will, Jane, Don, Mike, Scott, and Rick

The Trip "Out"

About our trip out here. (They always say "out" here). It was almost too good to be true. We did, however, have some misgivings in the beginning, as we left Washington, DC in a snowstorm. It was January 16 — Scott's eighth birthday. Will's wonderful Chinyanja teacher, Samson Mbvundula, was there at the airport to see us off at 6:45 a.m., having ridden several buses at that awful hour in a snowstorm. Needless to say, seeing him there made emotional Mom all teary. And again later, when we landed in Malawi and Samson's father was there to greet us.

The flight from Washington, DC to New York, where we were to change to the plane for London, was very rough and just awful; both Rick and Scott were sick (Rick all over his good shirt, of course) all the way. New York was having a blizzard so we gave everybody airsick pills. I took a tranquilizer and weakly assured the boys that everything was dandy, all the while holding a bag under Rick's green nose as he kept on being sick even on terra firma. *This* was the time — but the only time — I thought, "What are we doing?"

We took off two hours late after de-icing, and after the first ten minutes of bumps and burp bags the rest of the trip was perfect. Rick turned from kelly green to chartreuse and slept, and Scott rallied, helped by the fact that he could open his birthday presents all the way to London. He was completely surprised when the stewardesses came down the aisle with a birthday cake, singing, "Happy birthday, dear Scott."

I "hung out the laundry" (Rick's shirt, which I had washed in the airline washbasin) by my trusty safety pins on the back of the seat in front of us. My purse may weigh a ton, but I am Prepared For Emergency. Then, recovering from the idea that Rick's reply to people asking what he saw on his travels might have to be, "the bottom of a burp bag," we ate our way across the world to London. When I was a child I used to wonder what all those people up in planes were doing. Now I know. They are chewing.

The lights of London were beautiful; we'd gained five hours, so by the time we'd checked into our hotel and decided to go out and eat it was only 8:30 p.m. by Washington time, but 1:30 a.m. by London time. The looks on the faces of the British said, "More crazy Americans — taking little children out at this hour." Then Mike's astute comment upon observing all the teenagers with Beatle hairdos (long hair), "They're staring at us. Does that mean that our short hair looks as funny to them as their long hair looks to us at home?" Our first encounter with being "the odd ones."

The next day we went sightseeing in London and that evening flew British Airways all night to Nairobi. We landed at Rome first for an hour, then at Khartoum in the Sudan just at dawn for another hour. This was our first look at Africa. Khartoum looked dry and flat but interesting, with many Arabs in flowing white gowns. We landed in Nairobi about 10 a.m.

Nairobi was another world for us. We stayed at the famous old New Stanley Hotel in the center of everything. The boys' eyes nearly popped out of their heads when they saw their first safari party getting ready to go out with guns, pith helmets, and tons of gear. Late in the afternoon we had a driver in a little mini-bus take us to the Nairobi Game Park where we saw our first big wild game animals.

These African drivers in the Game Park are something else. They take off over the open fields, over rocks, up and down gullies, *anything* so you can see animals right up close. We got up to herds of giraffes, within six feet of sleeping lions, chased four cheetahs, saw gazelles, zebras, storks, and best of all, we were lucky to come by five lions who had just made a kill. We watched, transfixed, while they snarled and devoured a wild pig only about ten feet away. We stayed *in* the car, however. We saw a long list of other animals, such as wildebeest, impala, and "hortwogs," as Scott called the warthogs. It all seemed like a dream.

We left Nairobi the next morning with hopes of going back again. It is an interesting and lovely city. The flight from Nairobi was by East African Airlines, a smaller plane but a smooth, wonderful flight. We landed at Mombasa in Kenya and found the weather much warmer and the landscape very tropical with lots of bright flowers. We landed next at Dar Es Salaam in Tanzania and nearly melted. The Tanzania Minister of State happened to be aboard the plane and a huge crowd was there at the airport to greet him with dancing, singing, chanting, and beautiful flowers. It was very exciting for us to see.

Finally, Malawi. We landed at Chileka Airport, which is about ten miles from Blantyre. We couldn't believe it could be more beautiful than the places we'd seen but it was, and is.

We're Here!

February 2, 1965
Blantyre, Malawi

We're *here* and can scarcely believe how fast the days have flown by. We've seen and done so much it's hard to know where to begin. I started a letter a week ago which got longer and longer and longer, so we finally decided to keep it and just send excerpts home — so this will be a short letter, at least by comparison.

First and foremost, Malawi is simply beautiful and we just love it! Since this is the so-called rainy season, everything is a lush green. I say "so-called" because, contrary to our former beliefs, it doesn't rain all day or even every day — just short hard rains every now and then, with sunshine in between. Even from the plane as we flew down the east side of Africa we could see that Malawi was the greenest country by far.

The scenery is a feast for the eyes wherever you look. Blantyre surprised us by being quite hilly — rolling hills surrounded by mountains that suddenly jut up here and there. Everything grows in great profusion here, with grass, shrubs, flowers, trees everywhere. I even have the wild feeling that old Brown-Thumb Jane might be able to grow something here. Incredible.

We're living in the Peace Corps Field Center here in Blantyre until we can move into the house of the man Will is replacing, Gordon Nelson. The Nelsons don't leave until March 4, and after that, the house needs some paint and repair, so we will be here quite a while, and the boys are in ecstasy! The Field Center is a wonderful, huge old house used as a hostel by the volunteers when they come into town and is kind of like Grand Central Station with never a dull moment. It has three enormous dormitory-type bedrooms, each with its own bathroom (one of these bedrooms commandeered by the Lotter family) a very large living room; a gigantic kitchen with a twelve-foot table; and a dining room which houses a ping-pong table and a motorcycle!

The house is very old and could use lots of repair but it's comfortable and we think it's great. I'm typing this now on the front "khonde" (veranda), which is roofed and so big we were curious and paced it off. We found it to be eighty-seven feet long and eighteen feet wide. All the ceilings in the house are about twenty-five feet high. It is really quite a place and must have been a real mansion in its day.

The gardens are what we love the most, though. We're on a hill where there are acres and acres of grass and flowers. There are lots of trees, many with blossoms and some which are entwined all over with vines. There are ferns, moss-covered rocks, and not a spot of ground without green, except for the driveway. The boys especially like the part that really looks "jungly." They have a "Tarzan swing" tied to the tallest tree, and they swing out from the top of the hill on this thirty-six-foot rope — pretty breathtaking. I'm afraid I haven't lived up to my role of "Me Jane" yet, but am trying to muster up the courage to try it. The pressure is on.

Many of the trees here are new to us, although there are eucalyptus and evergreens which we know, and we've found out the names of some in the garden. My favorite, even without the red blossoms, is the flame tree, which has limbs and foliage growing out horizontally from the trunk. It looks (at least to me) very African. We saw lots of them in Nairobi and they are just beautiful. We also have lots of jacaranda, frangipani, and mango trees. The flowers we work so hard to grow at home just grow wild here in huge clumps: chrysanthemums, dahlias, roses, tiger lilies, and lots of others, the names of which I wish I knew. All this around us, and off in the distance — though not far — those mountains looking so dramatic the way they suddenly rise up from the rolling hills. Mother Nature must have had a ball making Malawi.

Will and I sat down last night and tried to put down our most vivid first impressions of Malawi. First was the beauty of it. Second was the friendliness of the Malawians. They are wonderful people, very dark, very handsome, warm-hearted and friendly. If you smile at them they always smile and speak. The third thing that struck us right away was the number of people along all the roads — walking. Literally thousands of people walking mile after mile. The women wear brightly colored dresses with full skirts, and most have baskets on their heads, babies on their backs, and several other little children following behind. The men generally wear shorts and always wear shirts, usually white. Very few people have shoes. For the majority of Malawians, "footing" is the only means of transportation other than the rickety bus, which is much too expensive for most of them. They are probably either bringing their produce into town from their villages or "footing" home. Some have bicycles, which they usually ride right down the middle of the road. Fourth, there are so few jobs all over Malawi you become painfully aware that the two things that are monopolizing the minds of 99 percent of the men are food and employment. Hunger and joblessness. A great number of Malawi men go to South Africa to work in the mines for very low wages, as there are so few jobs in Malawi.

We'll never get used to the beggars on the streets, the hungry children, the steady stream of men coming to the door asking for work. Yet in spite of the poverty and hunger, they appear happy. It really makes us think twice about civilization. We go through little villages of mud houses with thatch roofs and see people who have so little, and we hear laughter and see smiling faces. We can't know how they really feel inside, but we can't help but think about how many well-off Americans are unhappy — and with so *much*.

I was the one who was going to come here and have no domestic help, you know. I was going to Do It All Myself. However, the Field Center came with a full-time housekeeper and a gardener-caretaker-night-watchman, and it's the strangest thing, but I've had no trouble whatsoever adjusting. I've hardly shed a tear over not doing the dishes or the ironing. Our housekeeper's name is Saidi (pronounced Sigh-ee-dee) and he is a joy. He hustles around, always smiling, teaching us Chinyanja while doing all the dishes, setting the table for every meal, doing all our washing (on his scrub board, in the bathtub) and ironing (on the ping-pong table), as well as all the cleaning. His ironing is something to behold, from Will's shirts and my dacron blouses to the boys' socks and underwear. Just perfect. Stanley, the gardener-etc., is equally sweet and loves to bring me flowers from his garden.

Just when I was bolstering myself to have to Do a Dish on Saidi's day off (good grief), there was smiling Stanley at the sink, ever ready to fill in on the housekeeper's day off. They are both such good workers and their children are the constant companions of our boys. Saidi's eldest boy, Michael, is fourteen and very bright. Don has taught him lots of games, one of which is Monopoly, and Michael turned right around and beat him. Tuition is so high in the schools for Africans here that Michael can only afford to go to an overcrowded "night school" in a church for two hours a day. Here is where we can help. We are not supposed to "overpay" the help, and believe me their wages are low, but no one has said we can't pay school tuition for their children.

[This "not to overpay the help" was to keep British-U.S. relations on keel. Not an actual Peace Corps rule, but a "suggestion."]

Saidi's second boy, Lewis, who speaks only Chinyanja, is eight and he and Scott can play all day, somehow managing to communicate. It's a delight to watch. Rick is with these children all day and has learned a surprising amount of Chinyanja with just the right inflection.

Boyyy — I just erased two sentences here with two carbons so I could defend myself. I'll never do *that* again. But I will defend myself, having reread that last paragraph. You are no doubt picturing me lying around reading novels and eating chocolates, being fanned, waited on hand and foot. Well, it's not just that the Malawians need the work — *we* really do need them. Just the simple matters like doing the shopping consume at least twice the time they do at home.

Although I find the shopping fun and am amazed to find that you can get almost everything here, you have to go to many different stores to get all the things you want, all the way bargaining with the vegetable sellers outside on the sidewalks between stores. This is fun, but you don't get anywhere very fast, especially since I have to stop and figure out all the pences, shillings, two-and-this and four-and-thats.

And I do the cooking. (My!) We have had from two to five extra people for almost every dinner. With no frozen foods or packages of cake mix, it does take a lot of time. We have had many "interesting" fallen cakes and I'm now realizing that not only have I been doing the cake recipes from memory — but I have been using British measuring cups and spoons, which are not the same as American. Also I have not been making adjustments for the higher altitude. But I think I'm catching on now.

With ten people for dinner it's a real help to have another pair of hands to string and cut fresh beans or shell peas — to say nothing of washing all those dishes. Also, with no washing machine yet, and everything having to be ironed in order to prevent the putzi fly infection, suffice it to say everything just takes a lot more time than at home and is nearly always more complicated.

About the putzi fly: This is a fly that lays eggs in damp places, favorite spots being in wet laundry hanging on the line. You can't see the eggs or the larvae, but heat kills them. Therefore, unless you have a clothes dryer, everything needs to be ironed. Everything. This means even socks and underwear. *Especially* underwear. If you just innocently put on clothing not heat-treated, the eggs imbed in your skin, later hatching into little worms, which grow into bigger worms, maggots really (sorry — gag). First you get a sore and think it's a bad mosquito bite. Then it gets bigger and quite sore and red. Once you figure it out, you have to actually dig out the worm. But you never forget to iron anything after that. We heard about a PCV who put on a pair of underpants after they dried on the line, and the Peace Corps doctor had to dig more than forty worms out of her derrière. Yech.

Culture Shock

February 6, 1965

Culture shock has come in two varieties — neither of which has anything to do with Africans. The first is the *driving*. Will's. I'll never get used to roaring around a corner on the left side of the road. The Peace Corps owns both right and left-hand drive vehicles, so when Will is driving a left-hand drive on the left side of the road I'm just sure he's too close to oncoming traffic on the right side, and when he's driving a right-hand drive on the left side I'm sure he's too close to the curb on the left side. He's also steering with his left hand while simultaneously gesturing with his right hand at the beautiful scenery — and I'm a wreck! All the time he's claiming all is well, but I finally had my greatest moment the other day when I said (for the fourteen millionth time), "Will, you're sort of close on the leffffttt —" and we drove up over the curb. Marvelous.

For a little added excitement there are all these people on bicycles loaded down with vegetables, veering from side to side on the narrow roads. It requires nerves of steel and a heavy hand on the horn to make it. I'll never get over our first time out on an African road with Fearless Father at the wheel. We had the big International Carryall truck with four-wheel drive, and it seems as if you're up about six feet from the ground. Tight skirts are *out* here, ladies. There is no way you can get in — or out — in a tight skirt.

After many hair-raising close shaves, stopping for petrol (gas), not understanding the money, not being able to get the Carryall in the right gear (with an audience of about ten Africans peering in all the windows), going the wrong way on a one-way road with people shouting something unintelligible at us in Chinyanja, we finally found our way back to the Field Center. I was so relieved — and surprised — that we were still alive, that all I could think of was to get *out*. I did. In the dark. All I can say is that it's a lonnggg way down to the ground but my knees are healing now.

Culture shock #2 is the British schools. The Headmaster's very first words to the boys when we introduced them, were, "You boys know we use corporal punishment here, don't you?" Later we had to explain that corporal punishment meant that the teacher could hit them for punishment. At their stricken looks, we quickly assured them that it would only be used on the second or third offense, and certainly only for misbehavior. Since none of them had had behavior problems in school, it would not be a problem. (*Wrong!*)

The boys' classes have been changed several times as it's hard to figure out how to place Americans in school here, and poor

Mike came home all upset after his first day with a new teacher. He had been hit hard on the head and called a "stupid fool" for poor handwriting! A misspelled word on a spelling test merits a swat on the seat with a "tacky," a large, flexible tennis shoe which really stings when used to swat. All this, plus trying to learn math with pounds, shillings, and pence makes school quite an adjustment (understatement of the year). It's an adjustment for American parents, too.

The boys look so cute in their uniforms though (great consolation!) — gray shorts, shirts, and kneesocks, with royal and white striped neckties and blue caps. The "cute" part is definitely their mother's opinion. When I took the boys into town to get their uniforms, they were horrified and weren't even going to come out of the dressing room to let me see. Scott, being only in the second grade, didn't mind so much, but Don and Mike, suave twelve- and eleven-year-olds, were not going to be caught *dead* in these "stupid" uniforms.

[Would you believe that two-and-a-half years later when I said I'd send to the U.S. for Levis for them to wear for the trip back home to the States, guess what they preferred to wear? The "stupid" shorts and kneesocks!]

Mike (eleven) and Scott (eight) go to St. Andrews Prep School, which has "standards" (grades) one through six, and is just a few hundred yards away. Scott is in standard two and Mike is in standard six. Don (twelve) is in standard seven, which would be seventh grade in the U.S., and is in St. Andrews High School, which is outside of town. He rides his bike the three miles to and from school.

School starts at 7:25 a.m. and is out at 12:30. If they want, they can have sports until 4:00 p.m. They all have swimming three times a week, even in the first standard. They also have French, and Don has Latin and algebra as well. Guess they'll get an education beaten into them. Literally. Last week was bad, but this week they are all happier and seem to be doing O.K. Mike is determined to be a "tough American" and show that teacher he can do it and can take it, and we're proud of his attitude, but it chokes us up to see him having to go through this. The other teachers are not that bad, and the headmasters are pretty good. Will has let them know his feelings on the matter of corporal punishment, which may not have helped but sure made us feel better.

The Peace Corps staff here have all been wonderful to us. They came out en masse to meet us at the airport when we arrived. The wives have helped me shop, and they have all had us to their homes and have made us feel especially welcome. We have already had lots of wonderful times.

One of the most fun things we've done was to go on a Sunday picnic and swim at a beautiful spot called Likabula, on a river at the base of Mount Mlanje. There were ten of us crowded into a Land Rover for an hour over dirt roads (twelve on the way back, as we picked up some PCVs), and we went through many little villages, with children and chickens scattering out of the way.

Mlanje is the highest mountain in Malawi — 10,000 feet — and the top is almost always shrouded in mist, giving it a lovely but sort of eerie look. Everything was that lush green and there were many unusual wildflowers. It was a wonderful day. We all got sunburned, so now we don't look quite so much like newcomers. Everyone is tan here unless they just arrived.

We have inherited a big, wonderful dog. She is called a Collie-Alsatian here, but in the States we think she would be known as a German Shepherd. Her name is Cheena, and she is expecting momentarily. She is the sweetest, best-natured dog we've ever seen (excuse me, Sparky in California — we still love you) and she's a good watchdog by sheer virtue of size. We are also getting two kittens soon. Instead of people here talking about their cats being good "mousers," they talk about their cats being good "snakers." We haven't seen any snakes as yet, but we'll be prepared — or maybe the kittens will have to grow up a bit first?

Nguludi Mission

February 12, 1965

Whenever Will has to drive anywhere, Ricky and I eagerly leap into the Land Rover to go. We want to see absolutely everything. We had only been here one week when Will offered to drive Mack McKinnon, one of our older PCVs, a man in his sixties, out to a mission called Nguludi, with some special crutches he had designed and made. This mission is about a forty-five-minute drive out of town from here, most of it on dirt roads. What a lucky break for us to see this place so soon after we've arrived. I've been wondering where I could put in some volunteer time, and now I know. And, better yet, now I am.

Nguludi is a wonderful old Catholic mission which has a hospital with a hundred forty beds, an out-patient department averaging two hundred people a day, and an orphanage with twenty to thirty babies. The orphanage is what I'm really excited about.

The whole mission is run by only ten nuns and one doctor, a young Irish woman. The sisters, all of whom are nurses, are training young Malawian women to help and are teaching them nursing skills, but all the rest of the usual hospital work of caring for sick patients, giving shots, pulling teeth, delivering babies, even setting bones when the doctor is not there, is handled by just the ten of them. The work they do and the equipment with which they "make-do" is unbelievable. In the orphanage, for instance, they have made their own incubators out of wooden boxes lined with hot water bottles (which have to be refilled all the time, of course). They're crude, but they work and have saved many babies.

The day we took Mack out there is a memorable one for me — both seeing this mission for the first time and getting to know Mack. Mack is a real character, seemingly a crusty old guy on the outside, but with the proverbial heart of gold and all soft inside. We're already good friends. He told us he had been an engineer with General Electric, raised a large family (eight kids!), retired, was widowed, then joined the Peace Corps. He is teaching metal work and welding at the Technical College in Blantyre.

Mack has been going out to Nguludi for about a year on his days off and *loves* inventing things for the sisters at the mission: special metal beds, crutches, wheelchairs, etc., and he constantly surprises and amazes them. In fact, that day that we went out with Mack and his special crutches was a big education and surprise for *me* as well.

First off, I have to confess to some embarrassing and ignorant assumptions. Not being a Catholic and never having ever spoken to or even *seen* a nun up close, I hate to admit it, but I had this idea (blush) that only holy words and religious sayings came out of nuns' mouths. Well, we drove up to the mission and Mack got out of the Land Rover with these special metal crutches. A nun in white habit came out to greet us and when she saw these wonderful crutches she excitedly exclaimed, "Well, Mack! For Pete's sake!"

I couldn't have been more surprised if she'd said, "Well for shit's sake!" Excuse me, but I'll never forget it. Shows how much I knew. I learned very quickly that these nuns were actually mortals and quite earthly, with wonderful senses of humor — just a whole lot more dedicated and unselfish than ordinary human beings like me.

The orphanage at the Mission, though, is the place that grabbed my heart. It was love at first sight for me. All those adorable babies with no mothers. There is one American nun, Sister Mary Joy, and only about three young Malawi girls to feed and care for all twenty babies. This Sister Mary Joy is a real inspiration. She is young, vivacious, very pretty, witty, and she just adores each and every one of those little babies. What an enormous job she has. Twenty babies! As soon as we walked into the orphanage and met Sister Mary Joy, she picked up a baby and put her in my arms — and I was hooked. (She knew what she was doing.)

All of the babies are children of Malawian mothers who have died, usually in childbirth. In African societies an aunt or grandmother commonly raises orphaned babies, but in the cases of these babies, the nuns have taken them only when there is actually no one in the family who is able to raise them. Sometimes a baby's father will come back to reclaim the baby when it's old enough to walk and easier to care for. If not, then the babies are taken to another orphanage after about the age of three. So these babies at the Nguludi orphanage are all really little ones. There are several six-pound six-month-olds, some having arrived at the orphanage weighing only three pounds. Sister Mary Joy says she will save them "by hook or by crook and lots of love," and she does, too.

I asked Sister Mary Joy if she could use some volunteer help. The words were barely out of my mouth when she eagerly said, "We just can't give these little ones too much loving care and holding!" That's all I needed to hear. "Loving care and holding" I certainly can do.

I thought that helping the orphanage might be a good project for some of the Peace Corps staff wives. I talked first to Joyce

Leach, who loved the idea, so now she and I go out to Nguludi
every Wednesday morning to help with the babies. She succumbed
just as I did.

Last week when we got out there, one of the sisters said, "Wait
until you see Sister Mary Joy's new running shoes!" She runs
everywhere all day, the mission being quite spread out. The shoes
are new black U.S. Keds from her aunt in New York, and she
adores them. The nuns all wear white habits here because they are
cooler in this hot climate, so Sister Mary Joy's new black Keds are
quite noticeable and (to me) quite un-nunlike, but (to me) very
Sister Mary Joy-like. She is so vivacious, I wouldn't be at all
surprised if she had been a cheerleader in high school. I'll have
to ask her someday. I think she is from Texas, and I don't know
how long she has been a nun. I always wonder about the past lives
of nuns, but I don't know if it's proper to ask. Except for the
Malawian nuns, all of the sisters at Nguludi are either American
or Canadian, and I have enormous respect and admiration
for them.

The Mother Superior, Mother Catherine, has been there
for twenty-eight years. She has been home to the U.S. only twice,
the second time returning with the oldest dental chair I've ever
seen — with velour upholstery, yet. Somehow she managed to get
this huge thing all the way across the world, so she could pull
teeth better.

Here I need to describe Mother Catherine, so you can better
envision the scenes on ships and airports with this enormous
chair. Mother Catherine is about five feet tall, petite, soft-spoken,
sort of "sweet little grandmother" looking. Who would ever
imagine the strength and determination inside that little person?
Or who could imagine this little lady driving like a bat out of you-
know-where on these African roads? We tried to follow her one
time, and she left us far behind in a cloud of dust.

So the Nguludi Mission and orphanage are my special projects
and inspiration, and I can hardly believe my good luck at finding
them so early in our two-year stay. In between Wednesdays, Joyce
and I are going to make new crib sheets for them with a borrowed
hand-crank sewing machine. The other Peace Corps wives are
chipping in on the material for them. The possibilities for help out
there are endless. For example, there weren't enough safety pins
for all the diapers, and some diapers (nappies) had to be tied on
— so, needless to say, safety pins were the first things we bought.

Now Wednesday is my favorite day of the week.

Settling In

Will has now decided that maybe he'd better think twice before he takes any more overnight trips here. He just went on a little two-day trip, and when he left he had a wife, four kids and a dog. His *trip* was just fine, but when he came home he had a wife, four kids, ten dogs, and two cats. That ought to teach him. Cheena had given birth (under Scott's bed) to nine puppies; and our friends had given us our promised two fluffy kittens, Seymour and Charlie Brown. We are now living in the Peace Corps Field Center *Zoo*.

Because it's school vacation, a great deluge of PCVs, especially teachers, were in town this last weekend. All our new animals, not to mention all of *us* living here in *their* hostel, created much chaotic fun. All twenty-two extra beds were quickly taken, and we started hauling in cots, put some PCVs on the floors, then removed all the couch and chair cushions for more beds — bodies everywhere!

Our boys were enchanted when the T.B. unit PCVs all decided to bring their motorcycles in and take them apart on the porch here. Heaven for little boys. These Peace Corps health workers are issued motorcycles, on which they ride double with their Malawian counterparts, to go out into the villages in the bush to test people for tuberculosis.

Adding to all the confusion of the people, puppies, kittens, and kids, was the continual roar of motorcycles on the porch. Our tape recorder was also going full blast almost twenty-four hours. This tape deck has really been the best thing we've brought with us. The weekend was great fun. This is certainly a good opportunity for us to get to know the volunteers.

Right now there is a charming sixty-eight-year-old woman, Helen Montgomery, with us here at the Field Center. She has just finished two years in Malaysia as a Peace Corps Volunteer and is taking about six to eight months traveling around, even hitch-hiking, before going back to the States. She is a retired schoolteacher from Illinois and a lovely and interesting lady. Such an inspiration. A couple of weeks ago we had two ex-PCVs with us for four days who had just finished two years in Nigeria and were also hitchhiking all over Africa. Interesting people turn up from everywhere.

Some of the T.B. guys told us the cutest story the other day. They were out in the bush the week before, and while they were giving injections a lady appeared in the line with a brand new baby on her back. When they asked her the baby's name, she said she hadn't named it yet. They asked, in Chinyanja, if she would like them to name it. She was delighted. They named the baby America, and she beamed with pleasure. When they returned a week later to the village to check results of T.B. tests, they took that mother a new baby-carrying blanket — which the women use to tie their babies on their backs — with "America" embroidered on it!

The names some Malawians choose are priceless. They love English-language names, and some will just take them from anything they see. A friend's gardener's son is Limited, and I met a girl today named Scholastic. Then there are Time, Witness, and Kodak. Scott has a friend named Corn Flake. It makes me read labels and box tops with a new slant.

This is a great place for bug collectors and little (and some big) boys with jars. Just when I've sort of forgotten we're in Africa, and am daydreaming and minding my own business, along comes some monster crawling across the floor or down the wall, and I remember *fast.* Many of the PCVs are collectors; one in particular is in charge of the local museum. One day I opened a tea canister in the kitchen thinking a nice cup of tea would taste good — and there lay a two inch dead beetle (no tea). I do think beetles are interesting, but I like a little warning when they're in my tea canister. Upon hearing my surprised yelp, a PCV casually said he just "forgot" to tell me that he was saving this especially odd creature for Terry for the museum. Now I hold all canisters at arm's length before opening.

I spent an interesting but goose-bumpy afternoon helping a PCV knock down huge spiders from the eaves of the porch and placing them in jars. Our Mike has adopted one of these lovelies for his own and keeps it in a jar on his desk. We're finally beginning to get used to seeing lizards run up and down the inside walls. I even think they're kind of cute, and since I know they eat spiders, I now think they are especially cute. Spiders have always given me the heebie-jeebies.

Outdoors, very large ants are everywhere, and many of them bite. It's not a good idea to sit down in the grass, inviting as it may look. Out in the countryside you see anthills ten- to twelve-feet high. Fascinating. A handy bit of information is that the clay tennis courts here are made especially with the dirt from anthills because it is so fine.

Our air freight arrived after about a week, but our surface freight has yet to come. It should have been in Beira (Mozambique) on the fourth of this month. We're doing OK, except that I didn't know the weather would be so warm now, and our summery clothes are all in that shipment. It's not too uncomfortable, just a little sticky.

The Prime Minister's dress code is interesting. Women here, not just Malawi women but *all* women, cannot wear jeans or any type of long pants or shorts. Skirt hemlines have to be *below* the knee. These are Dr. Banda's laws — and we hear you can be arrested if you are seen in these outlawed types of clothing! At home in the States I *live* in jeans and shorts, so my big sacrifice here is to have to wear skirts or dresses all the time. At least they're cooler than jeans.

We are having fun picking up furniture to furnish our house, if it will ever be ready for us to move into. We are buying all African things. The kind we are getting is rattan and wicker, and we love it. Besides, it's cheap. Just about everything in our house will be handmade by Africans. Some of it looks a bit rustic, but it has a certain charm and seems ideal for our family.

After only three weeks Will has seen pretty much of this country, although there certainly is a lot more to see. His trip last week was to Port Herald *[now Nsanje]* in the southernmost part of Malawi, on the border of Mozambique. This is not the most desirable part of the country. Hot, swampy, humid, lots of flies, bugs, and mosquitoes, and lots of disease, especially malaria. Such a contrast to this area around Blantyre.

The PCVs down there need lots of moral support. They certainly are doing hard Peace Corps work. Not that the PCVs up here don't work hard too, but how much easier it is to work hard when the weather, surroundings, and food are decent. The Port Herald PCVs try to get up here on weekends to rest (and eat!). These are the guys I really like to cook for. Since their diet doesn't have much variety (about their only meat is goat), they go wild over my cooking, no matter how mediocre, and I *love it!* You should have heard them rave about my cake, which actually was a dismal failure — all of a quarter-inch high in the middle. I love cooking for these guys.

The other day Will went north to Fort Johnston *[now called Mangochi]*, which he found very interesting. We all went up to the Zomba Plateau last Sunday. This is the top of Zomba Mountain, a beautiful area with fantastic views, forests, and streams. It is about a one-and-a-half-hour drive from here. The road to the top is very steep, and the Land Rover was ideal with four-wheel drive on the steep hills. Now we are all at least starting to get around to see the Malawi countryside.

* * *

February 19, 1965

Well, as I was saying, lots of things happen every day. Will just took off for Washington, DC because a PCV had to be terminated and accompanied home very suddenly. My, what a surprise when Will came home and said, "I'm going to Washington, DC tomorrow." They will fly straight through, all day, all night, all day again. It will be physically tiring, to say nothing of the emotional strain. This is the sad side of the Peace Corps. Guess I can't say more except that when there are two hundred sixty young people, every once in a while someone is bound to foul up.

Will left with a large suitcase filled with African mementos to take to our families, and a very long shopping list from all the staff wives here so Will could *fill up* the large suitcase for the return trip. Surprising how fast they could get lists together.

Adjusting?

February 19, 1965

Yesterday we really hit the *jackpot*, with no fewer than eight letters from home! I couldn't get home fast enough from the Peace Corps office where our mail comes in, I was so excited. Will is on his way to Washington, DC, so the boys and I read them all out loud, and then I read each and every one over again later in the afternoon. Thank you, dear friends and family. I will try to answer some of your questions.

Yes, we do have electricity and running water. Since the electricity is 220 volts and our American appliances run on 110 volts, we have to use converters. Big heavy things, but they seem to do fine. However, the first time I gave Will a haircut with our electric clippers, whew — I nearly balded him, they went so fast, even with the converter turned down to its lowest. The water in Blantyre is OK to drink, which came as a great surprise to us. What luck. However, anywhere outside of Blantyre, it must be boiled.

Yes, fruits and vegetables are wonderful here. Bananas, pineapple, papaya, mango, guava, and all kinds of new things for us. We buy them either in the big open African market, which is wonderfully colorful, or from street vendors.

There is a very nice sort of supermarket called the Kandodo (pronounced Kan-doe-doe) and I have been astonished at all the things you can get. The red meat here is mostly beef and is good and very cheap. The fish, especially one called "chambo" is delicious. None of the meat or fish is wrapped or under glass though, even in the stores, which takes a little getting used to for Americans. In the open market the meat is right out in the open. Bread is also unwrapped, but is really delicious. It's actually so good that I'm not even going to try baking my own, which I'd thought I'd have to do.

My noble "real hair shirt Peace Corps" intentions of true sacrifices, such as not having any "help" in *my* house, baking all my own bread, scrubbing my own floors, etc., are rapidly dissolving.

There are two nice dress stores, a very good drug store, and two excellent restaurants. Many of the merchants are East Indians (from India) who have countless shops with all kinds of beautiful fabrics and dry goods. However, Malawians are having more opportunities to own businesses now that about forty percent of the British have left since Malawi won its independence from Britain in 1964. Most of the grocery stores are owned by Malawians. The Barclay's Bank, which we use, is managed mostly by Malawians, but, of course, is owned by the British.

The Zenith short-wave radio, er, excuse me, "wireless," is perfect. We listen to Voice of America every morning and evening, our *only* news, and get just about every country we want. Yes, there are three libraries in Blantyre, the best of which is the USIS (U.S. Information Service). There are also three theaters in the area, which have three-year-old American films. Fine for us.

Tennis is great on the clay courts, as the bounce is slower and I can *get* to the ball — well, at least more than on fast-bouncing hard courts. The clay does get shuffled up some, so there is always the risk of a bad bounce — therefore you have to keep your sense of humor intact. You don't even have to chase the balls, either, as there are young "ball boys" hired to do this, if you please. Ball boy jobs for young boys are much sought after.

We can see that we will probably have to join the Blantyre Sports Club, especially for the kids, as it has the only swimming pool and the only tennis courts. They say that the Sports Club is "integrated," but we don't see much evidence of it. However there is no other choice. Maybe we can help change things — who knows? The boys really need these activities now, especially Don and Mike, as they *so* dislike their schools. Scott, however, has a very nice teacher and seems to be happy. Thank goodness. Rick, of course, at three-and-a-half, is oblivious and happy as a clam playing around here with his new African friends, puppies, and PCVs.

Yes, sadly, the school situation is still not good for Don and Mike. The dark ages for sure. Mike has more bruises now, actual black and blue bruises, for instance for drawing a line in the wrong fashion in a long division problem. Boy, will they ever appreciate Davis schools when they get back!

It's not only the schools that are making the adjustment difficult for the boys, though. Many of the British here just don't like Americans. It's as simple as that. I really think the boys are going through culture shock — but not the kind we expected — and it has much to do with the British here. The boys love the Malawians and have lots of Malawi friends with whom they play, but they just simply are not accepted by the British children. There are very few American kids here. One bright spot for Mike, however, is that he loves rugby and always manages to get chosen first for the teams.

It feels uncomfortable for me too, when a smile is not returned by a British person. I'm not used to this. There are some friendly ones, and this is mean to say, but I confess that I'm getting so that I actually like to make the unfriendly ones feel uncomfortable by smiling at them. They seem not to know what to do. Probably only confirms their opinion of "callous Americans." I guess we don't endear ourselves on the tennis courts either, by laughing and giving actual outward displays of pleasure.

Other little everyday-living-in-Africa items: You should see our water heater here at the Field Center. It's outside in the back — a huge converted oil drum full of water on top of a tall fireplace in which a fire must be kept going all the time. You see why we need household help? And Stanley, the gardener, is out in the hot sun right now cutting the grass by hand with a machete. See why we need a gardener?

In African families the oldest girl is given responsibility for the younger children at a tender age. Little Emmy, the six-year-old daughter of Stanley, the gardener, carries her little one-and-a-half year-old brother on her back all day and is such a good little mother. It's hard for me to imagine this in the U.S., on the part of either mother or child.

We spent a delightful afternoon with the family of Samson Mbvundula (Will's Chinyanja teacher in Washington, DC) in their village, which is actually called "Mbvundula Village." It's about ten miles out of Blantyre, near the airport, and is a typical Malawi village of mud houses with thatched roofs. Their house, however, was whitewashed and tin-roofed, as Mr. Mbvundula's brother is the village Headman. They were friendly and cordial and overjoyed to have first-hand news of Samson.

Samson's father was a teacher and now is more or less retired and has cattle. The amazing thing to us was that not only is Samson studying in the U.S. (audio engineering), but he has a brother in medical school in Indiana, a sister in nursing school in Britain, another brother working in the Malawi government, and then a little sister still at home. Needless to say, Mr. Mbvundula is rightfully very proud of his family. You never know what might come out of a "typical Malawi village."

Don met a "witch doctor" on a trip with the Nelsons. Although this man said he was not a "medicine man" (we haven't learned the differences yet), Don brought back a headache remedy, which is stuff you mix with motor oil and rub on your temples. Also, some stomachache medicine that you rub into cuts on your hand. We haven't tried them as yet.

Will and I went to an American Embassy party and met all the foreign ambassadors. Now we have to learn fifty names and positions for a reception tonight given by the Peace Corps. At least, if learning all these names gives me a headache I'll know what to do to treat it.

Mas and Other Family Additions

February 20, 1965

We've decided that we are much too much work for Saidi, the Field Center's houseman, to do alone. Poor man. To begin with, the Peace Corps Field Center is huge. PCVs are in and out all the time. Then, add six permanent guests (and menagerie), and I think Saidi's good nature is being severely tested. Since we'll have to hire someone when we move to our own house anyway, Saidi has brought his uncle over to help. So now we have our very own houseman. His name is Mas and he is almost too good to be true.

Mas is at least in his forties, I'd guess, since he's been a housekeeper for twenty-seven years, mostly in South Africa. Many Malawians go to South Africa to work, usually in the mines, but many as household help ("houseboys"). He does everything beautifully, is quick to see how we like things to be done, and is really good-natured. He's in the kitchen at 6 a.m. and is still in the house right now, at 10 p.m., ironing. I have to *make* him take time off in the afternoons to rest. Most of his time is spent over a washboard, or the ping-pong-table-ironing-board, or hanging out the clothes, bringing them in when it rains, and then putting them back out after the rain. At least at the other house we'll have a washing machine, a dryer and an ironing board, so it should be easier. It bothers me to have Mas work so hard, yet when I did a little ironing the other day (imagine!) he looked so hurt and crestfallen, as if maybe I thought he couldn't do a good enough job, that I felt terrible. He's quite shy and sensitive, so I want to be especially careful not to hurt his feelings again.

Also, I want to teach him to cook. All those years as a housekeeper, and he was never allowed to learn to cook. He is pleased as punch, and should be able to get a better and more interesting job when we leave. He's smart and is already learning a lot, and is fun to teach. Mas is Muslim and always wears a little white skull cap (which probably has a Muslim name, but I don't know what it is called). He's very sweet and we just love him.

One problem we have with Mas is that after working in South Africa for so long, he keeps calling Will, "Bwana" (Master). "Yes, Bwana." Will just hates it, and would rather be just plain "Will" or even "Hey, you," but Mas just can't seem to do that. We're finally settling on a happy medium, which is "Bambo" (pronounced "Bombo") and means "Mister." Mas is so eager to please us, but this old servant-master thing is a hard habit to break.

* * *

Monday, February 22, 1965

Well, naturally, since forty new beds arrived and we got all set up for the weekend rush of PCVs, only about eight or ten came. Such is life. With Will gone, it is surely nice to have the Volunteers around the Field Center. They play games with the kids, and we all play cards or some other game in the evenings and listen to tapes. Two PCVs who had finished two years in Ghana were here for the weekend.

Also we have our first expectant-mother PCV. She and her husband are both teaching here, were married during training in the States and are expecting in July. They chose to stay and carry on. She had a million questions, having had no one to talk to about having a baby except her husband, who knows even less than she does about how to have or care for a baby. Barbara is a very sensible, level-headed young woman, I think, and should be able to cope with this. Teaching way out in the bush, caring for a brand new first baby — she'll have to be a special kind of person. The Peace Corps doctor is keeping a watchful eye on her, however, so she is in good hands.

We have added another pet to our menagerie. He's a chameleon with about a four-inch body and a six-inch tail, and doesn't look at all like the ones you see at home. The ones I've seen at home are smooth and kind of chartreuse. This one looks exactly like a miniature dinosaur or a monster on a horror show. He's not at all smooth, sort of bumpy, turns from chartreuse to polka dots, to stripes, to coal black when mad, and how can I possibly do my fine imitation of him with a typewriter? Well, when he's mad he goes "Haaaaaaahhhhh!" in a very terrifying manner. He has been a real show to watch. We are having to force-feed him though, as he won't eat. So we get him mad so that he opens his mouth wide to go, "Haaa" — well you know — and we pop in a wounded but alive fly or grasshopper. This morning I gave him one of the last of our half-dead pollywogs. He lives in a bucket with Torty Steekotz, Ricky's tortoise, which we keep losing and finding again.

* * *

Wednesday February 24, 1965

Here it is Wednesday, and Wes Leach, Peace Corps staff member (husband of Joyce), just came by to tell me Joyce is sick, so we can't go out to the orphanage today. Such a disappointment. I'd go out alone except that I'm not sure of the way yet. Also the little

Peugeot, which we bought for me to get to town to go shopping, and I don't always see eye-to-eye about how it should be driven. And on the way to the orphanage you have to cross a bridge with no sides, and with a river below. Yikes!

Last week Joyce and I were stopped by a police roadblock on the way out there. Apparently I must have looked very suspicious to the police (isn't that exciting?) because after they had politely searched the whole car, they asked to look through my purse. Joyce even said,

"Don't you want to look through my purse too?"

"No, thank you, Madam."

This struck us so funny. It does cross my mind, however, that I am still carrying that twenty-five-pound Absolutely-Equipped-For-Any-Emergency Purse, and it's quite possible they thought it contained all sorts of weapons, which is what they are looking for.

By the way, if you should read about any trouble here in Malawi, it is only between the Malawians: the Government and some rebels. There was an incident up at Fort Johnston last week, in which several Malawians were killed. That is far away, and only Malawians are involved. If we should hear any shooting, you will find us under beds until it's all over. If you read that anything happens in Blantyre, you can envision all the Lotters eating their meals under beds. However, we honestly don't anticipate any trouble here. Furthermore, this city is crawling with police.

Our Very Own Galimoto

About our little second-hand car. I don't think I've told you much about it yet. It's our very own "galimoto" — Chinyanja for car, in case you've forgotten. It's a funny little French car, a Peugeot, about a '52 model, which looks like a combination of a '38 Ford and an oversized Volkswagen bug.

Here are its good features: it was a good buy; it gets thirty-five miles to the gallon of "essence" (French for "petrol" or gas); all six of us can fit in, which is a trick with most of the small cars; it's a pretty powder blue; and it gets me to town to shop, which is its sole purpose in life. Its questionable features are:

1) It has no key. This means that you can't lock it. It also means that no key is required to start it. Anyone could just step in and drive it away. Therefore, this necessitates much grand dramatic pretense of locking all the doors whenever we park it.

2) I'm now beginning to get used to the steering wheel residing on the right-hand side of the car, and driving on the left side of the road, although I'm still terrified every time I make a right turn from the left lane.

3) The gearshift lever is on the left side of the steering wheel, with an identical-looking lever on the right side of the steering wheel — where I am used to shifting — but this one on the right turns on the lights, and if pushed in — honks the horn. This means, of course, that when I go to shift, if I actually do remember to shift, I automatically reach for the wrong lever (on the right) — and the lights go on and the horn honks and the engine stalls!

4) *Everything* is the exact opposite to my way of thinking. When knobs are pulled out, everything is off. When you want these knobs to do anything, you push them all in. Crazy.

While Will was away I absolutely had to master driving here. As I said before, the schools and the driving have been my culture shock. The very first time I soloed, I had to drive it home from downtown because Will was away. I had thought I could remember how to start it, but sat there pushing and pulling knobs for about half an hour, feeling totally foolish, before it finally somehow started up.

I didn't know about that headlight business at the time, and in all my fiddling around trying to start it I'd inadvertently gotten the lights on. For the life of me I couldn't figure out how to get them off. African boys all gathered around the car as usual — you can't do anything here without an interested audience — saying, "Madam, push this," "Madam, pull that," though none of them has probably been inside of a car, much less driven one.

Finally I just gave up and drove home with the lights on, causing at least fifty people to gesture at me and shout something in Chinyanja, which I presume was about the lights. Luckily, second grader Scott came home for lunch and actually knew how to turn them off. We would have had an awfully dead battery. Now who would dream the light control would be on the *horn* (or "hooter," as they call it here)? And how did an eight-year-old know that? This was just the first of many incidents with the little car.

It and I have had a real personality conflict until just recently, not agreeing at all on how it should be driven. I was even considering learning French to see if it would help. We are on pretty good speaking terms now, but it was on one of those days that we weren't speaking that I had another funny experience.

With all the kids in the car it took one of its notions to stall (for the umpteenth time) at the top of a hill at a stop sign, in spite of the fact that I'd actually shifted with the gear shift and not the horn. It refused to start (again) so I finally let it roll back parallel to the curb. Still wouldn't start. The kids and I then decided that I should let it roll back down the hill to the bottom, where I could back it up around the corner and then coast forward down another hill, put it in gear and get it started in compression. Well, this was a fine plan except I'd gotten it too close to the curb and it wouldn't budge. Stuck. Really stuck.

Don and Mike tried to push it up and away from the curb but couldn't budge it. Then a kind African gentleman saw our plight and came to help. Still couldn't do it, so he called for his friends to come. They poured out from everywhere, and of course with all this great crew of smiling, eager help, the car literally leaped up the hill and free from the curb. So I smiled, saying, "Zikomo (thank you), zikomo," nodding and waving good-bye — but in their eagerness to help they started *pushing* me down the hill. Backwards! I was shouting, "Stop" — didn't know the Chinyanja word for it — "*stoppp!*" and they smiled and nodded and pushed harder and faster. I was scared but got laughing so much I could hardly see, and I can't steer backwards even when I *can* see.

Rick started to cry in the back seat and Don and Mike were doubled up with laughter on the sidewalk. I was afraid to put on the brakes for fear they would suddenly grab and all fifteen men would come sailing through the windshield. We were really gaining momentum going backwards right down the middle of the street. By some strange miracle no cars happened along at that time — and I finally managed to outdistance my helpers and roar backwards around the corner at the bottom of the hill.

When I could finally get my own hysterics under control, I did manage to point it frontwards down the next hill, put it in gear, and get it started in compression. Don and Mike ran down the hill and jumped in the car, still laughing. We drove straight home, where I collapsed in exhaustion and fits of giggles.

Just another day with Galimoto and me.

We're Still Here

March 25, 1965

We're still living in the Peace Corps Field Center waiting for our house to be ready. After more than two months of living here in the Field Center with people in and out all hours of the day and night, it will probably seem pretty lonesome once we move. It's only a five-minute walk from here, however, so we hope to entice people over for pancakes or something. Food is wonderful bribery.

[This was THE PLAN THAT WORKED. 90,000 pancakes later, I can fully attest to it!]

The other house is undergoing major repairs, including rewiring, painting inside and out, and screening windows. The houses here have some funny features. I can't imagine who planned them. Neither the Field Center nor the other house has a single closet. They both have walk-in pantries, which are great, but not *one* clothes closet — or cupboard, for that matter. You have to use those big, ugly portable closet things which are usually dark wood and stand out like sore thumbs.

Today I discovered that the kitchen doesn't have a sink. Was I embarrassed that I hadn't noticed this before! Off the kitchen there is a kind of laundry area, a nice sunny room, and I'd thought, "My, how nice — an extra sink out there." It didn't register that it was *the* sink and there wasn't one *in* the kitchen. Can you imagine? (Either that there wasn't a sink in the kitchen, *or* that I didn't notice?) Oh well. The longer I'm here, the more reasons I find for having household help, that's for sure.

The school situation for the boys is about the same. Pretty grim. However, Mike, in standard six, is now playing rugby and soccer on Saturday mornings, as well as on school days, and just got a new pair of rugby shoes, so at last things are looking up a little for him. Scott is the happiest in school and still likes his standard two teacher.

Don is in standard seven, which is the first year of high school and is the same as seventh grade in the States. He is the only American in his class and still is not accepted by the other kids. His biggest outlet is tennis after school and on weekends. Unfortunately, only girls play tennis in St. Andrews Secondary School, otherwise he'd go out for a tennis team, which would be a lot more fun for him. His game has really improved, and he and Will have been beating lots of men's doubles teams, with Don winning as many points as Will. Will has been coaching some African high school-age boys in tennis. They are quite good, and Don has been playing them once or twice a week.

Rick usually goes with me wherever I go. When he's playing with the little African children here, he speaks half English and half Chinyanja. It gave me quite a start the other day when I heard him say something in Chinyanja that I couldn't understand. My three-year-old saying something I couldn't understand — to people who did understand! Funny feeling.

Will is giving a three-week clinic on teaching physical education for the African teachers from all over Malawi. He is really enjoying this. They are working principally on tennis and basketball right now. Nothing at all has been done in the schools here with physical education, so it's a wide-open field. He is also taking Chinyanja instruction for an hour every other day and studying hard every night.

At the time of my last letter Will was back in Washington, as I recall. The trip over wasn't much fun, as it was a sad mission — taking a PCV who had to be terminated back to Washington, DC. But the trip coming back was great, and I am still bright green with envy. He went via Paris and somehow managed to be "stuck" (oh sure) there for thirty-six hours. Poor thing. This was all complicated by the fact that he didn't have the proper visa to re-enter Kenya after his thirty-six-hour stay in Paris and Air France wasn't going to let him get on the plane from Paris to Nairobi.

Apparently it got pretty funny, with some very excited Air France officials doing much arm waving and rapid-fire spouting of French (none of which Will could understand) interspersed with suspicious glances at Will. Ten minutes before flight time they were still arguing and finally said, "Non, Monsieur cannot board." Monsieur would have to wait until Monday — and this was Friday — to see the American Embassy about a visa.

Will said, "OK. Then you get my bags off that plane and Air France must pay my hotel and meals for the weekend." (What nerve!)

Then much louder and more rapid French, and just minutes before takeoff the one (the only one) who spoke English said, "Follow me," and they sprinted at top speed, Will encumbered by attaché case, cameras, and overcoat, down corridors, through gates, and across runways. Just before the steps were going to be taken away, Will puffed up the stairs, collapsed into a seat, and they took off! He felt like an international spy or James Bond, at the very least.

Ironically, once in Nairobi he had no trouble at all. On this trip he had landed in Athens for an hour, then Djibouti in French Somaliland for another hour, then was in Nairobi for another day (such hardship). He went to the Nairobi wild game reserve and got some wonderful pictures with the new camera. He was gone for ten days altogether. Were we glad to have him back!

Sister Mary Joy

Monday, March 28, 1965
7:30 a.m.

The kids get off to school every day by 7:00 a.m., as does Will.
Rick and I are up and dressed, have had breakfast, and I've had my
third cup of coffee and listened to Voice of America; Mas has
already done the breakfast dishes and is now changing all the beds;
Saidi is doing the washing, having done the ironing at 6:00 a.m;
Stanley, the gardener, is hosing and sweeping the front porch — a
constant job, as we still have three of the nine puppies. And it's
only 7:30 a.m. It all still seems unreal. The stores open at 7:30 a.m.,
and often Rick and I are through with all the shopping by 10:00,
even though it takes a couple of hours to do it. What a different life
this is for me.

The Nguludi Mission is still the favorite project of our family. I
go out every Wednesday to the orphanage, and it is my favorite day.
Our whole family went out on a Sunday a few weeks ago to take
Sister Mary Joy, the nun who runs the orphanage and whom we all
just love, a birthday cake. It was so much fun because she was
totally surprised and had no idea we'd known it was her birthday.
We told her that Noah, one of the babies, told us it was her
birthday. She's thirty-one.

The cake, though delicious (chocolate), looked as if it had been
decorated by three-year-old Rick, it was so crudely done. But just
try writing "Happy Birthday Sister Mary Joy" with a "decorating
tube" made of a rolled up piece of not-stiff-enough paper! Then,
making it look even funnier, the only candle we could find was one
big regular household candle, so it really looked quite humorous.
She loved it and thought it was very funny.

Sister Mary Joy told us the other day that the last sister of their
order had been rescued out of the Congo just last week. She had
been separated from the rest of her mission and was alone for four
months at an orphanage. When the helicopter finally got to her,
she refused to leave unless the pilot would take all of her orphans.
Seventeen of them! The pilot about had a fit, saying, "But Sister,
we've been trying to get to you for four months — !"

She just kept handing him babies, saying, "Not unless you take
all my babies." He did.

When Sister Mary Joy told us this story, she was holding little
Lucy, a baby who had weighed only three pounds when given to
her, and of whom the doctor had said, "This one can't live," and
ordered last rites. Sister Mary Joy didn't put that baby down for

forty-eight hours, and somehow *made* her live. She is now six months old, weighs six pounds, smiles, and is coming along really well. So Lucy is really very special to Sister Mary Joy.

Then she said to Lucy, "Lucy-Bucy" (she has nicknames for all of the babies: Lucy-Bucy, Anna-Banana) — "when that helicopter comes, *you* will be the first to go!" Sister Mary Joy is one of the most inspiring persons I've ever known. What a real joy to be able to work with her.

Three Volunteers just dropped in for coffee and to see if Will has been getting ready for rugby. They are organizing a U.S. Peace Corps rugby team to play all the teams around here, and they're so excited. Is Will getting ready?!! Every day he's been running and running after work. Saidi and Mas thought he'd lost his mind the first time they saw him running like crazy up and down in front of the Field Center. It's beyond their comprehension to run just for the heck of it.

To confirm Mas' and Saidi's theory that we are quite crazy, there was a Peace Corps costume party Saturday night, to which everyone went. It was a "Come as your Favorite Villain" party. A lot of the PCVs were getting ready here at the Field Center, and by the time we left for the party Mas and Saidi were in stitches.

Will and I went as the "Headmonster" of St. Andrews and his wife. Will glued on a mustache, wore shorts, kneesocks, Scott's school tie (which on Will was about six inches long), Don's school hat (which even looks funny on Don), and carried a big *stick.* I wore my primmest high-necked clothes and Don's black school shoes and school kneesocks. We ended up having to do taxi service to the party, as the PCVs have no transportation and usually walk everywhere — but in all these wild get-ups we were afraid they'd get picked up by the police. One PCV came as an alarm clock (get it — villain?) and another guy came as a motorcycle (they are always breaking down). It was lots of fun. Hope the news of what we wore doesn't leak to the school.

Yesterday we went over to the "other house" to see how things were progressing and just happened to be there at the twelve o'clock noon changing of the guard at the Prime Minister's house next door. The bugle blew, and we all raced out to watch. Will even got up on the roof on the pretense of checking the chimney. My — it is really a spectacle. And they do this at least twice every day.

We stood right outside the gates of the Prime Minister's courtyard and watched. There were six uniformed guards with rifles, three replacing three; twelve uniformed other staff with a different uniform, six replacing six. The ones with rifles marched just like the guards at the Tomb of the Unknown Soldier in Washington, DC, a very serious event which we had all just seen, with high stepping and heels clicking. The Malawians looked terribly handsome and polished in their uniforms, also with high stepping and heels clicking, but there was one big difference — as they marched toward us, *they* smiled at us.

Also at the Prime Minister's compound were three police cars to chauffeur away three dignitaries. I was hoping to catch a glimpse of Dr. Banda Himself, but have yet to see him. Wonder if I could run over and borrow a cup of sugar some time?

French!

March 29, 1965

Poor Mike. With absolutely no inkling of any foreign language except some Chinyanja, he has been thrown into a third-year French class and is totally floundering. The teacher couldn't care less. Even though he's in standard six, Mike knows nothing about conjugating verbs, as he has never had *any* foreign language in school. Every bit has been a struggle, especially homework at night. There was no book issued to him for reference, so we went out and bought one.

Last week when he came home with thirty-six sentences to translate from English into French, among them the future tense of verbs he didn't even know the *present* tense of — I said, "This is ridiculous," and sat down and wrote a note to the teacher, who is the Headmaster, unfortunately.

It was a very nice note (I thought) explaining that Mike had had no French nor any foreign language at all, and I wondered if there was any way that he could be placed in an elementary French class, or should we get a tutor, or what might he suggest? Then, cleverly (I thought), I added that I really thought that the situation was much like "asking a child to do multiplication when he didn't know how to count." (Don't you think that's quite clevah?)

However, it really backfired in our faces. He not only made no effort to help Mike or to answer my note, but he said in front of the class, "This French is too difficult for Lottuh." From then on he would not call on Mike, even when he raised his hand, and Mike says it's just as if he's invisible. He isn't given any papers or anything. He just has to sit there and be embarrassed.

Well, I wasn't going to take this lying down. I fired off another note, saying that Mr. Walker must have misunderstood my note, that didn't he think there was some happier solution than embarrassing Mike in class? So things went from bad to worse, and Mr. W. wrote a very sarcastic note back on his veddy formal British school stationery, saying that Mike didn't have to take French at all, etc. Missed the point entirely. We want him to have French. Now Mike is furious at me for ever writing in the first place because things are so much worse than before. Oh dear. Poor Mike. But I keep telling him that if some American mothers don't complain about this system, it's only going to get worse for the next ones. I'm sorry he has to be the fall guy, though.

On a happier note, we are having fun gathering up African

mementos for our house. Will came home with a ten-foot python skin for one of the boys' rooms! We have a great assortment of African drums made out of skins, and some made from huge gourds. Ebony carvings here are beautiful, and we've been able to get some. We hope to move into the house in a week, and when Will flies to Salisbury, Rhodesia, on business, I can go along to shop for items which we can't get here. That should be fun.

We have some more entries to add to our list of interesting African names. Today I met a cute young, very very black Malawian girl, whose name is White. Did I tell you about Frighten and Fraction? They applied for work the same day at the house of a PCV, who wished he could have hired them both. Then there are Kidney, Sorry, Green Ford, and Blue Gum. And, of course, Scott's friend, Corn Flake and Rick's friend, Robot. We later figured out that Robot probably is Robert. We sometimes do not understand the Malawians' pronunciation of English. "Er" ("ur") sounds are difficult for them, as are most L's, which they frequently interchange with R's.

One day Scott came into the house and said, "Mommy, there is a man in the yard, and his name is Garbage!"

Delighted but unbelieving, I went out to find out for myself. After passing the time of day, I casually said, "What is your name?"

And as clear as could be (I thought), he said, "Garbage."

Hardly able to keep a straight face until I got back in the kitchen, I laughed until I cried and in between wiping my eyes and blowing my nose, I managed to ask Mas, "Is it really true that that man in the yard is named Garbage?"

"No, Madam. His name is Cabbage, and he is my brother." Uhhhh. What could I say?

On a more serious note, we've been following the events in Selma, Alabama, as well as we can with the limited news we get here. We were just sick about that Unitarian Minister being killed. By the way, it got front page coverage in all the African newspapers with a 4x6 picture of him in the *Malawi News*. We have been getting *Time* magazine, the overseas edition, and we read it from cover to cover. Will is sometimes able to get hold of a *New York Times* in town too. Voice of America is probably our best source of news, but it doesn't always come in clearly. We feel very far away.

There are some people here who just can't quite comprehend the motives of the Peace Corps and are sure there must be some underlying reason for anyone wanting to do this sort of thing. One day a man, who happened to be a Dutch priest, gave one of our hitchhiking PCVs a ride. The priest asked what this fellow was doing here. The PCV answered that he was a U.S. Peace Corps

Volunteer and that he was teaching in a school out in the bush. The man asked how many U.S. Peace Corps Volunteers there were in the country, and the PCV answered, "About two hundred and sixty."

"My!" The man was so surprised. Silence. Finally he said, "My, there must be just terrible unemployment in the United States!"

Our Own House

Finally we've moved into our new house! Of course it's not really new, but at least it's new to us and is *ours* for the two years we'll be here. The outside is not painted yet and looks patched up (is) but the inside is all newly painted an ivory color and looks clean and fresh. Quite a change from the former bright blues, greens, and pinks of various walls here and there. The house has lots of windows and sunshine and we love it — in spite of its not being the boys' dream of a mud-hut-with-thatch-roof-out-in-the-jungle.

I'm brightening things up with colorful African fabric cushions and pictures on the walls, and I'm sewing curtains like mad. The hand-made African rattan and wicker chairs and couches and the big round braided corn husk rugs look perfect. We've been picking them up whenever we've seen them for sale, often along the roadsides.

The boys are thrilled to have their own rooms. So are Mom and Dad. *Especially* Mom and Dad. We've all been in one room for almost three months. Scott and Rick share a room with bunk beds, but Don and Mike each have their own rooms. Mike's is a tiny converted sun porch just off our bedroom, but it is his very own, so he's happy. Don, at twelve, insists that he is grown up enough to read half the night if he wants to without anyone yelling at him to turn off the light — so he is delighted to have a room alone, finally.

Mas has moved his family into one of the little houses out in the back that were built to house household help. He has a very shy, quiet wife who speaks no English at all, and a cute little son named Saidi, who is Ricky's age, just three. We're all getting to know the garden man, Raphael, who more or less came with the house. He worked for the Nelsons, the former Peace Corps family who lived here, and the Peace Corps kept him on to take care of the grounds. He also speaks very little English but seems friendly and works hard.

So here we are — finally really settling in. It feels so good. The only thing is, though, after living in the Peace Corps Field Center with so many people around all the time it seems a little lonesome. I hope we'll have lots of visitors. Pancake breakfasts might lure them?

Going out to the Nguludi orphanage every Wednesday to help Sister Mary Joy and the other nuns is the high point of every week. Joyce Leach and I have such a good time and feel we are really helping. If nothing else, we have four more arms to hold and love the babies. Those babies simply can't get too much love. Every week we try to take some needed items out there — safety pins, bottles, nipples, crib sheets that we make, ground-up food for the babies and sometimes cookies for tea with the sisters.

Sister Mary Joy is always so grateful for anything for her babies. I think *she* really needs four arms, as she is always carrying around two babies. One day she was holding two babies at once and trying to feed one of them, but they kept snatching her wooden cross from the front of her habit and clonking each other on the head. Then they would cry. Finally she took the cross off, very carefully laid it on the floor beside her chair, and, typical of her sense of humor, very seriously said,

"Excuse me, Jesus." Joyce and I, each also holding and feeding babies, about fell off our chairs laughing.

We've gotten to be such good friends with Sister Mary Joy that Joyce and I are talking about trying to get her to come into town someday to have lunch with us and see all our kids and each of our houses. She never takes any time off, though. She works so hard (too hard!) and seems never to rest, and yet is always fun and upbeat. She is truly amazing. If she sits down at all, it's to hold one or two babies.

We're hoping she could justify coming for lunch by combining it with errands in town. We'd be able to drive her back and forth, and it would be such a treat for us. We'll have to wait and see what she thinks. She'll probably say she'll only come if she can bring one or two of her babies!

The "Best-laid Plans — "

Tuesday, April 19, 1965

Joyce and I are so excited because Sister Mary Joy is actually going to be able to come in tomorrow for lunch. We're going out to work at the orphanage in the morning and then we'll bring her into town with us. First we'll have lunch at Joyce's in Limbe and then dessert at our house in Blantyre. I've made my special chocolate cake because we found out that Sister Mary Joy loves chocolate cake. Then we'll take her to do her errands and drive her right back to the Mission. She'll only have been gone from the Mission a few hours.

Sister Mary Joy has met all my boys, but she hasn't met Joyce's son Mike yet. Joyce's Mike and our Mike are both eleven and are buddies. In fact, the Leaches are taking our Mike with them to Salisbury, Rhodesia, in a week when Wes has to do some Peace Corps business there. They will fly and both Mikes are excited about it. We do wonder if their excitement might have anything to do with the fact that Rhodesia has TV? (Malawi has none.) Nooo, couldn't possibly.

I'll wait to mail this now until I can tell you about the lunch with Sister Mary Joy. Joyce and I have been knocking ourselves out cooking delicious things.

* * *

Wednesday night, April 20

About the "best-laid plans" — what a shock. Joyce and I went out this morning to Nguludi in a great state of excitement about our lunch date with Sister Mary Joy. When we got there we found out that she had become seriously ill last week and by last night was so sick they had to take her by ambulance to Queen Elizabeth Hospital in Blantyre!

Joyce and I were there all morning today with the babies, but it was hard to concentrate. We're so worried about Sister Mary Joy that we haven't even cared or talked about the lunch. Some of the other nuns are also helping in the orphanage, especially the Malawian sisters.

Tonight after dinner I picked a bouquet of violets from our garden, wrote a get well note, and went over to the hospital to see how she is. I was shocked to see how terrible she looks! I guess I didn't realize how really ill she is. I only stayed a minute in her room and just said, "Sister Mary Joy, I'm so sorry you're sick."

She was kind of delirious, and I'm not sure she recognized me, but she looked at me and *smiled* and said in a little weak voice, "It will go away." So typical of her, sick as she is, to smile. They think it's malaria and perhaps hepatitis. Awful combination. We are worried sick about her. It seems to have happened so fast. Joyce and I were with her just the day before she fell ill, and she certainly appeared fine. Scary.

While sister Mary Joy is ill, Joyce and I will go out as often as we can to the orphanage to help. Unfortunately, Joyce will be away in Salisbury for a few days next week, but now I think I can actually manage to drive alone out there — sideless bridge and all.

Tragedy

Monday, April 26, 1965

I have some unbelievably awful news. Sister Mary Joy died. I simply can't believe it. I can hardly write, my hands are shaking so hard, and I can barely see through my swollen, streaming eyes.

She died this morning at 6:00 a.m. It was cerebral malaria, the worst kind of malaria, complicated by a case of hepatitis which no one, including herself, knew she had. The mission doctor was away last week, and with Sister Mary Joy being the kind of uncomplaining person she was, no one had any idea how very ill she was until last Tuesday night when they had to bring her by ambulance to the Queen Elizabeth Hospital here in Blantyre.

From then on it was a nightmare for me, going back and forth to the Blantyre hospital, distraught with worry, driving the nuns in and out from the mission to Queen Elizabeth Hospital to care for her twenty-four hours a day, and trying to help at the orphanage. Those sisters never left Sister Mary Joy alone for one single minute.

Friday was the most terrible day — a day to blot from memory. I'd gone by the hospital about 7:45 a.m. on my way out to the mission to see if any of the sisters needed a ride out to Nguludi and to find out the latest on Sister Mary Joy. We'd heard that she had responded a little to some treatments on Thursday night and so we were all newly hopeful.

But that Friday morning I was standing outside Sister Mary Joy's room when Sister Eileen came out of the room with a kind of dumbfounded look on her face. I will never ever forget her words.

"Jane, they don't expect her to live." It was like a bad dream. A horrible nightmare. I just couldn't believe it. I can't.

We all knew she was gravely ill, but no one expected this. It was simply beyond comprehension for all of us. I just fell apart. And so here was sweet Sister Eileen, who had probably been Sister Mary Joy's best friend since they had gone to high school together, having to take me into another room to console *me*. It was an absolutely horrible twenty-four hours. It was as if we were all moving around in a bad dream.

What a help I was that day at the orphanage — "the weeping wonder" — trying to make the babies happy. You know how successful that is. They've been terribly short-handed because of needing some of the sisters to be at the hospital with her all the time, plus their having to get some sleep between shifts. Joyce and I have spent every day out there in the orphanage since they first took Sister Mary Joy to the hospital. They need help at Nguludi so much that some of our PCVs went out and spent their whole school vacation working in the orphanage, running the hospital switchboard there all night, and helping with the hospital records. They were superb.

Amazingly, though, Sister Mary Joy lived four more days until this morning, just hovering near death. She had been unconscious ever since that second night in the hospital, Wednesday. I didn't know it then, but Sister Albertine told me later that apparently I was one of the last people to whom she spoke, even though she might not have known it was me. That gives me such a strange feeling and I can't stop thinking about it. She was just too precious to me.

Today is a special Feast Day for Catholics. Sister Mary Joy was always talking about how much these special days meant to her, even telling me about a friend who had died on one of these days and how important that had been. So, I guess if she had to die, at least she died on one of these special days that meant so much to her.

The sisters called on Sunday morning at 7:30 for help with driving, the day before Sister Mary Joy died. I was happy to be able to relieve Mother Catherine, who has been running the sisters in and out. It takes about forty-five minutes to get out to Nguludi. Luckily, I'm no longer scared to drive it.

Poor Mother Catherine. She talked to me for about half an hour yesterday about how responsible she feels about Sister Mary Joy, that she should have known how tired Sister Mary Joy was, and on and on. She just needed to talk, I think. It didn't seem to do any good when I said that it certainly wasn't her fault, that no one knew that she was this sick, so I just listened. Imagine *me* being a listening post for a Mother Superior. I just love her and feel so sorry for her.

You could probably tell by my letters how much I loved Sister Mary Joy. I feel as if I've hardly begun to tell you all about her though. I've never known anyone like her — ever. She was the most completely loving, compassionate, and unselfish person I've ever known. With her sparkling smile, twinkle in her eye, and wonderful sense of humor, she constantly gave of herself. Why did this have to happen?? When there are so many evil people around this world, why would Sister Mary Joy, of all people, have to die? Everyone who ever met her loved her.

The sisters have been offering me all sorts of what I would call "platitudes" like, "God gives and God takes," and "she was just too good for this world," but I find them hard to swallow. Actually, I think they are all having a hard time coming to grips with this one, too. They have been really wonderful, though, and seem so strong. I've only seen one of them actually cry, although I know they've all been just beside themselves, first with anxiety and now with grief. Except for Mother Catherine, all of the sisters are probably in their thirties and are just incredible. I feel very close to all of them, especially now through all of this tragedy. I do wonder, though, how they deal with their grief so well.

I just got back from the mission and am still so numb I'm moving like a mechanical zombie or something. We (family) are scheduled to go on Wednesday up to the lake for seven days. I've done no planning or packing at all, as I've been either out at Nguludi or the hospital every day since Sister Mary Joy got sick. The funeral is tomorrow and I'm dreading it. I guess I'll start packing for the lake after that. My heart is just not in it.

The Funeral

The funeral was this morning, and I feel as if I've been dragged through a knothole. It's almost 5:00 p.m., and I really don't feel like packing for our trip to the lake tomorrow, or getting dinner on the table — or writing this letter, for that matter. Nor do I even have *time* to be writing this, but I got to thinking that you might worry about cerebral malaria and hepatitis and I wanted to reassure you about us.

I found out some additional information on Sister Mary Joy's case. Apparently she must have been suffering silently for some time, as they found that she had a very bad liver condition, no doubt due to hepatitis. Her face had such a deep tan from the African sun that she appeared to glow with good health, the suntan obscuring the tell-tale yellow skin color caused by hepatitis. Because she was the kind of person who would never even mention that she didn't feel well, no one had the least idea how ill she was. We guess that her body was weakened by the hepatitis and just couldn't fight the cerebral malaria. It's frightening to realize that she was only really visibly ill for twelve days before she died.

Now here is where I want to reassure you. If anyone has anything in this family, especially me, we *all* know about it. If I have even a little splinter or a hang-nail, *everyone hears about it*. I have never been known to suffer in silence, nor do I plan to. Also, we are all taking extra malaria suppressants. With mosquitoes being the carriers of malaria, we have nets over all of our beds, are going through bottle after bottle of bug repellent, and are waging deadly battle with any hapless mosquito that chances by. So please don't worry.

As soon as Sister Mary Joy got really sick, you could see the yellowish cast of her face, which was the clue that she had hepatitis. When I saw her face on Saturday in the hospital, she had such a yellow color. On Sunday I didn't see her face, but I saw her feet when the doctor was changing the intravenous tubes in her ankles, and even her feet had this color. Her deep suntan had fooled everyone.

The funeral was really beautiful, and I didn't think I'd ever be able to say that about any funeral. I hate funerals. There were about four hundred people there. Out of all of those, there were only eight of us who were not either nuns, brothers, priests, or black. The nuns, brothers and priests were all dressed in white.

The old Nguludi church was packed. There were hundreds of Malawians, most of them having walked miles and miles to attend. The Archbishop performed the High Mass, which lasted about an hour. There was a lot of singing, and all the pews were filled. The sides and back of the church were lined with Africans — mothers with babies on their backs; men, many dressed in rags. They were all her friends and had come to pay respects to the friend they had lost. Everyone who knew her loved her. Sister Mary Joy would have been so touched to see that packed church.

After the mass was the long procession from the church to the graveyard. It was a beautiful sight; long lines of people, most dressed in white, slowly winding down the trails amongst the trees and tall green grass. With the mountains as a backdrop and the Malawian sisters singing softly in Chinyanja, it was an unforgettable and deeply moving scene.

The church service was hard enough for me to get through, but the hour at the graveside was nearly my undoing. The sun, even though it was only about 10:00 a.m., was getting hotter and hotter, adding physical discomfort to my already emotional wreck of a person. After the ceremony, they lowered the casket down into the grave, and each person picked up a handful of dirt and passed by the grave, gently dropping it in, some murmuring soft goodbyes. That almost did me in.

The only thing that made the day bearable for me was knowing that it was all so beautiful and appropriate for Sister Mary Joy, especially seeing all the Africans there. I kept thinking, "If this had to be, this is the way she would have liked it." I wished that her family in the States could have been there.

Today started by my driving a carload of people out to the Mission at 7:00 a.m. before the funeral. There were two nurses from the Blantyre hospital who had needed a ride to the funeral; Mack, our wonderful sixty-four-year old PCV who loved and did so much for Nguludi; Carol, another PCV; and also Don and Scott, who were going to be taking care of the babies during the funeral.

I had figured out that we had a big problem in the orphanage with the funeral being at 9:00 a.m. — *who* was going to stay with and feed the nineteen babies, of assorted sizes and ages, who always get fed between 9:00 and 10:30 a.m.? Everyone who had ever worked in the orphanage and was familiar with the babies wanted to be at the funeral, of course. So I recruited Carol, a PCV who had never been out there, and Don and Scott. Although only twelve and eight, the boys have been out there with me so much that they know all the babies, their names, habits, which bed is for which one, and how to feed them. Mike would also have gone to help, but he was on the long-planned trip to Salisbury with the Leaches. Joyce had to miss all of this.

When we got back to the orphanage from the funeral at about 11:00 a.m., Don was calmly standing there with tongs, taking nipples out of boiling water to put on the bottles into which he had poured formula — heated just right — and Scott had just finished washing all the dishes from the feeding of the cereals, etc. Three of the bigger babies were sitting on their little potties, Carol was changing two more, and they had all been fed. A few were crying in their cribs, but after all, there were nineteen of them. Carol said she was just amazed at the competence of Don and Scott. Don had even changed some diapers — and six of those babies weigh only six pounds. They really came through, and I was certainly a proud and pleased Mom.

I can't help but reflect on what a life-learning experience this was for our boys — playing a part in the two extremes of life: death on the one hand, and new life on the other.

Our Peace Corps Volunteers really came through, too, in this time of crisis. Before Sister Mary Joy's illness, three PCV teachers had gone out to Nguludi to help during their school vacation as part of their school vacation projects. One of them, Ann Hardy, whom Mack always calls "The Georgia Peach," has literally taken over the orphanage now and is simply amazing. Little did these PCVs all know that they would end up holding the whole place together. The other two were there to build a tennis court for the sisters, but ended up digging the grave and fixing up the graveyard for Sister Mary Joy. What a grim switch. They all did hospital records, ran errands, helped in the hospital, went to the orphanage to help feed and hold babies whenever they had any time, and were real godsends. Mother Catherine and all the nuns are so very grateful.

After the services, when we were all standing around in kind of a daze, Sister Jean came up and put her arm around me, and said, "Well, Jane — we have our own real angel up there now. And boy! Am I going to ask that angel for lots of favors — pretty soon you won't even know this place for the improvements!"

But what I can't stop thinking about is — that angel is only thirty-one years old.

The funeral was an experience both beautiful and awful. I don't think I will ever get over any of it. Sister Mary Joy was such an inspiration to everyone. I had thought that one of the most meaningful things about my experience here in Malawi would be knowing and working with her for two whole years. However, I'm immensely grateful for these three months. I will never forget her.

[Now, more than thirty-five years later, retyping this letter and crying all over my computer, I can honestly say that those months knowing Sister Mary Joy were, in fact, my most memorable and meaningful experiences in our twenty-seven months in Malawi. And it's true – I have never gotten over it.]

Trying To Recover

Friday, May 7, 1965

We had a week at the lake after the funeral, and if I *ever* needed a change and vacation, that was the time. The shock of Sister Mary Joy's sudden illness and subsequent death, combined with my going out to the Mission every day for quite a while, has left me pretty tired and wrung out. It's also left me no time or energy for letter writing.

Will had to go to two conferences. One was at Lilongwe, about a four-hour drive from here and only two hours from Lake Malawi. The other one was at Salima, which is on the lake. At the lake we stayed in a little thatch-roofed rondavel (round, whitewashed sort of adobe bungalow) right on the beach. It slept the six of us and even had a bathroom. It was idyllic.

Lake Malawi is absolutely gorgeous. It looks like a giant Lake Tahoe, but without all the people and neon lights. Clear blue water, long stretches of sandy beaches, perfect swimming conditions, all of our meals served in a dining room, tea brought to us in our bungalow at six a.m.(!), ten a.m., and three p.m., the latter usually right on the beach. What a life.

The Volunteers were such fun to be with and played with the kids a lot. We all got quite suntanned and/or burned. It was a welcome change for me. I feel physically rested now, although I just can't stop thinking (and crying) about Sister Mary Joy. I guess one never gets over something like that.

As soon as we got unpacked from the trip to the lake I went out to Nguludi to see how things are. They are so short-handed and the sisters are still exhausted. I'm planning to spend much more time out there.

Our next "event" coming up is Ricky's fourth birthday next Sunday. I'm going to town now to get his present and shop for birthday cake ingredients. I'm afraid I'm weakening to cajoling, accompanied by big blue pleading eyes, and actually might (might!) buy that little tin drum he wants so badly. Hm. We'll see.

Ricky's Fourth Birthday

Sunday, May 9, 1965

We had Ricky's birthday party today and we're all pooped. He had only four little friends come, so it really shouldn't have been so bad, but you know how kids' birthday parties are — exhausting for mothers.

The other children were terribly shy. One two-year-old American, Lauren Wallace, daughter of a Peace Corps staff man, and three "limeys" (as our boys call the British here). They were all so quiet and shy, I couldn't believe it. However, Rick made up for it by singing happy birthday to himself in his *loudest* voice, not once but twice, *pounding* on his new drum, running full-tilt around the living room, and bellowing in gleeeee. I think those shy kids were just scared and overwhelmed into stunned silence. No one but Rick ever uttered a sound — and he never stopped.

About this drum. Yes, I succumbed. It was all Rick asked for for his birthday. (Asked?! He'd been begging and pleading for it ever since the first day he had seen it in the window of Patel's Dry Goods shop downtown weeks ago). We even got it two days early before his birthday. Africa must be affecting my brain, I think. I mean, what mother in her right mind would pull such a dumb stunt as to buy her kid, especially a four-year old, a *drum*??

Even worse, as a PCV pointed out to me, "But Mrs. Lotter, that drum looks so awfully durable. Couldn't you have found one that had a *cloth* rather than metal part you beat on — you know — like you could accidentally put your foot through or something?"

Well, I'm sure that's what our neighbor, Prime Minister Dr. Hastings Kamuzu Banda, is thinking about now.

I got this stupid thing (or should I say that I stupidly bought this thing?) on Friday, and I had nearly lost my mind by Friday night. I made Ricky play it *outside* on Saturday. I thought the novelty would wear off.* I also thought that the Prime Minister was out of town. Well, it didn't and he wasn't.

About two p.m. a uniformed armed guard from the Prime Minister's compound came marching down the driveway, to the

---

[Reading this thirty-five years later I have to laugh – the "novelty" has NEVER worn off. Rick has never stopped drumming and is now a music educator and successful professional drummer (with a strong African beat). I think he was "imprinted" as a small child with the sounds of African drums.]

wide-eyed astonishment of Rick and Mike, and said, "Would you please not make that *noise?* The Prime Minister is trying to sleep."

He actually was very nice and Mike said, "Pepani, pepani" (sorry). Rick, scared to death, put away his drum.

However, Scott wasn't there at the time, so he didn't know about this little episode, and I had gone off to play tennis and had taken Ricky with me. A little while later, probably about the time Dr. Banda was just getting to sleep again, Scott spotted the unguarded drum and decided to give a little drum virtuoso concert on the front porch. Again the guard comes marching down the driveway. Again a scared kid puts the drum away.

But of course by today, being all of one whole day later, Rick forgot and while waiting for his birthday guests to arrive busied himself by performing a grand drum number on the front porch. This time the frustrated guard went to our landlord, who lives on the other side of the Prime Minister's house, and said, "Would *you* mind telling that little boy that the Prime Minister is trying to sleep?" So our landlord, Mr. Gattrell, phoned us (to my embarrassment) and repeated the request. But this time it was at four p.m. How are we ever going to figure out the Prime Minister's nap schedule??

It seems to me that *somebody* (or something?) has to *go.* Will it be the Prime Minister — or — the drum? It will be a battle, for sure. Perhaps an international incident. Who knows??

And I Only Stalled It Once

May 10, 1965

You will never guess what I did on Thursday. Mack, our sixty-four-year-old PCV who makes all that wonderful equipment for the Nguludi Mission Hospital, needed a ride out there in a truck with some big metal frames that he had made for steam tents. Since I was going out there anyway and Will had just taught me how to drive the new one-and-a-half-ton pickup truck, he got permission for me (me!) to drive it out there with Mack and his new offerings.

This truck is really a bear to drive — even the guys admit this. It's a new four-wheel drive, with the steering wheel on the *right* side, and is a terribly stiff thing to shift. When I shift into first, my left arm is completely stretched out as far as it will go. Just stepping on the gas pedal was enough to have given me a cramp in my right hip that lasted for two days when I learned to drive it up at the lake. And *I* actually drove this huge thing all the way out that awful road to Nguludi. And back again. And *I* do not really love to drive. Anything.

And I only stalled it once! That was when we approached the little narrow sideless bridge over a river that scares me to death even in our teeny little car. I guess I got rattled. I got it started again, but then I really didn't know exactly where the wheels were under this big thing. Mack looked a little pale, but said he wasn't really worried (heh heh). We inched our way across and somehow made it to the other side — then I realized I'd held my breath all the way.

Earlier, on one of the one-way roads with people on either side of us on foot and on bicycles, I had said, "Mack, do you think I come too close on your side?"

"Naw," he said, "You just took the fuzz off that fella's sweater, but that's OK." We and equipment made it out and back, but I was so exhausted that I slept for two hours when I got back and then went to bed at 8:30.

They are still having an awful time at the mission, as several of the sisters are sick now — I think probably from exhaustion and the emotional strain of Sister Mary Joy's death. In addition to going out there last Thursday, I'm going out again tomorrow, Monday. I do just love those babies, and it's really fun to see how they respond to love and attention. Just the littlest bit of holding and attention makes a noticeable change in them. It's so rewarding to see them improve and develop.

Strange and surprising things, sometimes awful, do happen

though. I happened to see Sister Damien in the butcher shop here in Blantyre and asked her how things were at the mission. She said, "Well, Anarese is terribly sick." I had just been there the day before and had happened to pay a lot of attention to Anarese, feeding and bathing her, and then rocking her to sleep before putting her down for her nap. She is about fifteen months old. She woke up two hours later with a fever of one hundred and five! I had left by then, but I'm sure she didn't have a fever when I put her down. If any, maybe ninety-nine, but surely nothing to indicate she was that ill. I just couldn't believe it.

This is what these babies often do. Since most of them are born small and ill, of mothers who die, their resistance is really low, and they can get terribly ill very suddenly. We have to watch them so carefully. One of our little tiny ones died while I was gone last week. He was so darling, and I was just sure he would make it. You never know. It's heartbreaking.

The crew all left for school and work at 7:10 this morning, and Mas has washed both the car and the truck — without even being asked! He was in the kitchen at 5:30 a.m., sweeping and mopping and setting the table for breakfast. He's always in by 6:00 a.m. He's a wonderful worker and is working out very well. We still have some communications failures now and then, but that's to be expected. We finally don't get peanut butter on the table for breakfast, but somehow not for lunch either. However, that's minor.

The other day I asked Mas for the salt and pepper at dinner and he brought in a roll of aluminum foil. (???) We couldn't quite figure that one out. Hours later I remembered that he calls aluminum foil "silver paper," and when I think about it, I guess "salt and pepper" sounds a little like "silver paper." This is only a small portion of how my day goes.

So, Rick and I are off for the Mission now, and I will mail this on the way.

Sister Mary Joy Memorial Fund

May 25, 1965

I'm spending about three days a week out at the orphanage, which means that I get little else done. But I just love it out there, and the sisters are so appreciative and really need us. We don't know when a replacement for Sister Mary Joy will come. Between Joyce and me, at least one of us is out there nearly every day.

The other day when I went out, I was pretty shook up to see that a lorry had gone off that sideless bridge just about fifteen minutes ahead of me! Some men were injured, but not too badly, and had already walked the mile or so to the Nguludi Hospital, arriving just ahead of me. They were lucky. But now it will only cause worse nightmares for me about driving across that thing.

A couple of weeks ago I wrote a long letter to Sister Mary Joy's parents. I told them all about the funeral and how beautiful it was, how everyone loved her so much, how much she meant to me, and how the sisters had never left her alone a minute during her illness. I wrote much of what I wrote to you about the funeral. I also told them what Sister Jean had said about having "our very own angel up there." I told them that I, too, like to think of her up there in her "running shoes" (those black U.S. Keds her aunt had sent her), taking care of all the little ones up there, and watching over all the little ones here in her orphanage! It was such a hard letter to write. I feel terrible for them.

Will and I wanted to do something, somehow, for Sister Mary Joy. We couldn't just simply let her go. So we've set up a "Sister Mary Joy Memorial Fund" with the Barclay's Bank and a lawyer here in Blantyre. The money will go to the Nguludi Orphanage. I've written to her family to let them know about it, and many of the PCVs are writing letters to their families also. Any amount we can raise will help, as the needs are endless — from safety pins and bottles and nipples to cribs and maybe even a water heater.

Already I'd hit up our Davis neighbors in Sunset Court for things for the orphanage before Sister Mary Joy was even sick, and from letters we're getting now, it seems that Davis is already going all out with "Money for Malawi" and several other drives. Good old Davis. If anyone is interested, or if you know of anyone who has some old money just lying around wanting to be put to good use, just send it in care of me!

Winter is setting in now. Doesn't that seem funny? It's still sunny in the afternoons but pretty chilly at night and in the mornings. Raphael, the garden man who kind of came with this house, has been building a fire in the fireplace for us every night before dinner. After much experimenting and nearly smoking ourselves out, we've discovered that he is the only one who can do it. This is our only source of heat. We've gotten out our jackets and sweaters now and have put extra blankets on all the beds. I just bought Rick the most beautiful warm ski sweater, if you can imagine, in the Kandodo store right here in Blantyre. Doesn't this all seem odd for Africa?

Will is the only one who has personally met our neighbor, Prime Minister Hastings Kamuzu Banda, but the boys and I have finally actually seen him — and this only by running out when we hear the bugles and sirens as he comes and goes. His guards try to keep things quiet for him when he's here, and for some strange reason, they don't seem to appreciate small boys with drums and firecrackers.

Firecrackers are especially a no-no here, and the boys all *know* that. With the constant threat of a rebel uprising, and living right next door to Dr. Banda, I couldn't believe it when I heard firecrackers going off in our yard — followed immediately by three guards knocking on our door. How mortifying! Drums are one thing, but firecrackers are quite another. Don, being the oldest (and commanded by a furious mom), then had to write a letter of apology, saying that he really *did* know better, and drag himself over to deliver it. We may not have met Dr. Banda, but he *knows* we're here.

Hmm. I see that he is just back from a short trip, so I must go hide away Rick's drum until the Prime Minister goes on another trip. While he was gone for two days, Rick drummed like crazy. We hear Dr. Banda is going to Europe for a month soon, so we think we'll have a big party, and Rick says he's going to play his drum every day.

I'll try to get a letter off soon. My time seems to disappear with all these extra letters to write about Sister Mary Joy, as well as going out to the mission at least every other day. Today was one of the few days I've been home all day, and six different PCVs dropped in at different times to visit. I loved it — however it's now 9:30 p.m. and I started this at 9:30 a.m.

Now It's a Home

Today is cold and damp. In the winter, which has just started here, there is what is called "chipperone," a very light rain, almost a mist or heavy fog. It's not bad enough to keep the kids from playing out in it, but they do get cold and quite damp. Looks as if the sun is trying to poke through it now.

Our house is now a *home*. Will has put up a basketball standard in the front yard. To our boys, *this* is what actually makes a real home, of course. It's standard height, set in concrete, very sturdy, and placed right where Dr. Banda's floodlights light it perfectly for night basketball. We've been having so much fun with it. Some of the PCVs come by almost every day to shoot a few baskets or play "Twenty-One" with the kids — even with me (and I'll have you know I even beat a fellow at "Twenty-One" the other day!). Then Will put up a short basketball hoop for Scott and Rick in the back yard. So *now* we're really settling in.

Yesterday we had great excitement here. Our big surface freight finally arrived! It had arrived in Beira, Mozambique on May second and we couldn't imagine what had happened to it. In it are all our bikes, records (the record player has not been off since!), books, extra clothes, pots and pans I have been needing, etc.

The best part for the boys is the enormous box of sports equipment that our friend Bob Day had collected for the schools here. He put a big box in his drugstore in Davis, got a story in the local paper, got the Junior High kids collecting athletic equipment, and you should see all the wonderful stuff! Peace Corps teachers have been going through the sports equipment and the books for their villages and schools. Don is already buried in the books. Such fun.

The best part for me, though, is the big box of baby clothes from our Sunset Court neighbors for the orphanage. Sweaters and warm sleepers, diapers, among other so-needed things. We've already been able to give warm jackets, sweaters, and shoes to some of the kids around here, Mas and Saidi's kids, especially. Mas was almost moved to tears with a warm sweater for his little boy, Saidi. We feel like Mr. and Mrs. Claus. Scott gave his best Malawian friend, Lassim, a pair of shoes and a shirt. The shoes might well be his first pair. He was here again this morning, all beaming smiles in his new regalia.

Yesterday for our regular family Saturday morning pancakes we had quite a few PCVs. Don (our twelve-year-old chef!) had this great idea of having "pancake open house" on Saturdays, so we had been telling people to drop by for pancakes if they were in town. All we have to do is make sure we have plenty of flour, baking powder, sugar, eggs, milk, butter, and syrup makings. It's easy to have unlimited numbers of people this way. Don doesn't even have to look at the recipe now and just whips them up. We can cook sixteen at once with my electric griddle and electric frying pan, then just keep on making up more batches of batter. Much easier than trying to stretch a dinner or lunch for unexpected guests. When I *know* I'm having guests for other meals it's not really hard with Mas and Raphael to help peel, chop, set the table, and — best of all — to do the dishes. But some meals don't stretch well for extra mouths. Pancake breakfasts are the answer. We want as many PCVs as possible always to feel welcome.

Some of our pancake guests yesterday were three new PCVs who were reassigned to Malawi from Indonesia, where the Peace Corps has pulled out. Will and the boys had gone out to the airport to pick them up on Friday and the strangest coincidence occurred. Don, who never goes anywhere without a book in hand (he is on number thirty since our arrival here), was carrying his current reading, which happened to be *The Doughboys*, by Larry Stallings.

So here was Don, sitting in the back of the Land Rover buried in his book, when one of the new PCVs looked back to see what he was reading and exclaimed, "Oh, my dad wrote that book."

He was Larry Stallings, Jr.! Isn't that amazing? What are the odds of this happening? Incidentally, he's from California and went to Stanford. All three are really nice guys and will be sports specialists.

This last week was really busy for me, with my having gone out to Nguludi four days, and done errands for them in town here on another day. Two of the nuns were on a trip, then a third one got sick, and Joyce was out of town. Still no replacement for Sister Mary Joy. However, it should get better now, as the two who had been away are back, and so is Joyce.

On Wednesday I had a sore throat and didn't want to get near the babies, so instead I helped in the office doing hospital records and filing. It was really interesting. I certainly am learning a lot. I dare say, so might the sisters and other future readers of these records, because on some that I was trying to record, I couldn't read some of the handwriting. So Sister Damien said, "Just get it as close as you can, and we'll figure it out." I'll bet there are some never-before-heard-of diseases recorded at that hospital now.

Will is Duty Officer at the American Embassy this weekend.

First an "immediate action" cable came that he couldn't decode, and, of all things, he couldn't get hold of any of the Embassy people who could. Swell. Actually, he has told them that Peace Corps can't do this weekend duty any more because that's when all the PCVs come in to town and need to talk to him.

Last night he got a cable that the father of one of our PCVs has died. We can't reach her by phone or wire because the lines are temporarily out to the place she is stationed, way up north. Her father's death was not unexpected and she'd already gone on home leave when he was first ill. But still, every time the phone rings when Will isn't here I'm afraid it might be she and I'll have to tell her. Oh dear.

Well, back to the unpacking, which looks as if it will take forever. But what fun to give away clothes to people who go around in ragged tee shirts and raggedy shorts, especially in this cold weather. I think we'll leave most of our clothes here when we go home.

Caught In My Nightie

Friday, June 18, 1965

Mom Lotter, your letter came yesterday with actual plans for your coming to visit us here. So now we *know* you are really going to come sometime, and we are all so excited! You asked about a hotel where you might stay — Yes, there is a hotel here, and it is called "Lotters." It has excellent accommodations, an experienced cook, lots of entertainment and company. However, it is restful after 8:00 p.m. Usually. Highly recommended by Deputy Director of the United States Peace Corps himself. Can't beat that for a recommendation.

When we bought furniture for this house we bought bunk beds for two of the kids' rooms, a good single bed for the other, plus extra cots, so that guests could stay and all we would need to do is juggle kids around. We do hope that Pamp can come, too, and think you would enjoy so many things here, Pamp — the flowers, the woodcarving, etc. — to say nothing of your grandchildren. Anyway, you would *not* be "crowding our house," and even if you were (which you won't), it would be such a nice crowd.

You asked which time of year is best and we are thinking that maybe just after the rains in April and May, but that is such a long time off. You had mentioned fall, but we hear it is too hot. Aha! Idea. Come right now! The weather is perfect. Well, I know that's impossible, but it's fun to think about.

Our cold spell has turned into a beautiful spring-like week with blue sky and warm sunshine. It's so beautiful here. I love looking off at the mountains in the distance. There are a couple of them that we are anxious to climb, some being only half-day hikes to the top.

Will was away this week on a trip up north visiting PCVs. The other day Mike and I felt like going on a hike on one of these beautiful days. Don and Scott were both at friends' houses, so Mike and I took the dogs, left Rick to go to a park with Mas, and off we went. Since we weren't sure where to go, we stopped off at the house of some PCVs who also like to hike, to get their recommendations — and they wanted to come, too. These three guys are favorites around our house, not only because they are nice people, but because (maybe even especially because) they have motorcycles and can be wheedled by little boys into being taken for short spins up and down our road! They are health workers in the Peace Corps tuberculosis eradication project and are issued motorcycles because they have to travel so far out into the bush to visit remote villages, both to test for and give medication for TB. This group is the only group of PCVs to be issued motorcycles. Each PCV in this group (I think there are forty) has a Malawian partner who rides with the PCV. It's an incredibly important program, as there is lots of TB here.

We had a wonderful hike in a pine forest and the scenery there reminded me of the Sierras at home in California — the first time I've felt a bit of nostalgia for home. Interestingly, two of these fellows are also from California and thought the same thing. Somehow, it seems strange to me to have pine groves in Africa. We do have a small grove in our backyard here, but this was huge and looked, felt, and smelled like the Sierras. Mike and the dogs loved it, and we all had a great day.

Will came home on Saturday and was to play in a tennis tournament on Sunday in Cholo, about forty-five minutes' drive from here. The three PCVs we'd gone hiking with, Mike, Bill, and Les, came over on Sunday and baby-sat our four boys plus Mike Leach, so Joyce Leach and I could go watch the tournament. They *offered* to do this! They played basketball all day with them, even helped with homework, and of course were conned into short jaunts on motorcycles. What nice guys.

Raphael, our gardener, works in the house on Fridays on Mas's day off. He speaks very little English and apparently understands even less. Many Malawians don't actually speak much English, but seem to at least understand a lot. Not Raphael. I have to carry my Chinyanja dictionary with me all day, repeat everything three times — and say, "Mwamva?" (Do you understand?) "Inde, Madam." (Yes, Madam). But he doesn't seem to understand the very same words we use every single day, all the time.

Last Friday I had to go out too early to turn on the roast for dinner, therefore decided to put it in the cold oven and tell Raphael to turn it on at three-thirty. He does know how to tell time. Then I said to shell the peas and peel the potatoes and just leave them — that I would cook them when I got home at five-thirty. Three times I said this, and three times "Mwamva?" In Chinyanja, plus sign language. "Yes, Madam."

Well, I got home at five-thirty and the roast was cooking — but so were the peas and potatoes — *all* since three-thirty. "Done, Madam," said Raphael proudly. They certainly were. This is only one of many adventures with Raphael. I think it's a good thing I have a sense of humor, although I didn't laugh too hard when he washed my favorite dress — which used to be white with red polka dots — with the boys' blue jeans, and is now a dingy gray with sort of dull reddish polka dots.

Will was gone again last night and one of the dogs wanted out in the middle of the night. So I got up (grumble) to let him out. *Not* Cheena, however, as she is in heat again — but when I opened the door, awayyy Cheena went before I could grab her. I was so *mad!* Usually she minds well, but I called and whistled and threatened — in my flimsy nightie on the front porch at 1:00 a.m. Then slowly up over Dr. Banda's wall first appeared a rifle (pointed up, fortunately), followed by a police hat and black face. There I was — caught in the floodlights! However, he just grinned and discreetly climbed back down. Guess I'll grab my robe next time. I could just imagine them all giggling over there.

This also brings to mind that while Dr. Banda is away now, those guards are really having a blast. The guards' quarters are out in back near our back door, and we can hear loud laughing and singing and radios blaring. It's certainly not like that when the Prime Minister is here. Shall I tattle?

Going North

July 7, 1965

Finally I'm going to get to go on a trip up north with Will to see Livingstonia and the northern area. Will has to go up there to visit PCVs and has decided that this would be a good chance for me to go along to see this part of Malawi for the first time.

As if this weren't exciting enough, a PCV has to drive a Land Rover up to Livingstonia with some equipment, and Will thought that this would be a golden opportunity for Don and Mike, who have school holiday now, to see this part of the country, too. It's about five hundred miles up there, and people rarely drive that far. It's definitely not like five hundred miles of American highway.

Don and Mike leave tomorrow, Thursday, and Will and I leave on Friday to fly up to Mzuzu where we'll pick up a Land Rover, visit PCVs, and then meet the boys in Livingstonia on Saturday. The boys will fly back by themselves on Monday, and we on Tuesday. We are all very excited.

Will's two Peace Corps secretaries, Sheila Thomson and Sue Urbonas, have offered to stay here at the house with Scott and Rick after working hours, and all night each night. Mas and Raphael are here with them all day, so it should work out fine, especially since the boys just love Sheila and Sue.

Sheila was born and raised in Malawi. Her father was a tea planter here, originally from Scotland, where he and Sheila's mother now live. We all love Sheila's Scottish-British accent ("you must take your vitt-amins on shed-ule..."). She was hired by Peace Corps in the very beginning of Peace Corps Malawi. Sue is a PCV secretary and she and Sheila have become best friends. Every once in a while they come by to see if any of the boys want to go swimming or to a movie or some other fun thing.

[After we came home from Malawi, Will and I served as father and mother of the bride for Sheila when she married an American in Mercer Island, Washington. She'd met Dale Shirley when he traveled through Africa with a gymnastics team. We were very touched that Sheila asked us to stand in for her parents, who had not been able to travel from Scotland, and Will felt especially honored to walk Sheila down the aisle to give her away.

Sue (Davis) and family live in Baltimore and in a way, we have come full circle as families because their daughter, Meghan, was a veterinary student at UC Davis where we live, so we got to play surrogate parents for her. She is now "Dr. Meg" and is in practice in Pennsylvania.]

* * *

July 8, 1965

George, the PCV who is driving the Land Rover, picked up Don and Mike at 6:00 this morning. A VSO (the British volunteer equivalent of our Peace Corps) also went along. What a sight this Land Rover was! There was all this katundu (stuff) that has to be delivered to schools and PCVs all along the way, and since Will is going to be giving sports clinics for some of the schools, there were javelins tied on top, deflated volley balls rolling around, sleeping bags, suitcases, kids and their stuff — and of all things — poor George — a mother cat and two guinea pigs! I wonder if this comes under the heading of "above and beyond the call of duty?"

I've been organizing the food, casseroles and such, to be left here for while we're gone, plus food for the boys to take on this trip with George, and trying to pack our stuff as well. Mas is doing really well with the cooking now, and I'm sure he'll do fine. I've been encouraging him to do more and more so that he will be able to get a good job when we leave. He was sick yesterday and did I miss him!

Raphael is almost impossible to communicate with, and when I had so much to do yesterday it was not a good time to have *him* in the kitchen instead of Mas. For instance, I was making cupcakes for the boys to take today and had melted half a cube of butter for the icing and left the room for a few minutes — came back and found the bowl all washed and back in the cupboard and no melted butter. When I asked Raphael where the butter was, he showed me the box of butter cubes in the refrigerator. "No, the butter in the bowl —" I said. "Bowl clean," he said, proudly showing me the clean bowl.

Yeah. Oh well. I gave up. It was gone anyway, so I didn't bother pursuing it further and just started over again.

We've already had a few other go-arounds, as you know. But it seems every time I throw my hands up in despair with him, he goes and does some wonderful thing like waxing all the floors without my asking him to, or washing the car, or cleaning all the woodwork. Pretty smart, I guess.

July 6 was Malawi Independence Day and the reason for the boys being on "holiday" from school. It was very exciting around here. Malawi flags were everywhere, all up and down our street, in front of Dr. Banda's house especially, and all over town.

We went to the big celebration in the National Stadium that afternoon and were lucky to sit in the grandstands, right in front. There were tribal dancers from all the different tribes and areas in

Malawi, and it was really spectacular to see. There were about twenty different groups, each dressed in its own tribal garb — some in animal skins, some in a conglomeration of feathers and leaves, the women in beautiful brightly colored cloth dresses with each whole group dressed alike in its own fabric. The dancing was wonderful, all to drumbeat — lots of drums — and the steps were so complicated that if you saw just one person doing it you would think he was just making it up as he went along, but when you realized that there were fifteen or twenty of them doing this with perfect precision — it was pretty amazing. We were just fascinated and stayed all afternoon.

Our neighbor, the Prime Minister, made his grand entrance into the stadium standing up in the back of his gorgeous red Rolls Royce convertible, waving his traditional fly whisk, as they slowly circled the whole field. We still have not met him, although one day he actually waved his fly whisk at us!

Last week when he came home from his month's European trip we could hardly get out of our driveway for all the people lining the street waiting for him. They were lined up for miles and for hours, singing and clapping and waiting just to see him go by. I didn't get a thing done that day, there was so much to watch — and right in front of our house.

We have found out that the schoolchildren are actually *required* to line the roads and highways, often for hours in the hot sun, whenever the Prime Minister is to pass.

Sir Glyn Jones, the British High Commissioner, and Lady Jones made a grand entrance at the stadium in their big black limousine. That was fun because Sir Glyn, whom we'd just met at the Fourth of July American picnic, spotted Will in the grandstand and waved at us. Will had been in charge of the Fourth of July games (of course) that day, and Sir Glyn, who was a special guest, especially wanted to see an American baseball game. So Will got it all organized, and then he and Sir Glyn stood right behind the pitcher so Will could explain it all to Sir Glyn. When that just wasn't enough, Sir Glyn wanted to try hitting — and then running the bases! It was a kick, and everyone loved it. Sir Glyn really enjoyed himself.

Must go finish cooking and then pack. Scott is baking cookies right now, and they smell so good. He and Rick are excited about Sheila and Sue coming to stay.

To Livingstonia

July 13, 1965

Our trip up north surpassed all our expectations. We had such a good time, met lots of interesting people, and learned so much about the north. Don and Mike had a great time with George, the PCV who drove them up there. He is really good with kids, and they stopped all along the way at missions and schools, spending two nights in rest houses. They saw and learned a lot and were especially impressed with the Catholic brothers at the missions. They were very friendly, showed them all around, and best of all, according to Mike, "They all had motorcycles and big dogs!" (I mean — what could be more important to eleven- and twelve-year-old boys?)

Will and I didn't see the boys until Saturday noon when we finally arrived in Livingstonia. Our trip had been wonderful, too, although it started out a little funny. We'd thought we were booked on the DC3 up to Mzuzu but got to the airport and found out that we were scheduled on the little single engine plane called the "Beaver," a six-seater (including pilot) plane. Quite a difference from the larger two-engine DC3.

We had noticed that the airport personnel looked sort of surprised when we checked in with a javelin, a sack of shots (for shot put), discuses, plus our luggage, and seemed equally astonished that I was wearing heels and a nice dress. I had noticed that women who flew on the DC3 tended to dress up. Women are not allowed to wear slacks or trousers of any sort here, so a dress didn't look so odd — but heels? On the Beaver? Needless to say I wore Keds coming back. With deft juggling they did manage to get us and all our stuff in, and the flight was really fun.

The pilot flew so low most of the way that we could see everything below and even wave to people on the ground. Since a plane only comes in once a week, each place we landed — Lilongwe, Mzimba, and Mzuzu — became a big social event drawing crowds of people to watch the plane land. At Mzimba we noticed two white faces looking up from below, and they turned out to be PCVs. When we landed they invited us to stop on our way back down in a few days and have dinner with them and spend the night, which we did.

Looking down from the plane it was interesting to try to figure out the village patterns. The farther north we got, the more organized pattern there seemed to be. We were told that the Ngoni tribes, which inhabit the north, have a rather more structured society than the tribes in the central and southern regions. It certainly appeared so from the air. Another thing I noticed was that all the fenced cattle corrals had a sort of hump in the middle, looking oddly like brown bubbles from above. The pilot said these were for the cattle to stand up on to better protect themselves from leopards and lions. We didn't know whether to believe that or not, but it sounded dramatic and added to the fun of flying in this little plane.

We had a good visit with the PCVs in Mzuzu, spent the night there, then took a Peace Corps Jeep to drive up the long, mountainous escarpment to Livingstonia. There were only very small villages along the steep road, some perched precariously (I thought) on the mountainsides. There was dense growth and gorgeous scenery all the way up and then finally at the very top on a plateau — Livingstonia, overlooking Lake Malawi far below.

Livingstonia is important in the history of Malawi. It is one of the oldest missions in Africa and was named after David Livingston, who is said to be the first white man to have been there. The ancient church and all the old buildings are of red brick, lending themselves well to the picturesque beauty of the place. The church has a lovely stained glass window with a scene depicting David Livingston making friends with the Africans.

The Peace Corps has ten volunteers there. All the rest of the non-Malawi population are missionaries, totaling twenty-seven, including children. We visited and ate with the PCVs, but stayed overnight with a charming Presbyterian missionary family from Ireland. They have two little boys, but somehow made room for the four of us and were very welcoming and hospitable. There is no electricity after nine-thirty at night, which added to the charm, and we all sat up chatting by the fire. We loved it.

On Sunday morning Will, Don, Mike, and I drove to Nkata Bay. Now *there* is the place. It was the most beautiful place I've ever seen, and I've announced that I'm planning to live there in my next life! The crystal clear blue lake, lovely little bay, trees, flowers, even wild orchids, all added to the peaceful and magical charm.

There is one PCV couple there who are the only white inhabitants. Tom and Ruth Nighswander are in the TB eradication program, live right in the village in African housing and love it there. They seem like an ideal Peace Corps couple, if there is such a thing. They speak fluent Tonga, the language there, ride a Honda motorbike out to the surrounding villages to do their tuberculosis work, and the people love them.

We stayed in the Nkata Bay Rest House that night. The next morning we hiked with Tom and Ruth out to the nearest village to watch them give medications to their patients. It was inspiring to watch the interaction with the people and see the obvious affection the Malawians have for them.

We swam in the lake, had a glorious time, then drove to Mzuzu, where we spent the night before putting Don and Mike on the Beaver to return to Blantyre. They had missed school that day, Monday, and needed to be back for school on Tuesday. Then Will and I drove on to Mzimba to visit our four PCVs there. More wonderful PCVs, doing inspiring work. I just love getting to know these volunteers. We visited the school of the two young women who were teachers there, and then went with the couple, who were health workers, out to a village to watch them treat their tuberculosis patients.

There was a scene out there at the village we were visiting that really touched us. Bill and Gail VanWie, the Peace Corps couple, had been away for a couple of weeks, and there was a very old lady there who had been waiting and waiting for them to come back. She was terribly poor, dressed in rags, but had somehow acquired a chicken (live) that she wanted to give them. This was like a fortune for her, and her sweet, wizened face was just radiant when she gave it to them. Bill and Gail fully appreciated what a big thing this was for her and we all got choked up — I just had to walk away. There are so many of these little scenes that turn out to be the big things you remember — that make you realize it's all worth the effort. We were very impressed with all the PCVs we met on this trip.

We flew home on the Beaver from Mzimba. It was a marvelous trip — and I was anxious to find out how our home-based crew had fared.

Doors I Have Seen

[This is not from my letters, but from an indelibly-stamped memory I have. At the time it happened, in July of 1965, it didn't seem an appropriate thing to write home about, as it didn't exactly enhance the image of the U.S. Peace Corps Volunteer. And besides, Will was too mad. I wish, however, that I'd written it up at the time at least for myself, because I thought it was both horrifying – and funny.]

When we had asked Sheila and Sue if they would baby-sit for us during our trip up north, they had said that they would like to, but had planned to have a small party at their apartment and had already invited people. We said they could go ahead and have the party at our house. We totally trusted Sheila and Sue and just said to keep it "under control," and especially to remember who our neighbor was.

One of the party guests was Phil Durand, one of our "more mature" PCVs, an attorney helping Malawi set up a new judicial system. He was also a very talented cartoonist. We have many of his cartoons to this day and really think he missed his calling and could actually have been a cartoonist for a national magazine. At parties he was especially popular with all of us, drawing endless cartoons of people and events. We must have at least fifty of them.

As always, Phil was drawing cartoons at the party, but it seems that he ran out of paper. When the party was getting better and he still couldn't find any paper, he apparently got looking at our many white doors — perfect for cartoons — much bigger than just a piece of paper. Much better.

He started in on the door into the living room and did a quite wonderful drawing, complete with title, "A Man's Home Is His Castle," with an elaborate, tall, turreted castle rising from the bottom of the door to the very top, complete with moats, and four little boys and dogs, cats, and other animals climbing all over it. It was awesome.

However — it was done with *indelible felt pen markers.* Then Phil proceeded to do all the other doors in the house. Wonderful renderings of "The Baby-sitters," always with Sheila's bright red hair and Sue's blond pageboy. Unmistakable caricatures. The bathroom door had Sheila in the bathtub (only the red hair visible) with dogs, cats, other animals, bubbles, splashes. Actually now I can't remember the others (wish I had taken photos) — but no door was spared.

During the evening, however, someone must have pointed out that felt pens won't wash off — but this statement was apparently negated by another party guest who said that it *"would* wash off." So on every one of the elaborately decorated doors was written, "Gunsberg says this will wash off."

Well, we came home to two totally chagrined and embarrassed baby-sitters who had practically scrubbed their fingers down to the bone, with hours and hours of trying to "wash it off." They'd tried everything anyone suggested to get it off, even having gone to the "chemist" to buy something. Nothing fazed it.

It's really hard to describe our feelings when we saw the doors. No, I take that back. It is not hard to describe Will's feelings. *Mad.* We stood there in disbelief for a while. I, however, recovering from the initial shock (remember — this was the house that had all been recently freshly painted) just couldn't help but admire them. They were really incredibly good. And very funny. I had to be careful to laugh only when Will didn't see me, however. To me they were New Yorker-worthy.

Phil didn't dare show his face — to either the baby-sitters or, *especially*, to Will.

The inevitable confrontation came in the Peace Corps Office when Phil came slinking sheepishly in after Will's angry summons. I'm sure that Sheila and Sue were hiding. By the sober light of the next day Phil had no doubt figured out that this artistic endeavor had not been quite such a clever idea. I don't think that Will had to say much more than for Phil to go *right* out and buy paint and repaint every blankety-blank door *right now*. One look at Will's face was enough, I'm sure.

It took three coats of paint to cover it all. Apparently felt pens just bleed into the coats of paint. I did notice that Phil, strangely, kept coming to paint when neither Will nor I was there.

Years later at a Malawi Peace Corps reunion Phil drew a wonderful cartoon (on paper) of Sheila, Sue, and other PCVs, prostrate with grief, waving tearful goodbyes to a plane which had just taken off from Chileka Airport, with the words of Guy Gunsberg floating out to the departing plane — "But I tell you Durand — it *will* wash off... . " (Actually Phil stayed and finished out his two years.)

To this day, Sheila and Sue are still embarrassed. However, enough time has gone by that we all laugh about it a lot. Even Will. Recently Sue came to California to visit and brought us a present — a box of *washable* felt markers. We are going to send them to Phil at his distinguished law firm in Tennessee, where he is a well-known and successful attorney.

[Unfortunately, before we got around to sending the markers, Phil passed away after a long illness. Phil's family gave us permission to print this episode as well as some of his cartoons.]

CARTOON BY PHIL DURAND

New Director Comes
So Does Haile

August 19, 1965

Finally the new Peace Corps Director has arrived to replace Jim Blackwell, whose term was up. For a while Will was doing both jobs, Director and Deputy Director, while Jim was getting ready to leave. The new director's name is Mike McCone. He and his wife, Nini, are both from San Francisco and have three little boys, three, four, and five — to Rick's great joy. We even have some friends in common, although Mike went to Yale and Nini to Stanford. We discovered that Mike's stepsister, another Jane, was a good friend of mine at Cal. Small world.

The McCones were two years in the Peace Corps in Sierra Leone, followed by Mike's working in the Peace Corps office in Washington, DC, so he brings lots of experience to the job, and Will is really looking forward to working with him. Also, not the least important thing — they are both tennis players! We really like them a lot and think we'll have a great time together.

Earlier this month Emperor Haile Selassie of Ethiopia paid a state visit to Malawi. Such folderol getting ready for this. There were red, yellow and green Ethiopian flags everywhere. Our little road up to Kamuzu's house had twenty-six of them, mounted on white twenty-foot-tall poles — quite spectacular — and we felt like celebrities, just driving between them going up the hill to our house.

When Haile Selassie arrived in Blantyre the grand procession through town was a mob scene, especially because it was a command performance for all the schoolchildren. Stores and banks were closed, and the streets were lined with people, police and special guards. A motorcade of white-uniformed police on motorcycles preceded black limousines with dignitaries. Then Haile and Kamuzu, standing up in the back of Kamuzu's red Rolls Royce convertible — Haile, resplendent in his medal-adorned uniform, and Kamuzu waving his fly whisk. (Isn't it nice to be on such friendly, first-name terms with an Emperor and a Prime Minister?) We did get a good close-up view and photos as they passed right under the Peace Corps office window. We probably won't get too many chances to be only ten yards away from an Emperor and a Prime Minister at the same time.

Joyce Leach and I gave a dinner party together last night at the Leaches' house to welcome two new Peace Corps doctors and their wives and to bid farewell to the doctor who is leaving. I had taken one of the new Peace Corps doctors out to Nguludi with me yesterday morning, and he was just as intrigued as all the rest of us. Then Joyce and I both cooked all afternoon, and the party went well and was fun. Today we have to make two trips out to the airport to say goodbyes and then go to a wedding this evening. Not much time for thumb twiddling around here.

A couple of weeks ago we hiked up one of the mountains we'd been wanting to climb for some time. Will had just bought a new, (actually second-hand, but like new) Roleiflex camera in Salisbury and was anxious to try it out. Since Will was carrying Rick on his back up a steep part, Don put on the backpack with the camera in it. Then the most unbelievable thing happened. Don opened up the backpack to get something, sort of leaning over at the same time — and out and down went the new camera! I was climbing up below and saw it go tumbling and clanking by my disbelieving eyes. Awful. Not even registered for insurance yet, either. At risk of life and limb, I climbed down and retrieved it — crying all the way. We don't know if it's repairable or not. Seventy-five feet it bounced down the rocks!

We had another traumatic experience last week. We had to fire Raphael. Things had been building up for quite a while, as you may have noticed. Although we liked him personally, we just couldn't keep overlooking all the things he did wrong — over and over again — with poor Mas having to work even harder to do them over right. Three times he didn't come back after his day off, the third time for five whole days, so we just had to let him go. Old soft-hearted Will had to do it and hated it. We'd put it off for such a long time, hoping Raphael would shape up.

We no sooner let Raphael go than a steady stream of men asking for work started coming to our door. Bush radio at work, I guess. So we have already hired a new man, Phillip, to work in the house and help our greatly overworked Mas. Phillip is a big, strong, handsome, good-natured guy, and is seeming to work out really well. Also, we are trying out a new gardener whose name is Friday. It's a new cast of characters around here right now.

On a happy note — the boys got their report cards and despite the many problems, they all did really well. We are especially proud of Mike, who has had such bad luck with teachers (really mean ones who simply don't like Americans). He has "hung in there tough," as Will puts it, and did fine. Now when PCVs ask him how school is going, he says, "I'm doing OK." This is a real change, and we feel much better.

Guests, Tennis, & Snakes

Tuesday, September 7, 1965

It's been school "holiday" now for three weeks, so in addition to all our own kids being home, PCVs were in town from all over Malawi. It was Grand Central Station here. For some odd reason the high school gets four weeks and the other schools only get three, so Don is lording it over Mike and Scott at every opportunity.

To go anywhere in Malawi you almost *have* to come through Blantyre, so this is why we've had such a deluge of vacationing PCVs. A lot of these PCVs only get here once a year or so, and this was our only chance to have them over — so we've had dinner guests, lunch guests, breakfast guests, and house guests. I think we've had only one dinner without extra people in the last couple of weeks — but it's been fun and is the way we like it. Thank goodness for Mas.

Ironically the two house guests we had, at separate times, were staying with us because:

a) one thought it would be quieter here than at the Field Center.

b) the other was recuperating from surgery.

Both went back to their posts later for a rest cure.

No, actually we had a lot of fun, and I think they fared OK. The first one was Emily, our "Senior PCV," who is seventy years old, a retired college professor from a small eastern college, in Vermont, I think. She also taught for a number of years at Vassar. She is wonderful and a ball of fire, and hikes and hitchhikes all over the country. If only I could be like that at seventy! She even survived sleeping in Scott's lower bunk with Scott thrashing around above her, fighting snakes and leopards all night. This we didn't realize until Emily clued us in. Poor Scott — or poor Emily?? Anyway, Emily was here for five days, and we thoroughly enjoyed her.

Then a very nice young PCV from New York came for four or five days, right out of the hospital after an appendectomy. He was very easy to have around and shared Don's room, which worked out well as they both read all day and half the night. He did comment when he left that he'd hardly ever seen a house with so many people in and out. True, true. As one motorcycle left, another was coming in, to Rick's delight because he got his usual ride on the back of each one, up and down the road. Anyway, it was lots of fun but not very conducive to letter-writing.

Now school has started for the PCVs and for Mike and Scott.

Don is still home and taking advantage of every opportunity to "sympathize" with Mike and Scott that they have to go to school, do homework, etc. while he goofs off. Things are getting somewhat back to normal, though I'm not sure what "normal" is around here, and I see a quiet morning hopefully ahead of me. No, I hopefully see a quiet morning ahead of me.

This is big tennis tournament time here. First came the Blantyre Tournament, which was several weeks ago. Will lucked out and won the Men's Singles after some long, great battles. Then he won the Men's Singles Handicap, and he and his Malawian partner, Maluwa, won the Men's Doubles Handicap. Maluwa is a delightful young man whom we sponsor in the Sports Club. Handicap tournaments are especially enjoyable because the better players start out each game with minus points, and lesser players (like me) start out each game with plus points. It makes matches more even. Then Will and I lost in the finals of the Mixed Handicap (I was his handicap!) and I lost in the finals of the Ladies' Handicap. I felt very lucky to have gotten to the finals, and it was fun.

The National Tournament, which was next, has been very exciting, going on for several weeks. Last week the finals were played before huge crowds. Will played a local British player in the finals of the Men's Singles and after a long close match, four sets, (they play the best of five), he *won* the Malawi National Men's Singles.

Governor General Sir Glyn and Lady Jones, who were honored guests, later presented the large silver trophies. It's the first time any American has won any Malawi national tournament. It was very satisfying (to put it mildly). There were other Americans playing in the finals, and we thought we Americans would do better overall, but Will was the only one who won. He is playing the best tennis he's ever played and he especially likes playing on clay courts.

Tennis is such a big deal in this country. They make a huge fuss over it. There have been two big "Tennis Balls." Yes, that's what they call them. After the matches we all went home and got dressed up for the "Tennis Ball" which was held at the Limbe Club. Some of the players were quite pooped, having played all day. But it was fun.

They have the nicest tradition: the winners fill their trophies with chilled champagne and go around offering their cups to everyone else — very friendly and jolly-like. Well, at least we *thought* it was a nice tradition, believing the champagne was gratis — until Will came sneaking over and whispered, "Do you have some pounds in your purse?" Oh oh. And *his* trophy held at least a quart.

Will's National trophy was first awarded in 1902. He keeps it and the Blantyre one for a year, then they go on to the next winners. Both are huge and very beautiful. He has smaller replicas to keep. This winning gets expensive — we not only had to fill them with champagne, but now we find that we have to insure them. So much for winning tournaments!

We took the African men who had played in the tournament to the party as our guests. This was a "first" and worked out well. Everyone was very nice to them. You can probably imagine the background to all this. There are so many colonialists here who believe in "segregated" clubs. But we were terribly pleased that the Tennis Association President gave them a very nice welcome, had them all stand up, and said he hoped there would be more Malawians next year. We felt we had made some progress in our attempts to integrate the Sports Club. It's a small thing, but you have to start somewhere.

Maluwa went with us to the tennis party this last weekend also. Another first, as this one was at the Blantyre Sports Club, which is supposedly "integrated," but not that we had been able to observe. Maluwa couldn't be nicer, has perfect manners, and we just love him. Now if we can get more expatriates and others to invite Malawians, maybe things will get better. The only tennis courts and swimming pools are in the sports clubs here, and for the sake of the kids there's nothing to do but join, and then work to try to improve the situation.

The boys are a lot happier now, as three new American families with U.S.A.I.D. (U.S. Agency for International Development) just moved in down at the bottom of our hill. They have kids the ages of our boys, so they have new friends. It's really made a big change for our boys. The British children still will not accept Americans.

Prior to these American families' moving in, our boys actually had needed to try to get along with each other, and sometimes even did. (Would miracles never cease?) Now they don't *have* to get along because they each have new friends. So they don't, of course. Hmm. There are lots of kids in and out of our house now, friends staying overnight, and much activity. There are two treehouses and several clubhouses going. This makes a huge difference in the lives of little boys in a strange country. They still have lots of Malawian friends who come to play, as well.

Saturday we were eating breakfast when Scott's Malawian friend, Lassim, who has been his friend ever since we arrived here, came into the house all breathless. It seems that a lion had killed a man in his village the night before. He lives only about three miles away. The boys were quite excited about it. There we were, eating our perfectly civilized American-type pancake breakfast in our perfectly civilized (well, sort of) American-type house, making it easy to kind of forget where we are. But you remember fast when someone comes running in to tell you something like that!

A few weeks ago they killed a black mamba in the men's bathroom at the Field Center. We remembered that we were in Africa then too, and were awfully glad we weren't still living in the Field Center. The black mamba is said to be one of the most aggressive and deadly snakes in Africa, if not *the* deadliest. Its venom is almost always fatal. So far, we have only had to fight cockroaches and bed bugs here in this house, neither of which I relish, but I must admit they beat snakes and lions.

Will is busy as can be with his work. You probably are saying, "oh sure — " after all the tennis stories. You probably don't think he even works at all. However, this is my fault, as I seem to write about all the frills and fun, and not so much about his work. And tennis was on the weekends, although there were also Peace Corps crises then, too.

Actually, there is never a dull moment with 260 PCVs. Thirty new ones came in last week. The Peace Corps staff has to be sure everything is set up ahead for their jobs, housing, etc., and still take care of all the everyday problems that come up.

Something is always happening. For instance, a phone call came the other night at home, from a PCV who had just flown in from Dar Es Salaam from his vacation. It seems the PCV he was with had been apprehended by the Tanzania police and not allowed to board the plane for Malawi, as he had simply taken a picture of a Soviet plane. A commercial one at that. This, then, involved many calls and cables to and from the American Embassy here and in Washington, DC. The flurry of excitement did simmer down shortly, with the young man being allowed to catch the next plane. This is just an example.

I am still busy with the Nguludi orphanage and am so happy and grateful that money is coming in for the Sister Mary Joy Fund. We just can't thank all of you enough, not only for the money, but also all the diapers and things you've sent. All the sisters out at the Mission send their gratitude too.

The babies are so precious and are getting more and more responsive to love and attention. There is something especially appealing about a little baby who has no mother to love it. With this money coming in, we hope to improve the equipment and the conditions for the overworked sisters. Sister Mary Joy is never out of our minds and hearts. Now there will be tangible remembrances.

The Fund and More Puppies

September 8, 1965

A little baby whose mother died in childbirth was born on the day that Sister Mary Joy died. So guess what her name is? Of course — Mary Joy! She is a beautiful four-month-old baby now and naturally is very special to everyone. I took some pictures of her yesterday, and I hope they turn out. I hear that Sister Mary Joy's family is quite interested in her, and I thought I might send them some pictures.

The Sister Mary Joy Fund is growing, and I'm really getting excited about it. A lady from Philadelphia whom Will met just briefly in Paris has been corresponding with us, and a little while ago she sent us a *New York Times* clipping about the Nguludi Mission. Apparently it was in a lot of papers and was an Associated Press release. She asked, "Do you know this Mission?" Will wrote back a glowing (evidently) letter about how we surely did know it, told all about it, and mentioned the Sister Mary Joy Fund.

Now we just received a letter from her in which she said Will's letter was the most inspiring letter she had ever read. I wish I had read it. Will can't even remember what he said. She asked if she could send his letter to a newspaper. She and her husband were enclosing a small contribution to help the orphanage fund — one hundred dollars! Boyy. I just fairly flew out to the Mission to show Mother Catherine and the sisters, and we are all ecstatic.

There are two things we'd like to do first with the money. First, and most important, is to get a water heater so we can give the babies warm baths more easily. We have to heat their bath water in a kettle on the two-burner kerosene stove — for nineteen babies. Sometimes some have to have cold baths, which I just hate to give.

The other is to get a blender to make baby food with. You can't buy strained meat here at all, although you can get all the other kinds of baby food. I've been cooking ground ("minced") beef and putting it in my blender and taking plastic bags of it out to them for the babies. But if the sisters had their own blender they could do this themselves. They grow their own vegetables and could easily blend them as well. Too, in the future there might not be anyone like Peace Corps wives around who would be able do these things.

I really can't believe that I've only been interrupted once while I've been typing this and that was by the plumber, whom I was *really* glad to see. He came to hook up our new washing machine. Yahoo.

Announcement: Cheena had eleven puppies a week ago yesterday! Again. Two died, so we *only* have nine. Again. Her last ones are only six months old, you know. We kept one of them, Alipo, so we have eleven dogs now. She has had twenty-nine puppies in just a little over a year. We will for sure have her spayed as soon as she weans these. I know, I know — I said this before, but somehow lost track of time. The boys are planning to sell these pups this time and earn money towards buying Alipo's airline ticket home. Hmmmm.

The kids found a small snake in their underground fort in the backyard, and Friday, our new gardener, killed it. We don't know what kind it was, but it seems that most of the snakes here are venomous. The boys somehow lost their taste for the underground fort. Isn't that odd? This is the only one we have seen alive.

A boomslang was, however, killed in the Pecks' garden about half a mile away. The African boomslang is another snake with deadly venom. Dr. Peck is the Peace Corps doctor in charge of the Tuberculosis Eradication program. When his wife, Barbara, told me about the boomslang, I thought she said *she* had killed it, and I was overcome with admiration, as she is the one who hit a burglar over the head with a flashlight one night and told him to "just run along home." Actually — darn — it was her gardener who had killed the snake. Too bad. Would have made a much better story.

Another flash! It looks like Will will be going to the States in November for about three weeks. Staff overseas are supposed to get to Washington once a year to go through the mid-selection boards of the next Volunteer group. This one is at Syracuse, N.Y. Then they are expected to go out for one week's recruiting trip somewhere. Soooo — I've already started my shopping list for him and must get all our Christmas letters ready ahead of time so he can mail them there. Doubt if he will get out to California, but you never know.

Please send us news. We don't get enough here. We are sick about the Watts riots in L.A. We do get *Time* magazine, etc., but we would like more news and wonder how much we miss.

[After Will's parents got this letter, Mom Lotter decided we should have just about every magazine printed. We were thereafter deluged with news and sports magazines. And all of them got read from cover to cover and made a wonderful "library" in our living room for visiting hungering-for-news-from-home PCVs.]

Burglars and Other Funny Things

September 10, 1965

After a lovely and quiet morning, Will came home for lunch and said, "Guess what? I guess we'll have to postpone the Mozambique trip again until the first of October." I just went on eating my lunch. Nothing surprises me any more. "Be flexible in the Peace Corps," they say. You ought to see how flexible I am. This is only about the fourteenth time this long-planned trip has been postponed.

There are so many things to tell about here that I barely scratch the surface in my letters home. Really wish I had time to write every day. So many funny tales.

Last week the Leaches had a burglar. There are lots of them here in the nicer areas of Blantyre and Limbe. Violent crimes against people are virtually unheard of in Malawi, but there is property theft, principally in urban areas. Volunteers out in the countryside, which is 80% of the country, tell us they never lock their houses and have no problems in this regard.

Anyway, Joyce and Wes both woke up in the middle of the night, having heard something. They both thought someone was in their room. It was pitch black. Wes sort of slithered out of bed and stood there listening. Joyce was lying there scared spitless. Then Wes apparently realized that the burglar was outdoors outside their French doors, which were right beside the bed. But he didn't tell Joyce, who still thought someone was *in* the room.

The best thing Wes could think of to do was to scare the burglar. So, without warning Joyce, Wes suddenly ripped open the drapes, which were on metal rings on a metal rod (loud), pounded with both fists on the metal and glass doors (*really loud*), and *roared!*

To make it funnier to envision — Wes is very blond and sleeps in his nothingness. Well, he did succeed in scaring the burglar, who dropped his file and ran like crazy, no doubt thinking a white maniacal ghost lived there. But this is *nothing* compared to how he just about scared Joyce out of her wits! She was sure he'd been stabbed in the back by a burglar in the room. It wasn't until a little later that she thought it was very funny. Frankly, I can't control my giggles every time I think about it.

Another funny thing happened yesterday. Or I guess I just have an odd sense of humor. I took the car into a garage because the door on the driver's side won't open (again). I said to the mechanic at the garage, a nice Portuguese man, "It's so embarrassing climbing out the window all the time... ." Well, naturally I was just kidding, but he looked at me and glanced down at the dress I was wearing, and the expression on his face was just too rare. He actually believed me! So I spent the rest of the afternoon with the giggles again.

Some of the fellows in the health project just came by for coffee, and we got talking about snakes. It seems that some of the PCVs who are teachers up at Mzuzu in the Northern Region had a student who came running into their house, saying that there was a huge dead snake right out in the road. Since their science classes were studying snakes, this was going to be a great learning opportunity.

They got a box and went out to get the snake to bring it in to study it. It was seven feet long and about six inches in diameter! They brought it in and put it on the table, and the five of them started looking up in texts to try to identify it, turning it over and counting the ventrals, pointing out this and that identifying mark.

Peter, the PCV science teacher, is so near-sighted and has such thick glasses that he had his face about two inches away from the snake in order to point out its various body parts. They had just decided that it was a spitting cobra, when it suddenly flipped itself over from back to front! Then it reared its head up to about a three-foot height and opened its mouth — at which time there was a great exodus from the house, the snake hurling itself from the table right at the heels of the nearest fleeing PCV, who had to vault out an open window!

Spitting cobras are known to spit their venom with deadly aim at the eyes of humans — causing blindness — at a distance of up to seven feet! Outside they ran to shut all the windows and doors to trap the snake inside, then ran to the headmaster's house and got a rifle, and came back to find the snake crazily slithering from room to room, rearing up its ugly head, ready to spit.

To add to the craziness of the situation, Troop, one of the PCVs, had run into one of the bedrooms with his little dog, and every time he would open the bedroom door to try to get out, and thence out the front door, the snake would head for him and the guys outside would yell, "No! Troop — get back —" and he'd slam the door! He was really trapped.

They decided to shoot the snake right through the window glass. Their first rifle shot missed the snake entirely and knocked a leg off the table. Then they finally got the snake cornered in a bedroom (still from outside the house) and shot right through yet another window. This time they actually hit it, miraculously killing it! It made such a bloody mess that they had to completely repaint the bedroom, in addition to replacing the windows, but at the time that had been the least of their worries.

One of the guys said that the snake's head flew off and landed on the window sill, looking out at them. I don't know if I believe *that* or not — but it makes a good story. You know, I can't tell or type that story without getting covered with goosebumps.

Tomorrow is Mike's birthday, so I need to go shopping for a present. I find twelve-year-old boys hard to shop for, and there's nothing like waiting until the last minute. Maybe I can find a nice snakeskin or something.

Things are going a bit better at the orphanage right now, staffwise at least, so I'm currently only going out once a week. The only trouble is that I miss the babies so much! Another Peace Corps staff wife, Joanne Wallace, is going out once a week now, too, and when she goes out, I often take care of her little two-year-old daughter. Joanne is hooked on the place now, just as both Joyce and I are. All it takes is one visit.

Leopard Repellent

Because of the disappointment of our Mozambique trip having been postponed again, and the boys being so crushed that they would have to stay home the whole vacation (while all, simply *all*, of their friends were going on trips), Will decided to take all of us on a trip he was having to make on Friday to Fort Johnston. *[Fort Johnston is now called Mangochi.]* He was giving a sports clinic at the secondary school in Fort Johnston, which is up near the lake. After he was through giving the track clinic, we went for the weekend to a place on the lake called Cape Maclear. It was a heavenly spot.

We took the large Peace Corps pickup truck, which is ideal for trips like this. It holds tons of gear, and the boys love riding in the back. The weather was perfect. We're getting into the warm season now, but it's not yet terribly hot. The countryside is getting dry and dusty, but is still beautiful. The browns and golds of the hills in the background give a stark, dramatic effect to the mud and thatch huts.

Dotted here and there among the many brown tones are gorgeous accents of blooming trees, in a wild profusion of color. It's almost as if Mother Nature feels the scene needs a little jazzing up. The jacaranda tree is one of the most noticeable because it loses its green leaves and becomes a soft cloud of lovely lavender blossoms. The frangipani, which resembles a magnolia tree, is beginning to bloom now, as is the "orchid tree," another beautiful tree which looks just the way its name would indicate — a whole tree full of beautiful pink and white orchids. All these blossoming trees look dramatic and incongruous when everything else is dry and brown, and surely make the scenery interesting.

Another thing we've discovered when traveling in the dry season is that much more of the village life is visible. During the rest of the year the elephant grass and corn are so tall everywhere that you pass whole villages and see only the roofs of huts, if that. Driving along now through villages and seeing the women out pounding maize in the big pots or cooking over their open fires, we felt as if we were sitting watching a movie of African life.

All the little children run out to the road and wave and yell. The one thing that we don't like, however, is looking back at the people walking along in the enormous dust cloud that the truck makes, even though Will always slows down when there are people. On Sunday when people were all dressed up coming home from church, we felt terrible knowing we were covering them with dust, even though we were practically going at a crawl, but they seem to be used to it and smiled and waved anyway.

Every day we are reminded of how polite Malawian people are. The other day there was a little old man on a bicycle who just about fell off trying to tip his hat to us — for honking at him so we wouldn't hit him.

Cape Maclear at Lake Malawi reminds us of Zephyr Cove at Lake Tahoe, our favorite California lake, it's so blue and clear and surrounded by mountains. The sand is clean and golden, and there are almost no people on the beaches. It was almost as if we were on a little private tropical island of our own. This was especially so since school vacation is over, and there were no other vacationers there. However, it never does get very crowded at Cape Maclear. Our boys did "have to" miss school on Friday, which of course broke their hearts.

There is a hotel there which is really a scattering of small cabins. There is one larger thatch-roofed building which has the dining room and the office, as well as the living quarters of the lady who runs the hotel. Unlike the places we stayed in at the other beach, at Salima, these Cape Maclear rental cabins don't have thatched roofs, nor are they right on the beach, but they are close and you can see the lake.

This time we took our own food and did our own cooking so the boys would be sure to get enough to eat. We have found that very often children not only are supposed to eat at a different time from adults, but are given a different menu, sometimes even given cereal instead of "adult food" such as steak. Our boys take an exceedingly dim view of this custom, and so do we. Since there was a picturesque thatch-roofed, open-sided structure with a barbecue pit, tables, and benches, we found we could do much of our own cooking, and it was perfect. Our cabin had only four beds, so Don and Mike planned to sleep out in the back of the pickup.

The woman who runs the place, a Mrs. Kennedy, is a most fascinating character. She is around forty-five or fifty, has a voluptuous figure, long blond hair, is very tan, and wears a bikini bathing suit all the time. She has lived in Africa all her life, though in Malawi just the last eight years, loves animals, has had every kind of pet, and had pictures and tales galore. She had a leopard for nine years, as well as civet cats, monkeys, baboons, fish eagles, and anteaters, to name a few. She had a million stories that had the boys spellbound. Will was spellbound, too, but I'm not sure it was the *stories*.

We heard tell that she has had five husbands, but don't know if that is true. She does have five children, ages ranging from twenty-two down to six, all of whom are away now at schools. The night we arrived, as soon as she saw that we had our German Shepherd, Alipo, with us (Mike would have stayed home if we hadn't let him take Alipo), she came over with her Alsatian (German Shepherd) of the same age, and said, "Be sure to keep the dog inside at night because there is a leopard around, and it killed the mother of my dog one night just two weeks ago."

You should have seen the boys' faces! Strangely enough, the argument about who "would *get* to sleep out in the truck," magically changed over to who would "offer" to sleep in the cabin with Alipo.

Then this marvelous Mrs. Kennedy came over with a big bottle of ominous-looking black liquid and a huge cotton swab. After assuring the boys that leopards never went after little boys anyway, she said, "Just to be sure, I'll put this stuff on the trees around here. Leopards can't stand the smell and will stay away."

Leopard repellent!? Imagine! It did have a horrible smell, I must say, sort of a creosote and medicinal smell. Mike got some on his shirt, so all the clothes in the dirty clothes bag with it came home with this lovely aroma.

After much discussion, Rick, Scott, Will and I slept in the cabin with Alipo. Don and Mike settled down (more or less) in the back of the pickup. After listening for a leopard's snarl or screech and discussing how they really could sleep with their eyes open, they eventually fell asleep. Eyes closed. Fists clutching sling shots.

Will and I sat out on the porch for a while that night. Holding hands, we marveled at how lucky we are that we are here in Africa. The full moon reflected on the lake and the weather was perfect. No sweaters, no breeze, no bugs, the mountain behind us full of wild life, and best of all — the sound of African drums beating in the village nearby. There are certain times like this that you fully realize you are in the heart of Africa.

We never did see any leopards, but we did see a lot of baboons. Between Monkey Bay and Cape Maclear, Will had to stop the truck to let a whole pack of baboons cross the road. There must have been twenty or thirty of them, including mothers with babies hanging onto their backs. Later, when we were swimming in the lake, a big baboon came out on the rock to "people watch." The boys thought this was awfully funny.

Mrs. Kennedy is going to try to get us a baby baboon to raise. She says they are much better than monkeys; if you get them as babies they are the most affectionate and responsive pet you can have. However, we've been promised a monkey in December by a PCV who will be going home, so we're not sure what to do. Well, we'll see. If and when the time and animals come, we're hoping to build a big cage out in the back around a small tree.

The boys had a challenging time trying to stay upright in a dugout canoe. This is no easy trick, they discovered. The bottom is round and the ends are pointed, and it rolls over exactly as it looks like it would, being the hollowed-out log that it is. This dugout is the kind you straddle with your feet on the outside, the canoe being too narrow to sit in. When you fish, you just toss your fish inside. Now we have the greatest admiration for all these Malawians who speed along steadily and effortlessly in these things, even managing to *stand* and fish from them. The weather and water were so perfect that the kids were out swimming both mornings at 7:30 a.m., and Will even took a dip at 9:30 at night. It was a perfect weekend. And we'll never forget about leopard repellent!

Will is off again on a trip for eight days. He and Mike McCone left this morning on the Beaver, the small six-passenger plane that flies into the more remote areas of the country. They are going to Karonga and Chitipa, which are as far north as one can get in Malawi, to visit all the Peace Corps posts in that area.

But now, back to reality — I'm being bugged and hounded to take the kids to town, and I've been interrupted 5,974,859 times since lunch. Grrrrrr. Guess mornings are my only hope for letter writing. However, I must say that I didn't intend this to be so long. Must go so that I'll have time to do Mike's special belated birthday dinner of chambo, our favorite Lake Malawi fish, and apple pie.

Mr. Stonynose From Grimsville

September 16, 1965

Our landlord dropped a little bomb in our laps yesterday — of course while Will is away, which is always when bombs choose to fall. The landlord called to say he was serving us notice — ninety days to be evicted! I almost dropped the phone. It seems he has a new man coming to work for him who needs a house, and he couldn't find anything else for this man, so he will need our house.

I said (no, I *screamed* —), "But didn't we sign a lease?"

"Yes, but there is this clause with a three-month notice." This is our landlord who we'd *thought* was our friend, but who has suddenly become a cold-blooded businessman. He had seemed so pleased with us and with all the work we've done with his house. Well, of course.

Now that the Peace Corps has paid to have the whole place done over from stem to stern in preparation for many years of rental by Peace Corps staff, and it has never looked so good — I just couldn't believe my ears. He did say that he hated to do this. Oh sure. I just bet. But he also did say (perhaps catching just a hint of my not-very-well-disguised fury) that if we could find another suitable house for this man, then we could stay. Rentals are just practically non-existent here, and this is a real problem.

However, I did happen to know that our missionary friends, the Coxes, are building a new home and will be moving out of their rental. This would be the first available one I've heard of since we've been here. I quickly called Lois Cox to ask if their rental house had been promised yet and was relieved to find out that it hadn't been. So Lois and I deviously cooked up a little plan. Aha. Script and all. I hardly slept for worry and practicing our "plan."

This morning the landlord's man came. Before I even met him I just knew I wouldn't like him. Move us out of our house — indeed! Then when he actually did turn out to be unfriendly and cold, veddy British, it made it easier to really *hate* him. However, I acted civil. Sort of.

I took him first to see the Coxes' house. When Lois pointed out things like the shower, I said, "Oh, aren't you lucky to have a shower! And the closets, *closets* — my — I haven't seen a closet since I left the U.S. — and *storage space* — why, I should have brought over all our stuff to store here, you have so *much space* — !" He never uttered a single word, nor smiled. Mr. Stonynose From Grimsville.

Then we came down here to our place and he silently prowled all over. I was pointing out that there was no shower and only enough hot water for two baths, no closets or storage space at all, no sink in the kitchen — clear out on the back porch, if you can imagine! No comments at all from Mr. Stonynose.

Finally he said, "I'll let your landlord know in the morning which house I want." Not even a thank you. Both houses are the same size, the same rent and it obviously didn't matter a bean to him whether he was moving out a whole family if he took our house. I couldn't stand it. I let *blast* —

"I-just-want-you-to-know-that-we-would-be-just-*sick*-if-we-had-to-move-from-this-house-after-all-the-work-and-money-and-effort-we've-put-into-it-expecting-to-live-here-for-two-years-and-I-hope-your-decision-won't-be-too-difficult!"

We haven't heard yet from the Coxes' landlord, who lives in Salisbury. We're praying that he hasn't already promised it to someone. I'm not a bit sure that I could pull off my "flexibility" act if we had to move again. Pack again? Make drapes all over again? And besides, we really love this house now (in spite of no shower or closets or kitchen sink), and the garden is all done over and just going great guns, and we've just redone all the wiring to accommodate our clothes dryer. Oh, I can't stand it.

I'll write as soon as we know.

Atta Boy, Mom!

September 17, 1965

We think it worked! Our landlord did call this morning to say that his man decided on the other house — if it turns out to be available. We are now waiting to hear from the Coxes' landlord in Salisbury. There is time yet, apparently, as the man (Mr. Stonynose) isn't coming right away. Whew. Lois and I are patting ourselves on the backs and awaiting other future dramatic roles.

This is a good way to celebrate Don's thirteenth birthday today!

The boys have been as anxious as I, and when we got the word this morning, they used a wonderful term they'd used on me last weekend on our trip — to them the highest form of praise: "Atta boy, Mom!"

The "atta boy, Mom" story that I didn't have time to write about happened on the Friday that we drove up to Fort Johnston.

While Will was giving his track clinic in Fort Johnston, a bit of excitement befell me (or at least befell my passengers), as Will wanted me to drive the truck about fifteen miles out to a place called Malindi to give a message to some PCVs there. Two of the gal PCVs from Ft. Johnston came along to guide me, and the kids went with me too.

The first two blocks or so, I was trying to remember how to shift the gears on the truck and trying to convince the PCVs that I really did know how to drive it — heh heh. Before I'd fully refreshed my memory on how to do this, we'd rounded a bend and were headed down a hill, at the bottom of which was the Shire River and a little tiny "ferry" onto which — to my horror — I would have to drive this truck!

This "ferry" is a flat pontoon ferry, more like a big raft, which is pulled across the Shire River by a cable. It was filled with Africans on foot. The man had them all stand aside and beckoned me to drive on. Ulp. My passengers blanched. I was on the verge of telling the PCVs which kids did not swim well and would need to be rescued first, trying to ignore the fact that the Shire River has a reputation for its large crocodile population, when I decided just to act very brave and nonchalant.

The truck wheels had to go onto two little planks going from the shore over the edge of the water onto the boat. I hadn't the least idea where the wheels were, the truck is so big and high. After putting it in the wrong gear three times (not nervous at all) and hoping the PCVs didn't notice my shaking knees, I said a little prayer that the wheels were on the boards, and kept my eyes glued on the man beckoning me forward. Since he kept smiling, I figured we were on. Whew. What a relief — until the awful realization came that we'd have to do it again going back! Oh dear.

The road to Malindi was almost as bad, being windy (how do you spell that? — well, the road wound — well, it was a very *curvy* road) having many narrow, sideless bridges with the same kind of two planks that the wheels must fit on. I just couldn't believe I was doing this. I only *learned* to drive rather late in life and am Chicken Little at the wheel in *any* car — what was I doing??

My shaky knees were justly rewarded, however, when we finally got there, by all the congratulations of the fellows at Malindi and by the women saying that I had done great things for American Womanhood! Little did they know that *never* in my wildest dreams would I have done this thing if I'd known what was before me.

Will about died when he found out I'd had to drive onto one of those ferries and all those sideless plank bridges, with PCVs and all our kids in the back. One of the PCVs was new and I'm sure that ride was her first "culture shock."

The thing that really surprised and pleased me the most though, was the reaction of my own kids. They said, "Atta boy, Mom!" — my highest compliment!

"Weren't you scared??" I asked them —

"No, we knew you could do it."

Wish I had been that confident.

Just One Afternoon

September 23, 1965

What started out as a nicely planned and organized day a couple of days ago, went off and took a few detours of its own and got all out of my control. Will had come home on Monday from a wonderful trip upcountry, where he saw and learned so much. We were having two PCVs in for dinner that night, and Will was anxious to tell all of us about his trip.

I'd decided we'd have chambo (our favorite Malawi dinner), a rice casserole, vegetables, and that I would bake two apple pies. All easy for me except for the pies, which always take me forever, as I'm really more of a cake baker. So I did the shopping in the morning. Very Organized. Plan: start the pies right after lunch, knowing how long they take me. Fine. But some people dropped by after lunch. Still OK.

3:00 p.m. Still time. Then Mike came in from the backyard. Bleeding. He'd had a large wart removed from his arm the week before and had three stitches. It had all healed just fine and Will had just removed the stitches at lunchtime, as per directions from the doctor. It seems that Mike was playing with the dogs and Alipo had jumped up and his teeth had caught hold of the band-aid and also the edge of the incision and ripped the whole thing open again. It looked quite ugly and was about 1/2-inch long and almost as wide at the center. The Peace Corps doctor was out of town, so off we went to the hospital.

At the hospital the doctor on call had to cut away the healed stitches and scar tissue in order to re-stitch. For some reason the shot of Novocaine didn't take, and, although the doctor kept telling Mike it "wasn't hurting," I could tell it really was. Mike was pasty white and beaded with perspiration and whispering to me, "Mom, it *really* hurts." I tried to tell the doctor that Mike was really not a complainer and that I could tell it really hurt. He was from India and I don't think he understood much English, and I'm not even sure how much he understood about pain, telling Mike it "does not hurt." We got nowhere. Poor Mike.

So an undone Mike and a not-quite-yet (but almost) undone Mom returned home to resume the Organized Dinner Plan. 4:00 p.m. — still enough time. Just as the second crust was getting underway — a miserable anguished moan from Rick's bedroom — "Mommm, I'm gonna throw up — !" Drop pie — dash to bedroom. Not too late. Snatch Rick up from bed to run for the bathroom — whoops — too late. All over bedroom floor. Going to be more —

got to keep heading for the bathroom. Vain attempt to step over. Disaster. Mom and Rick lying in the midst of it all. Stunnnn.

Sure that I'd done no less than break my elbow, I yelled for Mas and Phillip, who luckily were in the house, and who hurried Rick on to the bathroom. Eventually the mess got cleaned up, and we got cleaned up and I really only have a purple elbow and a bruised shoulder.

Now Rick is in bed and it's only 4:45. Maybe we can still have pies. Guests not coming until 6:00. Oh no. They arrive early. They were hitchhiking and *got* a ride. Oh well, they're reading magazines in the living room and I'm doggedly continuing on with the blasted apple pies, which I'm hating by now. Finally get them in the oven and am heaving a sigh of relief (maybe I should have selected a better verb) when the kitchen door flies open and in comes Don. Bleeding.

"Hey Mom, I just cut my finger to the bone with my new Swiss Army knife!" Blood all over. At this point nothing could surprise me. "Oh? So what else is new, Don?"

I considered going out looking for Scott to tie him to a chair to avert more emergencies. We got Don all cleaned up, bandaged and sympathized with, and amazingly enough, dinner was delicious and even on time — and the pies were actually good. These two fellows did ask me if I had days like this very often.

After Will related his glowing tales of going all over in Land Rovers, on backs of motorcycles, seeing country not often seen by white people, visiting PCVs everywhere, such adventures — I said, "Well, this is a perfect example of the differences in a man's life and that of a woman with four little kids. We both have adventures. They're just different, that's all."

Ride, Anyone?

September 30, 1965

Will loves to give Malawians a ride when they are hitchhiking, if we have room in the vehicle. We are learning a lot while doing this. The way they "hitch" is not by the thumb, like we do, but rather by raising and lowering one arm. We have just had two "learning experiences."

The first happened up in Mzuzu when there were just the two of us in a Land Rover. A nice Malawian man asked us if we could give him and his wife and children (no number, but an implied "few") a ride just into town. Not far. "Of course," we said, only too happy to help, and only a little too naive as yet.

Well, it turned out that it was a wife, four or five kids, and you've never seen so much "katundu" (luggage and stuff). It seems they had just moved from Salisbury, lock, stock and barrel, and had lock, stock, and barrel with them — but sort of back in the bushes where unsuspecting hitchhiker-picker-uppers wouldn't notice. They kept coming out of the bushes, all of them with huge baskets on their heads.

Will decided he'd first take me into town and drop me off, and then would come back for them. About a half hour later Will, big grin on his face, came driving by where I was sitting on a store step waiting with a PCV. We about died laughing when we saw them. Little smiling black faces at all the windows, katundu piled up at least five feet high on the roof of the Land Rover — all topped by a bicycle!

They so seldom do get rides (I wonder why?), that they are really grateful when they do. We simply know now that we only stop for "one person" if we have room for three or four or more, plus katundu. Often one person will get in the car and then a few hundred feet away down the road, will say, "My wife is just down the road here with a few of my children —" and, of course, the scene repeats itself. They are not being dishonest, and I'd probably do the same if I were in their places, but now we are wiser.

The next day when Will stopped way out in the middle of nowhere for one lone man with the waving arm, Will (very wise now) asked, "Are you only *one?*"

"Well, there are two mai" ("mai" means woman or women), he answered. It never fails. We just laugh and cram them all in.

We are actually packing to go on the many-times-postponed Beira (Mozambique) trip. This is Thursday and we go on Saturday at 6:00 a.m. The boys are all excited about the nice beaches and a wild game park we've heard about. We'll come back on Wednesday.

Tomorrow is school "Open Day," so today and tomorrow will be very busy. I saw Scott's teacher in town and commented that Scott is very excited about the school program.

"Well, he's terribly important," she said.

"That's what he keeps telling us — and I'm so happy to hear it's really true," I confessed. He's the announcer and prop man and such. He polished his shoes tonight until I'm sure you can see him coming a block away. Mike is announcer for Standard Six, but he seems pretty blasé about it all. I doubt he's given his shoes a passing thought, much less the pass of a brush.

* * *

Friday, October 1, 1965

Guess what happened to the Beira trip again? Here we are, all set to go tomorrow and Will comes home from the office to get the airline tickets to *turn in!* There is a crisis in the Peace Corps office, and Mike McCone has to fly to Washington, DC — so guess who has to hold down the fort? The old Peace Corps "be flexible" motto is surely being tested. But actually, I hardly blinked when he told me. Luckily, not too many things were packed yet.

When I told the kids at lunchtime that we weren't going to Beira tomorrow after all, their reactions were very funny. Mike said, "Oh. I knew it. I never thought we'd really go and didn't even tell my teacher I wouldn't be at school on Monday." (Gosh.) Then Don came home, and when I told him, he said, "Hey Mike — I told ya so!" (Gee!) But Scott, having looked forward to the game park especially, cried. We explained that Will's job comes first and that's why we're here in Africa. When Mr. McCone has to leave the country Daddy has to be in charge. But I admit — it is a big disappointment.

* * *

Monday morning

To try to make up for the disappointment, we did, however, go on a wonderful picnic and swim on Saturday at Likabula, on Mlanje mountain. It's a beautiful river with natural pools, and we had perfect weather. We called the Leaches at the last minute to go with us, took lots of good food, and had a great time. We even took all the kids to a movie that night, too. Not quite the same as an African wild game park and a plane trip, but we tried.

Last week we took the boys and Michael, Saidi's oldest son who is fourteen, to see the movie, *"Sound of Music."* (Saidi is the houseman at the Field Center.) We are so fond of Michael, and this was his very first "cinema." He was on the edge of his seat the whole time. Watching Michael watch the movie was worth the price of admission! I'd had him come over to the house early so we could play the record of *"Sound of Music"* and explain the story. I fixed hamburgers to take to eat in the show, since it was a 5:00 p.m. showing — and this turned out to be his very first hamburger, as well. He was almost speechless by the time we took him home. What a wonderful movie to see for your very first one!

We've hired the new gardener we were trying out, to replace Raphael. His name is Friday Black Mussa (love it), and he works just half time, is about eighteen, and goes to school the other half of the day. He's a good worker, very anxious to please and does speak English. He's replanted many flower beds already, and things look much improved.

However (there seems always to be a "however"), the other day I looked out the window and saw Friday industriously taking apart the guinea pig cage that Don has been laboriously building for his new guinea pigs. Don had drawn up plans with great care and thought, and I'd driven him over to Limbe to get the wood (it's difficult to buy wood here), and he'd gotten the "wire" (screen) himself. We like to encourage the boys on constructive projects like this, and Don was very excited about it. He'd worked diligently on it all the day before but hadn't quite finished it before he went off to school the next day. It was only missing a door as yet.

At some point, Mike and I had been discussing how Don was going to make the door, while Friday was sweeping the porch and apparently taking in this conversation. He had already built us a very nice dog pen, and so I guess he thought he would *really* please and surprise us and "fix up" the guinea pig cage.

When I saw him taking apart Don's beloved masterpiece, I went tearing out there to see what he was doing — and he said, proudly, he was "making door!" Trying not to hurt his feelings (he's really very sweet), I said that it was awfully nice of him — but this was a special project that Don wanted to do all by himself — that Don had wanted to make the door a certain way — and only Don knew how he wanted it — and could Friday possibly put it all back the way that Don had left it — before Don would get home for lunch??

Oh dear. I hoped Don wouldn't notice, but of course he did because it was pretty messed up. And poor Friday felt terrible.

So then (of course there's more) I went all around the garden with Friday, admiring and praising all his hard work and hoping he would feel better. I did mention that when he had time, there were a couple of long spindly shoots on the bougainvillea waving about fifteen feet higher than all the rest of the bank of it. Did he think he could reach just those two and trim them off?

"Oh yes, Madam."

A couple of hours later I glanced out the bedroom window and saw an enormous pile of branches and beautiful blossoms. Again I tore out to the back yard. He had cut the whole gorgeous huge bush clear back to the bare trunk!

"Stop — stop"! (too late, of course) I yelled, nearly startling him off the ladder. This gorgeous bright pink/salmon-colored bougainvillea had covered the whole side of the house and was my favorite part of the entire back yard. I honestly felt like crying. Then I had to explain to yet-again wounded Friday, what I had *really* wanted him to do and that I knew he meant well — but — what was done was done. I hope it will grow back.

Just now while typing this, I absent-mindedly reached for my mug of coffee and almost drank Rick's mug of pollywogs. I was afraid of that when I saw him put them in that mug. What a way that would have been to start my day!

Tortoise; Tennis; Tree Fort

October 15, 1965

All the big kids, Will included, are off to school and to work, and Rick is busy taking care of his new tortoise in the back yard. Saidi brought him this tortoise yesterday from Zomba, with a string attached to a hole in his shell, so he and Rick go for walks. The Chinyanja name for tortoise is "kamba" so Rick named him Bambo (mister) Kamba from Zomba. He's about six inches or so long, about like the one he had before, but lost. Rick is very happy.

Our nine puppies are especially cute now and almost old enough to give away. They are a constant source of entertainment, and people are always coming into the back yard to see them. Friday's remodeled packing crate dog house is now graced with a "United States Peace Corps" sign that Scott nailed up, having acquired it when the Peace Corps office moved to a larger space a few weeks ago and replaced it with a new sign. Makes for many Peace Corps dog house jokes.

Yesterday and last night were big times for little old Blantyre. The international tennis pros, Lew Hoad, Rod Laver, Butch Buchholz, and Frank Sedgman came to Blantyre for an exhibition match. They are on tour and had an open day between Nairobi and Salisbury. Bill Hussey, Deputy Chief of Mission of the U.S. Embassy here and an avid tennis player, contacted their manager to see if some of them could play in Blantyre. We couldn't believe it when they all accepted. In a matter of just a few days, all the improvements that have been needed for fifteen years at the tennis club, including installing lights, miraculously got done.

The appearance here of these celebrities was not only great for tennis itself, but for our tennis facilities as well. Will and I had seen these players in 1961 at the Cow Palace in San Francisco, and we, along with thousands of others, were thrilled to see them, from probably around row 170 or something. Now, here we were in the middle of Africa, sitting right *on* the court, no, I guess a couple of feet off, watching these tennis greats and hearing every word they said.

And — guess who was the umpire of the singles match between Laver and Buchholz? Will. One of the PCVs there asked me if Will had ever umpired a tennis match before? When I answered, "No" (forgetting that he had called some little local matches in Davis), he said, "Well, there's nothing like starting at the top!" They play for money, so it's no haha matter. Will did a very good job; in fact,

I thought he did better than either of the other two umpires for the other matches, and I'm not biased at all, of course.

We saw great tennis. And what nice fellows those four are. After the matches the Husseys had a cocktail party and supper for the players, and we were invited. Bill Hussey about made me faint with excitement when he put Butch Buchholz next to me at dinner. Will sat next to Rod Laver. Imagine! Butch is the only American of the group (the others being Australians) and is a very nice person.

At the match that day there were seats for about eight hundred people, and admission was one pound ($2.80). Will bought tickets for the eight African high school boys who play tennis and had played in the Malawi National Tournament. They could never have afforded it, and would probably not have the chance to see tennis like this again. They really enjoyed it.

In the back of the program there is a page with little blurbs about five "Malawi Tennis Personalities," and one of them is Will. Now, when in the world would Will ever be in a tennis program with Lew Hoad, Rod Laver, etc. again?

Malawi, as well as all of East and Central Africa, is having very strange weather. October is supposed to be terribly hot, but we've really only had a few warm days and lots of cold weather. An African lady told me yesterday that this means that the rains will be early and long this year. Last night people had on sweaters and coats, and the day before it was raining and just horrible — in fact, we had been afraid that the tennis matches would have to be called off. What luck that it was OK for the matches.

We have had to hire another houseman to help poor Mas. Mas is so conscientious and works so hard that he has been getting skinnier and skinnier. He works too many hours, and I can't get him to rest unless he feels everything is done. It's just too much work for one person, so we hired Phillip. Phillip is big, strong, good natured, and a wonderful worker.

Who was that lady who was going to go to Malawi and do all her own housework??

I'm excited to find that we have $394 in the Sister Mary Joy Fund! I spent most of yesterday working on the books and on thank you letters. I also did a half day's work for the British Red Cross at the Well Baby Clinic for Africans and just loved it. I think little black babies are so adorable that now I'm beginning to think white babies look kind of pale and underdone.

The boys are enjoying having more friends now. The other night, Don and his friend Bill decided to sleep out in Bill's tree fort. Bill's family is one of the new American group just down the hill from us. Will and I had gone to a movie that night, and came home to find a note on the door, "Me and Bill are here." (He's getting excellent English training in this veddy English school). It seems that they *weren't scared.* Uh uh. It was just "too boring." We also found a burned-down candle, Frankenstein book, and knife in its sheath lying by the door.

However, it seems that Bill's folks didn't know that Bill and Don had come up to our house and thought they were still up in the tree house. In the middle of the night someone shined a flashlight in their bedroom window and woke them up. Thinking it was Bill and Don wanting in, Mr. Blackmun called out,

"Just a minute, Bill, I'll come and open the door—" Then when they heard footsteps running away, they realized it was a burglar! Can you imagine the burglar's surprise when someone yelled out, "Just a minute, I'll come and open the door" ?

Flexibility and New Pets

October 21, 1965

This is Flexible-Adjustable-Jane writing. Yesterday I wrote you too, but it seems that everything I wrote yesterday was changed by today so I burned it and am starting over. From now on, anything I say may not be true in the next hour.

Will *was* supposed to leave for Washington, DC next Wednesday, and for the Peace Corps Malawi training program at Syracuse University, followed *maybe* by some meetings in California. Now we find that his departure is postponed, but not for long, we think. Judging by the way things have been going around here — no one counts on doing anything at all until they're actually doing it. "Be Flexible!"

This morning, before knowing about Will's latest departure postponement, I zoomed over to Zomba. Hah. *That's* not even true. This car "zooms" along with the gas pedal to the floor — at thirty miles per hour. What I mean is that I *tried* to zoom because I was in such a hurry to get all my Christmas shopping done because I *thought* Will was going to the States next Wednesday and could take the gifts.

Zomba is only forty miles away but it took me more than an hour each way. However, with great determination and an additional few hours finishing up here in Blantyre, I almost finished our Xmas shopping. When Will came home at 6:30, I proudly boasted about how well I'd done with the shopping and had a great display of the Xmas items for him to take to the States on Wednesday. "Well," he said, "I'm not going Wednesday after all."

"Oh." That's all I said. See how flexible I am? "Oh."

Oh well, at least it's nearly done and who knows, maybe he'll call home tomorrow and say he's leaving right that very minute. Wes Leach was standing around the office yesterday morning and the next thing he knew he was on a plane for Salisbury. So we are all learning to be flexible.

Another f'rinstance on flexibility: Tonight a PCV came in about 5:30 and was playing around with the kids, and I said, (feeling lucky that we had a stretchable kind of dinner), "Can you stay for dinner, Tom?"

He said, "Well, as a matter of fact — Will *did* invite me." When Will came home, he told me that he'd tried to call me, but I was gone all day. Wouldn't it have been embarrassing if I'd said something like, "Gee, Tom, we'd love to have you stay for dinner but we don't have enough tonight — how about tomorrow night?"

Good thing we're flexible.

We have just added to the family again. And this is the cutest thing we've ever seen! It's a baby duiker (pronounced "diker"). A duiker is a small antelope. It's a beautiful little animal that looks exactly like a miniature Bambi. He is eleven and a half inches tall, weighs two and a half pounds, is very tame and so sweet! His little legs are long, about the size of pencils, and his tiny hooves are about 3/8 of an inch wide. We have him in a basket in the kitchen, where it's warm, and we give him a bottle of warm formula every few hours.

Will bought him from an African boy who brought him up to the office. Knowing the poor little thing would surely die if someone didn't buy it, Will paid the boy while lecturing him on how he shouldn't take baby animals from the mothers, etc. etc. Probably not too effective a lecture. The veterinarian told us these little animals are very hard to keep alive, but we're sure going to try.

Tonight after I gave the duiker his bottle, we put him down on the living room rug and watched him. After he walked around a bit he lay down and went to sleep. Then Cheena came in and licked him, lay down beside him, and they slept like that all evening. It was so cute and, of course, I didn't have any film in the camera. Such a picture it would have been — a big German Shepherd and a tiny baby duiker. Darn.

Now I've just given him another bottle, and he's asleep in his little basket beside me while I type. He's so teeny he can only drink about two ounces at a time. You should see his beautiful little face. I just hope we can keep him alive.

We still have five of Cheena's puppies, the two big dogs, and two guinea pigs, but Ricky's tortoise, Bambo Kamba From Zomba, went away the other day after Ricky untied him and we can't find him. We also have another dead snake, either a mamba or a boomslang, in a bucket waiting to be identified. Scott found it in our yard Sunday in his little "fort," and Mas killed it. This is the second snake they've found in the fort, so now for *sure* this fort is abandoned, at least by small boys. This snake is not very big, maybe fourteen or fifteen inches long — but I wonder where its mother is??

* * *

October 23, Saturday morning

The athletic equipment that the Davis Junior High School kids had collected and sent to us arrived a couple of days ago. It was so exciting! Don and Mike's Davis school had had some fund-raisers to raise money for Malawi athletic equipment. The Junior High principal then wrote to Will and asked what kind of equipment they should send. Among other things, Will suggested tennis rackets because the high school is just starting to teach tennis, the only Malawi school to do so, and has only two rackets. There were also basketballs, baseballs, mitts, bats, track shoes, and other wonderful equipment.

Will called the headmaster of HHI (Henry Henderson Institute), the African high school here in Blantyre, to set up a time for a presentation of the equipment. This is the largest high school in Malawi. The headmaster set up a school meeting yesterday afternoon where Don and Mike presented the equipment to the school.

It was held outdoors and the whole school was there. Don gave a talk about how his Davis Junior High School raised the money and got the athletic equipment, and said that it was a gift from his American school to this Malawi school. The headmaster gave a speech of appreciation, and our friend Maluwa, who is captain of the HHI tennis team, gave a speech of gratitude. There was even a USIS (U.S. Information Service) photographer there. It was a beautiful sunny day and a very nice ceremony. We'll send photos and letters of thanks to Davis Junior High.

Will is really going full-tilt these days, as Mike McCone has had to be in Washington, DC for some time now. All sorts of things have been happening. Things always do happen in a place like this with almost three hundred PCVs in this country, but it really seems especially hairy lately. Every day another crisis of some sort. Another PCV became politically involved and created a huge furor, especially since Dr. Banda found out and got the Embassy all shook up (to say nothing of Peace Corps) and had to be escorted home. Then a young PCV woman got really sick and had to be taken home yesterday by one of our doctors. Every day something.

We're hoping to get away this afternoon and go up to the Zomba Plateau to the ambassador's cabin, if no one else has reserved it. Our ambassador has left the country for a new post in Washington, DC, and any Americans can arrange to use the cabin when he's not using it. It has a phone, so Will could be reached in case of emergency, and it's only an hour and a half away.

We really can't leave the baby duiker, and we can take him there to the cabin with us. In fact, Will is going to the lake on Monday to a two-day conference, and I would love to go, but can't leave "my baby." Guess I have to be flexible even with new pets. Will is flying up, and I wouldn't want to try taking the duiker on the plane. Since I'm the only one he'll take a bottle from so far, wherever I go — he goes. The kids have tried giving him his bottle, but he just won't take it. It's sort of like having a newborn preemie. However, he's so adorable that he's worth it.

African Bees!

Friday, October 30, 1965

Last weekend we were able to get away to the Zomba Plateau to spend a couple of days at the American Embassy cabin. We took the baby duiker with us, and he is doing just fine.

The cabin is very rustic, comfortable, and restful. There is even a caretaker there who helps with the cooking and does the dishes and the cleaning, so it's especially relaxing for Mom. A large khonde (porch), furnished with big comfortable chaise lounges and a barbecue, overlooks a pine forested mountainside and valley. The fresh cool air and smell of the pines reminded us all of the California Sierras. It doesn't seem like Africa at all. We think the elevation is about 7000 feet.

We could hear the river below and decided to take a hike down there. There were huge lush ferns growing right to the river's edge, and it was like a shady paradise. The dogs, Cheena and Alipo, galloped joyously up and down and in and out of the river. The boys waded and threw rocks in the water. The first two days were just the kind of change and rest we needed.

And then — Sunday morning Will and the three older boys decided to climb up the nearby mountain. Rick and I stayed down at the cabin and had fun watching them climb. Every once in a while they would stop and wave at us. Then suddenly we saw them all jumping around and flapping their arms and we could hear them all screaming. Terrified, I cupped my hands and yelled, "What happened???"

Will yelled, *"Bees!!"* Unfortunately, I had just read a *Time* magazine article on African killer bees. I would have been plenty scared anyway, but now I had immediate visions of Rick and me being the sole survivors of the Lotter family.

Not really knowing what to do, I ran for the caretaker and told him to get all the ice out of the fridge and to fill both bathtubs with cold water. Then I quickly looked in the Peace Corps medical kit and to my relief saw that we had Benedryl (an antihistamine) to give them all.

They were running helter skelter down the mountain, all the boys screaming. By the time they got to the cabin they were all covered with bee stings and still had a lot of the bees inside their tee shirts and in their hair. It was truly a nightmare. We gave them the Benedryl right away, got their clothes off, and hurried them into the tubs of cold water (more yelling). Ice helped, especially on their eyes. One of Don's eyes was already almost swollen closed.

Mike had cauliflower ears. They all looked as if they had just been through a prizefight — and lost. Will had his fair share of stings, too.

We went back to Blantyre that day with a healthy respect for bees. No one had further complications, but no one is very eager to climb that mountain again either. It did rather put a damper on an otherwise lovely weekend.

This week has been even busier for me than last week. With the Peace Corps conferences going on up at the lake, everyone was up there except me (sob) — simply everyone. Will was there from Monday until Wednesday. Then for the rest of the week he was holding down the Peace Corps office single-handedly while the others were still up at the lake. I was holding up our end of the orphanage and Well-Baby clinic. The weather has turned warm now, so I feel as if I've been in a panting, perspiring race.

Interspersed with all these activities were the St. Andrews Prep School swimming "Gala" on Tuesday afternoon, in which both Scott and Mike were participating, and a birthday party for two Peace Corps staff kids. The swimming gala started at 2:00 p.m. and wasn't over until almost 5:00 p.m., with all the parents sitting out there in the broiling sun all that time.

Then yesterday for the birthday party (not at our house) there were fourteen kids between two and five years old, plus Scott, who had been asked to "help" and was in his glory organizing everyone. This party wasn't even at our house and it wasn't even one of our birthdays — so why the heck was I so pooped??

We also still have our pet chameleon. What a show he puts on! We have discovered that if we put an index finger up to his chest he apparently feels he must walk up it. So now we can take him up to windows that have flies on them, and watch while he first gets both eyes swiveled around together to zero in on a fly (each eye moves independently), then unwinds his curled up tongue, shoots it out, and boink — zaps the fly. This has become quite an entertaining pastime. Wonderful entertainment at cocktail parties. We have named him Willie Mays, after Will's favorite major league baseball player — because he catches so many flies.

About the coming trip to the lake, I said, "barring any unforeseen emergencies" because Gary Stewart, one of the Peace Corps doctors, and his family is supposed to be going to the lake with us, but Gary now has to wait to check out a possible appendicitis case with a PCV. Gary's wife, June, and their two children have already gone up with some PCVs, and Gary will drive up with us tomorrow, if all is OK with the PCV and there are no other emergencies.

The Stewart kids and Rick have a wonderful time together, as they are almost the same ages. Wayne and Rick are both four and Tammie is three. Incidentally, there are now fourteen Peace Corps staff children — twelve boys and two girls — and all but four of them are under five!

About Will's "supposed" trip to the States — again it is postponed indefinitely. Now I don't even blink when he says anything is postponed or changed or canceled. Maybe I'll blink when he actually gets on the plane, but not until it takes off.

Leopards and Launches

We just got back last night from such a nice three-day weekend up at the lake. How we do love that place. It's the most restful, beautiful spot you could imagine. It's very hot now, both here in Blantyre and at the lake shore. We spent most of our time there submerged in the water.

We had planned to come back from the lake early this morning, but decided to drive back in the cool of the evening last night, especially since the kids were so sunburned and had to ride in the back of the pickup truck. Even at 7:00 a.m. it's hot, and we were getting sunburned at 9:00 a.m. on the beach. It was fun watching for wild game while we were still in the more mountainous region near the lake, and the kids were awake and ready with flashlights. Then the kids slept the rest of the way and we got home about 11:00 p.m.

When we had arrived at Cape Maclear, Mrs. Kennedy greeted us again with her Alsatian, who had been Alipo's big buddy the last time. The dog was swathed in bandages and skinny as a bone. A leopard had gotten it just eight days before! Since we had *both* Alipo and Cheena with us, here we were with the leopard problem again — only double. Mrs. Kennedy is really lucky to have her dog at all.

Remember, I wrote that the mother Alsatian had been killed and dragged off by a leopard just a month and a half ago? This time the leopard had come at 5:45 p.m., in broad daylight, right down to the bar bungalow next to the beach and attacked the dog. It was especially surprising because there were people in there having drinks, and usually leopards are shy when humans are around. Someone grabbed a gun but couldn't shoot for fear of hitting Mrs. Kennedy's dog. However, they managed to scare the leopard away.

The poor dog has huge, horrible open gashes in her side. Since we had the Peace Corps doctor, Gary Stewart, with us, he ended up treating the dog while we were there. Peace Corps is not only flexible, but versatile!

This leopard problem again created the dilemma of who would sleep inside with the dogs, and it was so hot all night that no one wanted to sleep indoors. Mrs. Kennedy once again assured us that leopards don't bother people, but they do savor dogs. Finally, Rick and Scott did sleep inside, and the dogs had a whole extra room to themselves. This seems to amount to the fact that we paid for hotel facilities for two kids and two dogs. The rest of us slept on air mattresses outside. What a switch.

There were sixteen PCVs, the Stewart family, and our family, and it was loads of fun. We had hot dogs, potato salad, potato chips, and chocolate cake. How American can you get? All but our family left Sunday afternoon.

Then a family with *five* boys, ages seven to thirteen, arrived — what a great time for our kids. Monday, while we and the nine boys were on the beach, Mrs. Kennedy told us that the Governor-General Sir Glyn Jones and party were to arrive by launch for lunch. (That could work into something, couldn't it — like they could "lunge off the launch for lunch?" Hmm.) Soon a beautiful white launch came churning in with a party of five people, British flags on the masts, and white-uniformed African sailors on deck.

Don and Mike, who were playing in a dugout canoe, paddled out to meet them. Will took lots of pictures. The sailors carefully lowered a little boat over the side in preparation for removing the passengers. Then, before our fascinated eyes, Sir Glyn removed his jacket and shorts, displaying a bright blue bathing suit, clambered up onto the bow, did a beautiful dive into the water, and swam all the way in. Then Lady Jones, no young chick, appeared in proper bathing garb, topped off by an incongruous-looking old army fatigue-type hat, and gracefully climbed down the ladder and swam in, too. Their two companions and a young fellow, maybe a bodyguard, did the same.

While we were wondering who the little boat was for, a sailor climbed in and rowed a lone passenger in — a little Pekinese dog, who rode to shore in grand elegance all by himself. How I wish we'd had a movie camera. When Sir Glyn came dripping up onto shore, Will and I greeted him and shook hands. We were very pleased that he remembered us, and he introduced us to his friends, while mentioning Will's tennis.

The water was perfect, and it was such a hot day that they stayed and swam and talked for nearly an hour. We really got to see the other side of these people. Sir Glyn has always been easy to talk to. We've especially liked him since the Fourth of July picnic, when he told Will he'd like to see an American baseball game. But he not only wanted to watch, he wanted to play! Lady Jones has always appeared rather reserved to me, not smiling much and looking quite stuffily formal. But here she was, paddling around in the water in that funny battered hat, having the best old time. She said she'd heard we had quite a few boys, but was it really *nine*? She was very friendly.

Both Sir Glyn and Lady Jones got a big charge out of Rick,

who was floating around in his little tube with a huge straw hat on to protect his poor little sunburned face. Then when Rick had a ride in the dugout canoe, Lady Jones put her Pekinese in with him and both Sir Glyn and Will took many pictures. We all had quite a few laughs, and I'm sure I won't feel intimidated by Lady Jones anymore. It was a memorable weekend.

Will's trip to the States is canceled and we're so disappointed. Now I've really got to hustle to mail our Christmas things. And our shopping that Will was going to do — oh well. It's possible that he might get to Syracuse for final selection in December, but we just can't count on it. Because of a crisis, Peace Corps Director Mike McCone is still in Washington, DC, so Will has to stick around until he gets back. They can't both be gone at once. Our Christmas things for the family will undoubtedly arrive late now, but it can't be helped.

Duikers and Lunches

November 3, 1965, Wednesday

Will just called, and a visiting VIP from the State Department in Washington is coming for dinner. Oh my. Must rush to town and see if there is any chambo today — our favorite dinner, especially for anyone visiting for the first time. Chambo is the lake fish that you can't get anywhere else in the world, and it is so good. It tastes like chicken and even non-fish-eaters like it. Must hurry and shop and also must give our "baby" his bottle before I go.

That baby duiker is the most adorable thing! He takes his bottle well now, drinking six ounces. Now he'll let other people give him his bottle too, which is a big relief for me. He walks around the living room and loves to climb into the back of the cool fireplace and sleep. He gathers up his courage to make the leap across the slippery floor between the rug and hearth, and it's really funny. He improves every day.

We also have a little "potty" (a tuna can) handy and can tell when he needs to use it, by a certain way he stands when he needs to pee. We quickly set it under him and don't even have any puddles to clean up. It even makes him seem like he's potty trained! Very impressive when guests are here.

Speaking of our animals, I really had to laugh last night, as I was watching Mas and Phillip with all the various pets here. We had been barbecuing steaks in the back yard, and Ricky discovered that there were a lot of frogs around. He caught a nice big one and brought it into the house. Well, naturally, it jumped out of Rick's hands and was hopping around loose in the kitchen. Bedlam ensued. Mas, Phillip, Rick and I were all dashing here and there, then crawling crazily on our hands and knees. Finally the darned thing got under the refrigerator and, not without difficulty, they got it.

Mas and Phillip are always having to feed the dogs and puppies and the guinea pigs and the catfish and hunt for the tortoise, and bottle-feed the duiker, and not throw out the dead snake being saved in the freezer for Terry at the Museum. It all struck me very funny. What they have to put up with.

* * *

Thursday

Our dinner guest last night was a very nice older man on the State Department Foreign Service Inspection Team. How lovely it is to get food ready ahead of time and know that Mas can now cook everything beautifully. I can take a bath, look like a lady of leisure, be able to sit down and even have a drink with the guests, and know that the table will be all set, candles lit, wine chilled, and dinner dished up just right. I can just *sit there* and not even have to carry off a dish or ask for the dessert and coffee. Am I spoiled for life in the "outer world"?

There are now some dinners that Mas can do all by himself, especially roasts, mashed potatoes, gravy, and any vegetable, so we are making all kinds of progress. This accomplishes two purposes — it's great for me, and also he will be able to get a much better job when we leave. He's very proud of himself and deservedly so. I just wish that he knew how to read. It would sure help with recipes and/or reminders.

Mas is so willing and eager to do well, but just when I think I've made great progress with him, some communications failure will befall us and the results can be hilarious — or awful. When he misunderstands me, though, it's usually my own fault.

One day we were taking a picnic to the pool. Everyone but Scott likes tuna sandwiches. And those of us who do, like them with lettuce. So I said to Mas, "Make everyone except Scott a tuna sandwich. Make Scott either an egg sandwich or a peanut butter and jam sandwich." The result was many very nice tuna sandwiches with lettuce. Fine. And — one very interesting sandwich with egg, peanut butter, jam, and lettuce (I'd said not to forget the lettuce — but I'd meant on the *tuna* sandwiches). He also remembered that Scott loves honey, and so he put some of that on too. Well, at least he didn't forget anything.

Everybody but Scott thought it was awfully funny.

Birth In the Back Yard

Friday, November 12, 1965

Another busy week has gone by, during which I came down with some bug for three or four days and Rick seems to have come down with the same thing just last night. The baby duiker got sick, too, and we have been doctoring him. All three of us are on terramycin. Duiker and I feel pretty good today. He's been cavorting around the backyard with the puppies, and is now happily ensconced in his cage out in the sunshine.

Yesterday was a most unbelievable day, one I'll surely never forget. When we first got up in the morning, I commented to Will, "Oh boy, I sure won't have time to bog down today — so much to do."

I'd been "bogging down" each day since I'd been sick. The Peace Corps staff wives were giving a tea in the afternoon at the Field Center for the new Peace Corps doctor's wife to meet all the women volunteers and staff wives. Nini McCone and I were in charge of it, and I was going to bake cookies, arrange flowers, and do a zillion other things. Before I ever got to #1 on my list, Phillip came running in and said, "Madam, come quick — Mas's wife is starting baby!"

I ran out back, all excited — "OK, hurry! I'll take her to the hospital!"

The odd thing about this was that I'd dreamed just that night that Mas had come knocking on the window in the middle of the night, saying that his wife must go to "hoss-pee-tall." I'd intended to talk to him in the morning to tell him again to be sure to call us at any hour, whenever her labor started. But the baby wasn't due for another two weeks.

We've all been so excited since finding out she was pregnant because they have only one child, little Saidi, who is three. They have lost *three* other children. None at birth, one at one month, one at two years, and one at four years. The infant mortality here is staggering. I was *determined* that this baby would be healthy.

When I got out to their quarters in back, Phillip's wife, Delia, was standing outside the door. "She just had the baby, Madam!" Thank goodness Delia can speak English and could interpret for me. I found that Saidi's wife (Saidi, who is the houseman at the Field Center, is Mas's nephew) was in there with her, and for some reason they wouldn't let Phillip's wife in. I had her ask if there was something I could do to help, and to my surprise, they invited me to come in!

With shaking knees, wondering whether I'd know what to do, I pushed open the door to the tiny room. It was so dark I could hardly see at first, saw no one on the bed, then realized that Mas's wife was crouched down on the floor. She'd just delivered the baby and was passing the afterbirth. When my eyes adjusted to the darkness, I could see that it was a girl and she was lying on the cold cement floor. Saidi's wife was crouched down in the corner brewing a big pot of some strange kind of black stuff on a small open fire on the concrete floor. I felt as if I'd stepped into some other world, and back several centuries.

My first thoughts were to see if the baby was all right. I don't know what I'd have done if she weren't breathing or something. Luckily, she was breathing, wiggling, and whimpering. I ran back to the house and got some clean towels, and shouted to Phillip — "Put water on to boil!" (Like they do in the movies. We never did use it. I didn't know what to use it for anyway.)

Then I carefully moved the baby onto several thicknesses of towels, wrapped her up well, laid her on her mother's lap, and ran back into the house and called Will at the Peace Corps office to get the doctor. With amazing luck he was able to get Gary Stewart, our Peace Corps doctor, who came right out. Was I glad to see him!

The next half hour was a great lesson in midwifery for me, combined with dashing back and forth to the house for things like plastic to put on the bed, more towels, and scissors to cut the cord. To my utter and frantic frustration, I couldn't find any string to tie the cord, but luckily Saidi's wife found some.

Gary got the baby all cleaned up, got Mas's wife fixed up on the bed, and gave me instructions for "kneading" the mother's stomach every hour, putting antibiotic on the baby's umbilical cord, and taking temps. We both told her she must stay in bed. We also told Mas, who wasn't even allowed near, incidentally.

Feeling my great responsibility after Gary left, I kept going out to "do my job," but every time, I would find her sitting on the cold floor! I just could not get her to go to bed, and never did "knead" her tummy. She seemed all right, so I didn't try to force the issue. I felt quite flattered that they'd let me in at all, and really didn't want to be intrusive, especially in another culture.

Then I found out that they didn't even have a diaper ("nappie") for her. Absolutely nothing. So, having nothing at all here in the house, I rushed to town to buy nappies, little shirts, blankets, pins, baby powder, oil, etc.; dashed by the Field Center to tell Nini what was happening, and left her with *all* the work for the tea; brought the baby things back, only to find that the baby was lying on the floor on a piece of cardboard. So, again I dashed back downtown and bought a bassinet. We'd gotten one like it for Phillip's baby. Woven of cane, with wooden legs (very cute), it only cost eleven shillings and six pence, which is less than $2.00. African babies are usually on their mothers' backs, I know, which is ideal, but when they're not — on cardboard on the floor? At least it made *me* feel better buying a bassinet.

I actually made it to the tea on time, just as if nothing had happened all day! I even managed to give the baby duiker his bottles and medicines.

The baby is just beautiful, and weighs five-and-a-half pounds, which is about average for Malawian babies. Did you know that many African babies have light skin when they are born? She could almost pass for one of mine now. The skin apparently darkens later, maybe when they get out in the light and sunshine.

Having seen this birth — well almost — which actually had much better circumstances than those out in the villages, I can see why the infant mortality is so high. I've been determined right along that this baby should get good care. We've purchased prenatal vitamins for Mas's wife and made sure she's gone for checkups. I never dreamed that I'd almost deliver it!

I went out first thing to see her this morning and take the mother's temperature. The baby looked so cute, all wrapped up in a new clean blanket. But again, the mother was sitting on the cold floor holding her, even though I'd given them a big wicker chair so that she could sit comfortably.

Their African customs and traditions are so strong that even the more modern Malawians still combine the new concepts with the old. This morning Mas was discussing with me just how he had fixed a bottle for the baby, sterilizing it and using boiled water. And yet I knew, at the same time, about that "brew" (which, incidentally, Saidi's wife hid when Dr. Stewart came).

They usually come to us now before they go to the medicine man or witch doctor. We give such simple things as aspirin, band-aids, indigestion pills, or we treat burns. The other day, Saidi came over to tell me that my indigestion pills (sort of like Bisodol) weren't helping, and he wanted me to know that he was going to Zomba to a witch doctor. I forgot to ask him yesterday whether he was any better. We never say anything about their traditional practices, and many natural remedies are very good. We just try to help them before they resort to extremes that could be harmful. At least Saidi felt he should (and could) come and tell me. We have gone through two complete Peace Corps medical kits, which are amply supplied.

We didn't go out to the mission this week, any of us, because seventeen of the twenty babies had measles. The sisters didn't want us to take any chances. Can you imagine caring for seventeen fussy babies? They were coming down with it when I was out last Friday, apparently, as I found three with temps, so I must watch Rick for a rash now. It's the three-day kind, which is not so bad.

I did put on a few more gray hairs that day when I saw one of my favorite little babies, Alphonsina, who is six months old and only weighs seven pounds, have convulsions. It was terrifying. We have been giving her such special care. She almost didn't make it, but is doing OK now. Such a scare.

Mankwala

Monday, November 15, 1965

Friday (the day, not the gardener) was busy enough, with Rick being sick and my "patients" out in back, but more has happened since then. First, Saturday morning about seven or eight PCVs came over for Don's pancakes, and we had a lot of fun. The pancake idea was Don's from the beginning, and we have been doing it every Saturday morning. The first person arrived at 7:00 a.m. and we were ready, believe it or not. We had such a good time, and this is certainly a great way to be able to have any number of people over.

After the last ones left, I went out back to see how things were going and discovered that Mas's wife had a fever. The baby looked OK. I asked how the cord was healing, and said to be sure to put the antibiotic ointment on it several times a day. Since the baby was asleep, I didn't look at the umbilical cord though, which turned out to be a big mistake. It dawned on me later that they had also acted as if they didn't really want me to look at it, but I'm so paranoid about interfering that I didn't realize this at the time.

That afternoon I saw Gary and told him about Mas's wife's fever, so he said he'd come by in the morning. On Sunday morning when we went into the little house to see them, Mas's wife was sitting on the cold concrete floor (the nice chair I'd given them was piled up in a corner on the bed), and the baby was again on the floor (the nice bassinet I'd given them was piled on top of the nice chair I'd given them) — but at least the baby was on the nice blankets I'd given them.

First we took the mother's temp, and it was almost 101°. Then Gary pulled back the baby's blankets to see the cord, and we both nearly fell over. The cord and all of the baby from the waist down was coal black, smeared with this African "mankwala" (which, translated, is "medicine"). It's a horrible-looking, black, gritty, greasy-looking stuff, some of the ingredients possibly being charcoal mixed with ground-up leaves. I'm sure it is what Saidi's wife was stirring over the fire. This poor little baby's umbilical cord was just a mess, and was infected underneath, and no wonder! It made me feel really sick to my stomach. I found out that the death rate of infants here is 40%, which now doesn't surprise me.

Gary said we'd just have to clean that "stuff" off, and so we went into our house to talk to Mas, hoping that he'd understand. That poor man. How mixed up he must be. He's really caught between two cultures — the old African traditions so ingrained in him and his very traditional African wife — yet understanding so much about our culture now. Mas knows, for instance, how to care for Rick's skinned knee, cleaning and applying antiseptic. So here he was, understanding what we were saying about infection and keeping the baby clean, yet at the same time saying, "But all babies in Africa have mankwala."

Gary very kindly and gently explained the dangers, and I finally told Mas that this was "my very first girl," and I sure didn't want anything to happen to her. He's been so pleased that I am especially happy that it's a girl, that I think maybe my saying this convinced him that we could clean off the mankwala. He would talk with his wife.

He had a hard time persuading his wife though, and she wouldn't let us bring the baby into our house to clean her up, but she did let us do it out there. So we took pans of hot water out there and washed her thoroughly. Then Gary put lots of antibiotic ointment on her and gave me terramycin to give to the mother. I think that now they are doing all right. He also told them that when they were not holding the baby, they should use the bed for her — or at least not put her on the cold floor.

That night I really had qualms about having done all this because Mas came and asked if he could sleep on the floor of the laundry. He said that Saidi's wife was staying with his wife, and she wasn't letting him in. I felt terrible and wondered if I had unwittingly caused a rift in their relationship.

I was so bothered about it that I hardly slept that night. In the morning I had a long talk with Mas and explained that we understood how important his traditions were to him; that we weren't really meaning to interfere or trying to change his traditions — unless we saw danger for the baby. We did it then only because we care so much for him and his wife and children. He said that he and his wife did understand. I hope so. But I wonder.

By sheer luck Mom Lotter's box of baby things for the orphanage arrived on Saturday (thank you, Mom!), and I took a few things out for the baby. They need them as much as the orphanage, and there were plenty. Mas and his wife are very grateful and happy.

The big news around here is "UDI," the Unilateral Declaration of Independence from Great Britain, by the Prime Minister of Rhodesia, Ian Smith. We wonder how much effect it will have on us directly. Malawi depends so much on things from Rhodesia: food and many other supplies. Everyone expected it to happen, but not until the end of November or in early December.

The U.S. Consulate in Salisbury, the capital of Rhodesia, has closed down. Will had to call the Consulate and was able to talk to the one man left, who said it was bedlam in their office. I should think! All our pay and other things come out of Salisbury, and they don't know yet where they will relocate. Probably Nairobi, but what a mess.

Will is still busy as a bird dog. Mike McCone has been gone seven weeks now. It was hard enough for the two of them together to get all the work done, so Will is working long, hard hours.

Leopard In a Bedroom?

Friday, November 19, 1965

We are in the poultry and egg business! Or I should say, the boys are. This is their first real business venture, if you don't count Kool-Aid stands in Davis.

I think we told you that the boys have been trying to figure out ways to earn money to send Alipo home with us when we go. Well, they have each been putting in a shilling a week of their allowances, and then they sold Cheena's nine puppies for about $15 apiece and opened a bank account to go toward this. Now they have taken part of that money out and have bought eighteen laying hens and a cock, chicken coop, feed, and all.

They went down to town and bought a receipt book yesterday and have an account book all worked up. As soon as we know for sure how many eggs we get a week, they can get customers. Of course I will buy all my eggs from them, too.

The boys had done all the moving and building all day Sunday. Monday was the first day of business, and there were fifteen eggs! The boys are so funny and excited about it and still not used to the correct terms. They say things like, "that one did an egg," or, this one "made" an egg. Guess you can tell they're not farm kids. Until the novelty wears off, the poor chickens are probably going to lay fewer and fewer eggs, the boys are in and out of the chicken house so often. I tell them they're making nervous wrecks out of the hens.

Our yard is quite large and very long, so we put the chicken coop way out in back, quite a ways from the house. It's about fifteen or twenty feet from Dr. Banda's wall, which goes the whole length of our yard. But this part is not near his house at all. However, what we didn't think about was that there is a big floodlight on the wall near the chicken coop. Dr. Banda has lights all over the place, so the chicken coop is lighted all night. Actually, we hear this is supposed to make them lay more because they think it's daylight, but it also causes the rooster to start crowing at 2:30 a.m.!

Oh dear. June Stewart just came by to tell me that one of our babies at the orphanage, little Rebecka, died Wednesday night. I was there on that morning, and nine of the babies were very sick with measles, and we wondered if Rebecka would make it. She died that night. Two others are critical right now. Last December they lost four babies with measles. I'm glad I wasn't here then.

The sisters really have their hands full out there now, so I think I'll go out several times next week. Two of my favorite littlest ones are awfully sick now. I guess this is one of the bad things about getting so attached to these babies.

We were very surprised to receive a clipping from a California newspaper (amazingly, an Associated Press release) about our Mrs. Kennedy at Cape Maclear. It was also in the Blantyre paper, of course. She shot a leopard in her bedroom! Imagine — in her *bedroom!* And only two nights after we had left.

We remember that one of the nights at Cape Maclear when we were sleeping outside Will had awakened in the middle of the night. He woke me up, whispering that he had heard "something in the bushes." Don said he heard it too. Then we were all wide awake. We guessed that maybe it was a baboon. Now we wonder if it was the leopard. What a thought!

I love Mrs. Kennedy's answer to, "Have you ever shot a leopard before?"

"Yes, but not in my bedroom!"

Baby Naming

It's only 7:15 a.m., but the week ahead is looking so busy that I thought I'd better at least start a letter now while I can. Today I am going to baby-sit the children of the Cox family, our American missionary friends we like so much, who are moving into a new house up our road. Their four boys and a girl are two, three, four, six and eight. Also, Nini McCone is coming over with two of her boys, ages two and three. Ricky and I are awaiting their arrival.

Don and Mike gave strict orders to lock their bedroom doors before the kids come. They have so many things that little kids would just love to get their hands on (and sometimes do): models, neatly sorted stamps, breakable carvings, African spears, daggers, and arrows, spiders in jars, and all sorts of other enticing "playthings." Their rooms are veritable dens of temptation for two- and three-year-old boys. This could be quite a morning.

Last night we had such a fun party. We had twenty-four for dinner and co-hosted it here at our house with June and Gary Stewart. It was our first attempt to entertain some of the local PCVs. Will dug a pit out in the front yard and we borrowed a big grate and barbecued T-bone steaks. We set up card tables on the lawn, with colorful African tablecloths, under the frangipani trees. We have four beautiful frangipani trees in bloom now and they smell heavenly. Our front yard is in terraces, and Friday has planted flowers all along the edges of each terrace. Everything is blooming right now. It all looked great.

We'd invited all of the PCVs from "Harmony House," a large house where about eight of them live, as well as others stationed locally. We all ate lots and topped it all off by wonderful chocolate éclairs that June Stewart made. Everyone seemed to have a good time.

Next Friday we're going to do the same thing for the volunteers stationed at Zomba, in the ambassador's cabin on the Zomba Plateau. On Thursday, Thanksgiving, we are having six or eight local Volunteers who are just about to leave Malawi. It's going to be a full week.

You should see Will now. He's one big skinned-up mess. He's playing rugby and having a ball. His knees, elbows, nose, shins, and forehead all have scabs on them. My, what a rough game it is! The Americans have already had two broken arms in only three games, but they all seem to enjoy it anyway. These have actually been practice games, and they have won one, tied one, and lost one. Pretty good, considering that none of them really knows how to play.

Will is a regular madman out there and makes me shudder to watch. He loves to tackle, and I think that he's trying to make up for about eighteen years of coaching sports and not being able to play. He leaves poor stunned men lying all over the field. The PCVs get a huge kick out of it (at least the ones who are only spectators). Guess it's a great way to work out any frustrations, and there are plenty of those around here these days. I just hope Will makes it through the season in one piece.

Believe it or not, the morning went so smoothly that I even was able to fix a nice quiet lunch for the Cox adults and us, having fixed a picnic in the backyard for the nine kids (the school kids were all here for lunch). I'm typing at a table by a window in Scott's room, where I can watch all the cute little blond boys and their trucks in the front driveway.

I have to add a sad note here. Our baby duiker died very unexpectedly on Saturday morning. The veterinarian said this is very common. In spite of all my warnings to the children that this could happen, as baby duikers are really hard to raise, *I* was the one who was really undone by it all. He was *my* baby, and he was so attached to me and tried to follow me all over the house, slipping and sliding on the waxed floor. Also I think (know!) I became too attached to him, especially because he was so teeny and fragile, and I knew that there was the possibility that he might not live. Darn.

I had known he was dying when I put him in a little basket and tearfully took him to the veterinarian, who was very sweet and understanding when I came all unglued. He said, "These little animals are very difficult to raise. You'd better get yourself a dog. They are easier." I managed to blubber that we already have two dogs, and even sometimes nine or eleven, and it doesn't help any at all. "Duikerbok," as we called him, was lots of pleasure for the six weeks we had him. He gave us so much enjoyment that I'd try it again if one came along.

Now happy news. Mas told us that they never name a baby until the day the baby "is out," which is the sixth day after it is born. Until that time the baby is never taken out of the house. This, no doubt, is why they would not let us bring the baby into our house here when Dr. Stewart and I wanted to clean off that mankwala.

So last Wednesday morning Mas came in and announced with great ceremony and a broad smile, "Madam, the baby is out!" Since it was early and a chilly morning, my immediate reaction, forgetting this tradition, was to say, "Oh, I hope she's warm enough!" But luckily Mas laughed, and said that they had taken her right back in.

This was the day they were to name her, and guess what they named her?? Gulp, lump in throat — Jane. I was so thrilled, I got all teary, and Mas (such a gentle soul) got all teary, too. His wife is so sweet, and when I am there she just beams whenever she says "Janie." (They put an "e" sound on the end of many words.) So she's Baby Janie. She also has an African name, but they keep referring to her as Janie. I'm not *very* excited, as you can tell!

We are gambling that Will will get to Syracuse for final selection of new Peace Corps Volunteers the latter part of December, although we hope not at Christmas. He hasn't the remotest idea whether they will send him or not, but we are hopeful. We decided not to mail our family Christmas presents, planning instead to send them with Will if he goes. They would have gotten to you late anyway, so we didn't have much to lose under the circumstances. We thought it worth the gamble. If he doesn't go, we're hoping that one of the terminating PCVs can take them. Sooo — cross your fingers.

Spots, Itches, & School Speeches

December 7, 1965

We just came back from the airport having — brace yourselves
— actually put Will on the plane for Nairobi-London-Washington,
DC. He finally made it! Right up until he boarded the plane, I was
furtively looking behind us for someone to run up with a cable
saying, "Stoppp!" But at least he's off on the first leg now, and what
a relief for him.

Guess I got a little carried away on my Christmas shopping
because he ended up eight pounds over the allowed weight.
However, they let him go without saying anything, and at Nairobi
before the next weighing-in he will put some of the things in the
underweight suitcase of a PCV who is going home all the way on
the same flights.

My, such a rat race trying to get everything done. He had
meetings; I had wrappings; we both were up late doing the third re-
draft of our Christmas letter. He will have it printed in Syracuse
and put into the envelopes I've already addressed. Now I don't even
know what it said. Guess he'd better mail me one.

Later — 9:30 pm. I thought I'd add a little more to this before I
turn in, especially since something funny has just happened.

I'm keeping the Stewarts' two children for eight days, as June
and Gary have gone to a medical conference in Kampala, Uganda.
They are combining this with a vacation for a three-week total and
we've divided up the babysitting among the Peace Corps wives.
This week is mine. They are darling children. Tammy is three and
Wayne is four, as is our Ricky.

However, those three little kids have managed to set a whole
household (complete with full-time help, yet) and family on its ear.
But now that the Christmas things and Will are off, tomorrow *was*
going to be less chaotic. *However,* the "funny thing" that has
happened — Tammy and Wayne have just broken out with
something. They have spots all over. And all *three* of them have
fevers tonight. Isn't that a riot?

Lee Ellison, another Peace Corps doctor on our staff just came
by to see them tonight and said, "If it's chicken pox they can't leave
here, and you've got 'em for the whole three weeks — haha!" A
really fine sense of humah there, don't you think? And he and
Ruth are supposed to have part of the babysitting time, too. It may
be an allergic reaction to something, however. We'll see what
tomorrow brings.

This is par for the course when Will goes away. Two things

always happen: someone gets sick, and the car breaks down. Believe it or not, the car did, just last night. However, Will was still here and was even driving it, which was most unusual (both that he was driving it, and that he was *here* when it broke down).

The car couldn't make it up our hill. We got almost up to our driveway, but it couldn't make it. We rolled back down and backed into Dr. Banda's driveway, revved it up, and tried another run at the hill. Couldn't make it. Backed down and into Dr. Banda's driveway again. By this time I don't know how many guards were peering over the wall, watching and grinning.

Scott ran to get Mas and Phillip to help Will push while I steered. They made another run at it, pushing me up to our driveway which then goes downhill to our house. So there she sits. Will just said, "Have it fixed." (Typical!) Now I am annoyed at *both* Will and the car.

Last week when Will had left town for Mzuzu, I had to leave it at the bottom of a hill and hitch a ride home. I think it's not only old, but very tired. I do have the Land Rover, but I shouldn't use it except in an emergency, as it's for official Peace Corps use.

Tomorrow Mike has a big speech in the St. Andrews School program. He is giving the farewell address for the standard six class, and we are so proud of him! Isn't this hard to believe after his dreadful start in that school?

Now here is a good example of the chaos in our house: tonight Mike was practicing his speech for me, standing at the end of the living room. Approximately halfway through, I gave him a pointer about diction, and this happened to be about the fifteenth interruption (only the first by me, however) and Mike said, "Oh Mom—" and backed up and accidentally sat down and squashed Scott's Kenner set building he'd been working on for hours. This, needless to say, brought on wailing and howls from Scott and was all it took for absolute and complete bedlam to take over. Poor Mike gave up and went stomping off to his room, and that was the end of that rehearsal. But I think he'll do fine.

* * *

December 9

Well, after consultations with two doctors it's finally been decided that it's not chicken pox! They're not sure what it is. The kids have spots and temperatures and are itchy. They're not bites, either, but something erupting from inside. Very odd.

Yesterday I managed to leave three crying children with Mas and Phillip and escape to Mike's program. It was wonderful, and I must say that the British do things up brown. The auditorium was filled with people. In the front, facing the audience was a row of chairs with six children, Mike being one of them.

Standard six, Mike's class, did the whole program, announcing and everything. It was well-organized and went off like clockwork. There were three speakers, two girls and Mike. They gave a resumé of the year's activities and introduced the choir and the recorder group. Mike's part lasted about five minutes and he did beautifully. He looked so cute in his crisp uniform and his kneesocks, and he was all smily. I was so proud, and especially sorry Will was away.

Even the Chancellor of the University came, making a grand entrance in his black robes, and sat in the front with Mike and the other speakers. At the end of the program he gave out the year's awards. Everything is based on the results of the Cambridge Exams, and prizes are given for first, second, and third in each class, with additional prizes for effort, progress, etc.

Our boys didn't get any prizes, but did awfully well. Mike came in seventh out of thirty-nine! Scott came in tenth out of thirty-one, and Don thirteenth out of thirty-four. We're pleased with all of them. But think how the little guy who comes in thirty-fourth out of thirty-four must feel. This system might be fine for the top ones, but think how demoralizing for the bottom ones. Finally, our boys are all happier in school.

We keep thinking about Mike's famous ironic words a couple of weeks ago: that he has "learned much more this year than he would have at school in Davis, because here they *discipline* so much!" We were stunned. It's true that he has actually learned to buckle down and concentrate, but we hate to think it came about from fear of getting beaten physically. However, apparently it did work for Mike. Isn't that awful, though? All through school his teachers have always said he was capable of doing good work if only he would concentrate and pay attention.

I've been avoiding telling you yet another tragic thing. Last Friday, Alipo, Mike's beloved big dog, was hit by a lorry and killed. It was like a nightmare and something I'd had many a nightmare about because Mike and that dog were so devoted. Mike and I were both right there, although we didn't see the actual impact.

Alipo had run down our hill, having heard Mike shouting to me as I drove around the corner at the bottom of the hill. Mike was on the other side of the road with his friends, and Alipo came galloping across to greet him — right in front of a truck. The truck kept going, and Mike and I ran to Alipo, who was then still alive. Thank goodness there was no blood or anything, as that would have been so much worse. We got some men to help us get him into the car and we rushed him to the veterinarian, but he had died by the time we got there.

I just can't even type about it, it was so awful for Mike. He couldn't eat for two days and actually even got sick. He's better now, and the boys are going on with the money-raising, even though the chicken business was all to raise money to send Alipo home with us. It will now be either to get a good German Shepherd when we get home or, well I don't know what. We may get another dog here, although I'm for waiting. We do have Cheena. Think we'll leave the decision to Mike.

Alipo was such a good dog and so beautiful and obedient. We told Mike that we knew no other dog could replace Alipo, but that he could love another dog just as much. He's thinking about it. Alipo was supposedly all of ours, but, in reality, he was Mike's — a one-man dog. Golly, how am I ever going to survive raising four boys and all their pets? Awful. I had to wear dark glasses all weekend to cover up my red eyes.

The rainy season is here, though not full-scale yet. It is really hot and muggy and sticky. It's beautiful and sunny right now, but will suddenly cloud up with no warning, and amidst crashing thunder and lightning, buckets will pour down. Then, just as suddenly, the sky will clear up and be lovely again. It has done this every day. You don't dare go anywhere without an umbrella. Raincoats are too hot, and you end up being wetter on the inside than on the outside.

The other night Don and Rick and I went to the Christmas program at St. Andrews Prep School, in which Mike and Scott both sang. It was so hot, we were sitting there just dripping. At a *Christmas* program — and I was in my coolest summer dress and white heels. Seemed so odd, even with our being from California.

Will had an interesting traveling companion for his trip to Washington, DC. He took a *live tarantula* in a coffee can in his flight bag! This tarantula had a five-and-a-half-inch leg span. Some PCVs caught it in Lilongwe and thought it was so big that it should go to the Smithsonian Institute in Washington, DC, via Will.

I had the dubious honor of having to transfer this monster out of the cookie canister it had been delivered in by a Peace Corps driver (who left it and fled), into a coffee can, because those PCVs wanted their cookie canister back. Friday was reluctantly helping me. One of us would shake the cookie canister over the coffee can, which the other would hold. The biggest trouble was that both containers were opaque. We couldn't tell whether the tarantula had actually landed down inside the coffee can without looking into it.

Since we both kept trying to keep the containers at arm's

length, this made it next to impossible to see into the things. ("You look." — "No — *you* look!") I was covered with goose bumps, and I swear that Friday, who is very black, turned white. We could hear the tarantula scrabbling like crazy, hanging onto the sides, scaring us even more. Finally, somehow we got it into the coffee can and we both nearly collapsed. At times like this, I'm sure all of our household help think of looking elsewhere for jobs.

Then, to top things off for poor Friday, the very next day when he was hanging some things on the clothesline, a forty-three inch green snake dropped out of a tree right over his head and landed at his feet! He killed it with his panga, and it's in our freezer waiting to be identified. Someone said it's just a harmless green tree snake. I don't care how "harmless" it's supposed to be — forty-three inches is *big*. And *very* harmful to my mental health. And I wonder where its family is? Shudderrrr.

Thank goodness the three sick kids are all feeling better and the mysterious spots are going away. We'll probably never know what the heck it was.

"Mr. Ambassador, I Couldn't Disagree
With You More — "

December 9, 1965

Will should be in Washington, DC right now. He had four
hours in Nairobi, and was meeting with the Kenya Peace Corps
Director who is coming here Saturday to be the temporary duty
officer until Will comes back. What an earful Will will give him.
What a mess things are here.

The Peace Corps is on shaky ground in Malawi now for lots of
reasons, some its own fault, admittedly, but many beyond its
control or even understanding. Will has had four meetings in the
last few weeks with Prime Minister Banda, the last one just before
he left. That one was a bit more encouraging, thank goodness.
And then there is the American Embassy — but things are looking
a little better there now, too. Will has been Acting Director for
these ten weeks, and I'm sure there couldn't have been more
crises.

From London he was to go on to Washington, DC, where
Mike McCone was to meet him, and where they would be able to
spend the evening together. We're sure now that Mike won't be
allowed to come back — and he is really getting burned on this
whole deal. Not by Peace Corps, but by the State Department.
However, in all these ten weeks there has not been one single
official word on this from anyone. Only the letters that Mike
himself has written. When he suddenly had to leave ten weeks ago,
it was only to be for a few days, or a week at the longest.

This whole thing was over the U.S. Ambassador's going into a
tirade because the Peace Corps here in Malawi had let the PCVs
publish an article in their in-country PCV newsletter. This little
newsletter, aptly named *The Migraine*, is written by and for PCVs
here in Malawi. The editorial, written by a PCV, condemned the
Vietnam war. The ambassador summoned Mike and Will to the
Embassy. He shook the newsletter at them and said that this
article was *absolutely* unacceptable. He was furious.

Mike told the ambassador that he felt that the PCVs had a
right to voice their opinions about the U.S. in their own PCV
newsletter, and that as long as they said nothing critical of the
Malawi government or Malawians, they did not give up their right
to free speech about U.S. policy when they joined the Peace
Corps. The ambassador was livid and adamant about the whole
thing.

Then Mike said, "Mr. Ambassador, I couldn't disagree with

you more." Will's jaw dropped — partly in admiration — and partly in fear for Mike. So this was the start of the whole mess. The ambassador immediately cabled the State Department and requested that Mike be recalled! He had to leave the country within twenty-four hours. It was awful.

[A couple of interesting sidelights here: Our PCV who had written that editorial in The Migraine *was Paul Theroux, who is today a prominent writer in the U.S. Also, most significantly, we found out that the ambassador had a son in the military service in Vietnam at that very time. No wonder! However, Will was in total agreement with Mike on his stance on PCVs' freedom of speech. He also says it was that article by Paul Theroux that really opened his own eyes about our U.S. policy in Vietnam.]*

Nini McCone and their three little boys are still here alone. She is so good about it I can hardly believe it. I know she is just dying inside, but outwardly she is holding up amazingly well. We've been doing a lot of things together, going to movies and such. Such a wonderful person. She even kept the Stewart children for four days, insisting on helping when Gary and June were out of the country. We really like both Mike and Nini so much and are sick about all this mess.

After Mike McCone got to Washington, DC, another untimely thing happened that made things worse for Peace Corps Malawi, and therefore for Mike, since the buck always stops with the director. This was the alleged political involvement of one of our PCVs with the rebel party. Dr. Banda found out about it and was so enraged that he ordered the PCV deported immediately. It really was bad for Peace Corps. It was also unfortunate for the PCV, who was an excellent teacher and Volunteer with only a few months left to finish his third year. It is a strict Peace Corps policy that PCVs do not become involved with in-country politics.

[That Volunteer happened to be Paul Theroux, the same Volunteer who had written the anti-Vietnam war article.]

So we are in big trouble with not only our own U.S. Embassy, but the Prime Minister of Malawi. And it all comes down on the head of Mike McCone. It's so unfortunate for Mike, because he is really a good director and great guy. Now it's just a waiting game to see what will happen.

In the meantime, Will is going from Washington, DC to Syracuse University to the Peace Corps Malawi training program in a few days. He has to clue the new trainees in on the problems here. Final selection of the new volunteers will be completed on December 20, and he'll leave Syracuse for Malawi on that day. If he's lucky and can get permission from our State Department to fly back through Salisbury, Rhodesia, he'll be back in Blantyre the afternoon of December 24 — for Christmas Eve! He has to get special permission since the U.S. is participating in the international boycott of Rhodesia because of UDI (Unilateral Declaration of Independence). This means, among other things, that no employee of our government can go to Rhodesia. If he can't get the special permission to go through Salisbury, the only flight down here from Nairobi is on Christmas Day in the afternoon. Darn.

We have such exciting plans for Christmas Eve. We'll have a lot of PCVs in, and if Will doesn't make it, the kids will still have a great time. On Christmas Day we're having open house for PCVs late in the afternoon, with Christmas cheer and snacks. That will be fun.

Mother Catherine's Birthday

December 15, 1965

We had a cable from Will from Washington, DC saying that he and Tarantula both made it safely. Tarantula is now in residence at the Smithsonian Zoo. They were very happy to welcome him there, as he is especially large and the only one they have from Malawi. I really don't know how Will managed to get him (or her?) through customs. It was in his flight bag — however, in a coffee can with a *very* tightly taped-on lid.

Today I worked at the orphanage, and tomorrow I'm going to work at the Well-Baby Clinic in Blantyre. I'll be taking Joyce's place there every Thursday from now on, as the Leaches are getting ready to leave on January 8. I just hate to see them go. We have such a good time together.

Friday, December 17, is Mother Catherine's birthday, and Joyce and I are giving her a surprise party. All the nuns are in on it, and we've worked it out so that we will be out there on the pretense of sorting baby clothes at the orphanage.

Joyce and I are collaborating on the birthday cake, and the sisters are making coffee and tea. I'm making a chocolate layer cake, and Joyce is making her special icing. We'd asked the sisters what we could get Mother Catherine for a present and one of them suggested a record holder, because one night when they were playing some records Mother Catherine had commented that she really must get a record holder or all their records would get warped and ruined. So that was easy. We got a beautiful Christmas music record to put in it.

When we were in town shopping for the present today, who should come along honking her horn at us like mad, but Mother Catherine herself. She had a huge crate tied onto the top of the station wagon. She said that her aunt had sent her a check and she'd rushed right into town to buy a washing machine for the orphanage! She said, "Aren't I just terrible? The check just came in the mail today, and I've already spent it!" She was so excited to tell us that she held up traffic in both directions. She is just something else. How lucky we are to have our lives cross like this. It will be such fun to surprise her on her birthday.

* * *

Saturday, December 18

We pulled off the surprise party — Mother Catherine really

was surprised! It was a huge success and our cake was delicious. We had tea and coffee and lots of laughs and fun with all the sisters. Mother Catherine wondered how we knew she needed a record holder. We said that one of the babies told us.

Last night I got the giggles in bed because Will mentioned a man's name which brought to mind an embarrassing experience I had a couple of weeks ago. Will had said that he was going to an "Economic Seminar," which is really a men's poker party, at Mr. Foutouhi's house tonight. Mr. Foutouhi's whole name is Abel (pronounced "Obbel") Fazl (pronounced Fozzle) Foutouhi (pronounced Footooee). He is the Director of the U.S. Information Service and is a very nice man.

One day I was driving up a hill in town with Rick, when we saw Mr. Foutouhi walking down the hill. I said, "There's Abel Fazl Foutouhi," because it's kind of fun to say his name. As we rounded a corner just two feet from Abel's nose, four-year-old Rick leaned out the window and shouted, "Hi Ozzle Fozzle!" I was so embarrassed that I darn near drove right up over the curb. Now, of course, I just can't think of this nice man as anything but "Ozzle Fozzle." I can only imagine what he must think of us.

Our Christmas 1965

December 27, 1965

We had a great Christmas. Will got back earlier than expected, on December 23rd, with State Department permission to go through Rhodesia. We had a nine-foot-tall tree (for about 85¢), which is some kind of evergreen and not bad, though a bit more scraggly than we're used to. We decorated it with homemade ornaments, and it actually looked quite pretty.

The ornament business turned out to be another Mother-Fiasco, the idea having been that it would be "such a nice children-project." Ha. After the first half-hour it turned out to be a complete "Mother-project." And a nine-foot tree takes one heck of a lot of ornaments, I'll tell you.

We had our own family Christmas dinner on Christmas Eve with two turkeys, one eleven pounds and one five pounds. One turkey alone would not have been enough. They were delicious. We had everything except cranberry sauce. Most things are scarce and more expensive now because of UDI and no supplies coming from, or through, Rhodesia. We didn't have any PCVs in for that dinner because there were so many in town, and you can't single out just a few. Also we were going to have an open house for everyone on Christmas Day.

Christmas Day was perfect. We had Open House from 3:00 p.m. to 6:00 p.m., and about forty-nine people came, mostly PCVs. I've never baked and prepared so much food as I had the week before. Yeast rolls, cookies, ham, cheese balls, etc. It was loads of fun, and everybody seemed to have plenty to eat. We played Christmas carols on the record player and had decorations everywhere. The most-heard remark from PCVs — "Gosh, it really *is* Christmas!"

Will brought back tapes from home for us. His brother Dick teaches music at Oakland High School and directs the band. Dick had the Oakland High School band play some music and dedicate it to the "Peace Corps in Africa." So we played this on Christmas Day. It was just wonderful. What made this *really* extra special was, not only did we have a houseful of PCVs, but one couple, Fritz and Emily Sparks, had graduated from Oakland High! In fact, Fritz had actually played in the band there. All this was before Dick was teaching there, however. Fritz had also played football and Dick had taped a whole Oakland High School rally — and Fritz and Emily knew all the yells and songs. It was so much fun.

Also our kids' new toys went over big. Some people were trying to work Scott's new printing press, some were in Don's room listening to his new records on his new record player, and of course there were those shooting Rick's new guns and working the dump truck on the floor.

One touching scene was PCV Pete Johnson holding two little girls (daughters of British friends here) on his lap, saying, "Well, I have thirteen younger brothers and sisters at home." Imagine — he's the oldest of fourteen. It seemed that almost all the PCVs enjoyed being in a home with little kids at Christmas time.

On Christmas morning some African kids had come around to our driveway with a little musical band. They were an experience to hear and to watch. They were dressed up with cardboard hats, cardboard "spats" on their lower legs — attempting to look like the Kings African Rifles Band, which is the Malawi Army Band. There was a homemade guitar, banjo, penny-whistle, metal-can "drum" with a string attached which served as a bass, and many tin-can and cardboard "drums." They were accompanied by a joyous group of Malawian children who sang (very loud) and danced. It was a sight to see. Will took pictures, and we were sorry we didn't have a working tape recorder.

We asked them to come back in the afternoon when all the people would be here, but unfortunately that group didn't come back. Another older group did come, and they drummed and danced (and Will had gotten the Peace Corps tape recorder by then). One of them was dressed in a big mask and corn husks and was quite a sensation. They do this and hope for money or gifts, and we were prepared with little boxes of cigarettes. However, we really preferred the kids' group.

* * *

December 29

Well, that was the end of that letter. There I was, sitting in the sun in the backyard, all loveliness in my curlers, old shorts, and perspiration, when up roared two motorcycles. I only put curlers in my hair once a week but *always* get caught by visitors.

A couple of weeks ago Nini McCone came over and was quite amused that I was sitting at the table chatting and drinking coffee with three or four PCV guys with my head in my ridiculous voluminous hair-bonnet-dryer that has an equally ridiculous-looking big purple plastic flower right in the front. The bonnet part has a hot-air hose attached to a box-like electric thing which I have to plug into the electricity converter. Unfortunately, the converter happens to be in the dining room and is much too bulky and heavy to move. I must admit that it (and I) were pretty weird-looking, but what could I do?

[I probably don't need to point out that the '60s were before discreet small hand-held hair dryers were invented.]

That night a group of us was meeting here to go to the movies, and Nini walked in and sat down — wearing a huge shower cap with a big purple flower (live) dangling down her forehead!

One weekend during Christmas vacation it seemed that everybody was in town for one reason or another. The Field Center was overflowing, so we had four PCVs stay here with us. With Will still gone, Rick could sleep with me and free up one bed. Then with Don's top bunk, the couch and a cot in the living room, it all worked out fine. On that Saturday morning nine PCVs came for Don's now-famous pancakes. There were fourteen the week before, and it really is fun.

Sunday of that same weekend was eventful. I had played "taxi driver" to a rugby game in Cholo, about a forty-five minute drive from here. We all came back tired and the kids and two PCVs and I had just sat down to dinner when a call came that a PCV was very sick and could I get the doctor? So I bolted my dinner and — more driving — went to get the new doctor and led him to where this PCV lived, which was practically up on top of a mountain. When I came back, a bunch of guys had come over to listen to the Green Bay Packers game on our short-wave radio.

It was about 11 p.m. when the game was over, and I was too tired to drive anyone anywhere, so I said for them to take the car and bring it back in the morning. Most were staying at the Field Center, but one, Jim Seidel, was staying with Dr. Peck, who lives quite a distance away. Otherwise they would all have walked. So Jim dropped the guys off at the Field Center and drove to the Pecks' house and — guess what? No brakes!

He crashed right into the Pecks' garage, luckily not doing much damage to the garage, but breaking a headlight on the car. Then in the morning when he was taking the car to the garage to get the headlight fixed, he had a blowout! Both of those things would have happened to *me* the next day, or worse — could have happened that day or evening with all the people crowded in the car, or on that mountain. Scary. So I told Jim that I was sure glad it happened to *him* instead of me.

"Thanks. Thanks a lot!" he said. Well, he probably won't be wanting to borrow our car again soon.

New Year's Day 1966

January 1, 1966

The flying ants are attacking! These flying things are all over the place. They arrived on Christmas Eve and shed their wings all over my pretty Christmas decorations — a new and creative type of Christmas "snow"? How there can still be more of them really amazes me. I'd heard they were coming but surely wasn't prepared for what we got.

The night they arrived I looked at the table that I had just finished decorating, and there must have been a thousand wings all over it. They come flying in through all the doors, windows, and cracks in the house, drop their wings — which are about a half-inch long — and crawl away. Under lights, especially outdoors, there are *millions* of them.

Some people call them sausage flies, probably because they are sort of fat, and lots of Malawians *eat* them. Actually, I think they are termites. You see people putting buckets of water under outdoor lights so that they can collect them when they fall. They gather them up and pat them into cakes, sometimes frying them and sometimes eating them raw. They are considered quite a delicacy, and I've heard that they have a lot of nutritional value. Some of our PCVs have even tried them and say that if you don't know what you're eating, they taste pretty good. Crunchy seems to be the preferred style. Hmm? Let's see — for dinner tonight — shall I fry them? Or perhaps serve them on pasta?

Mike McCone finally came back just before Christmas! They left last Tuesday for a new assignment in Sarawak, Malaysia. We were so sad to see them go. Mike was gone for three months while Peace Corps Washington and the State Department were trying to decide what to do with him. All that time Nini and the boys (three, four, and five) were here alone, thinking from the very beginning that Mike would be back any day. She was so brave about it, always managing to smile, entertain, and do all sorts of things to keep busy. I would have gone flapping up the nearest wall after the first few weeks (days?). We all have the greatest respect and admiration for Nini. I'll really miss her, but at least we'll probably see them again, as they are both from California (San Francisco and Marin County).

Nini and Mike did the most amazing thing the night before they left. They gave a dinner party for all the staff and their children. Eighteen adults and thirteen children (all but four under five years of age!). Nothing was packed yet, the packers were coming the next morning, and they had to be at the airport to leave at 12:30 p.m. We tried to talk them out of doing this dinner party, but to no avail. I don't know how they did it. I did manage to take their boys to our house the morning they left, bathed, fed, dressed them, and got them to the airport on time, but this was just a drop in the bucket. They made it — amazing people.

Don and Mike are going on a trip next week that should be really great. One of our health PCVs in Karonga, all the way up north, invited them to come and spend a week. He works out in the villages and wants to take them along with him. So — and this is one of the best parts — we will put them on the train here in Blantyre and they will go (probably all day) to Monkey Bay, where they will get on the Ilala, the big lake steamer on Lake Malawi, on Friday. It will take three days and two nights by boat to get to Karonga. Then the following Friday they will fly back to Blantyre on the Beaver, the little single-engine plane that hops down, taking almost all day. How's that for a trip for a couple of twelve- and thirteen-year-old American kids? (I wish I could go.) The PCV they will stay with up there, Tom Popp, couldn't be nicer, so this is a real opportunity for the boys.

Last Sunday was a day of big celebration here, although we never did find out what they were celebrating. Mobs of Malawians started coming early in the morning to the Prime Minister's house and were outside all the gates and in groups in front of our house, singing and dancing. You could hear drums constantly. Then, in the afternoon he opened up his gates and let people into his courtyard. There were probably three hundred people in his courtyard and countless others outside. He and some other dignitaries sat up on his porch all afternoon watching the dancing of different groups and listening to and giving speeches. It was exciting hearing the drums and singing all day.

We went over to watch and take a few pictures. To our surprise, Dr. Banda saw us standing in the back of the crowd, leaned over, spoke to his chief guard, and pointed to us. The guard came down, worked his way through the crowd, and escorted us up to the front, where we could see and take pictures. It was terribly hot, so we didn't stay long, but it was interesting. And noisy. We went home and set up the tape recorder in our living room, stuck the mike out the window and taped the rest of it. The festivities next door were blaring all the rest of the day. Quite a few PCVs came over during the afternoon to see and hear and take pictures. I have a "watching stump" out in front — a tree stump with bricks on top, right next to the wall — think I'll start charging admission to stand on my stump and peek over.

Santa Claus brought Rick a pair of cowboy boots from Washington, DC, and he hasn't had them off yet, except to go to bed — and that under protest. He also has the pants, shirt, hat, holsters, and guns. The Malawians get a huge kick out of him. Most of them know the term "cowboy" and laugh and laugh.

We fixed up a stocking for Mas's little Saidi and filled it with most of the same things that we got for Rick — little toys, balloons, paint box, etc. We gave Mas and Phillip each a wristwatch, Friday a new shirt, and their wives and children gifts, too. Baby Janie is doing beautifully, weighs about ten pounds now, and is adorable. We gave her a sweater and a dress. With all these families to care for, it really took some thinking and shopping, but it was fun. Joyce Leach's housekeeper has *nine* children, so I shouldn't complain.

The Nguludi Orphanage fund is coming along so well. Mother Catherine gave me a pile of checks the other day that Sister Mary Joy's family and friends sent with their Christmas cards. I have to sit down and figure it out, but I know it must be over $500 now.

Our first purchase with some of the money came last week — the water heater! It came just after I'd given four little babies cold baths. There had been no hot water left in the kettle, and some of the babies had diarrhea and *had* to have baths right then — I just about cry when I do this. We also ordered ceramic tiles for the walls of the changing and bathing room because the walls were rotting from being washed so much. What an exciting day — just think — *hot* water at the orphanage!

"Director Will"

By now you've received the cable that Will is the new Peace
Corps Director for Malawi! We are thrilled and *relieved*. The last
few months have been an unbelievable strain for everyone — living
in limbo with no appointed director. Whew. Will had to send an
acceptance cable to Sargent Shriver in Peace Corps Washington,
and we had fun trying to figure out what to say. "You're kidding!"
"It's about time!" etc. He ended up with "Thrilled and honored to
accept Malawi Directorship. Nominate my wife for Deputy." I
thought that was pretty funny, but I do wonder if "Sarge" will
think so.

Wes Leach's plane took off at the very same time that his
replacement's plane landed here on Saturday. You can't get it
much closer than that, but it's a shame that they didn't get to meet
each other. We were all standing around red-eyed at the Leaches'
leaving (that was awful), so it was a good thing to have this new
young couple arrive to cheer us up. Keith and Phyllis Bravinder
and five-month-old Jennifer, an adorable baby, are also from
California. Keith and Phyllis were PCVs in Ethiopia for two years
and then trained Peace Corps Volunteers at UCLA for the last
year and a half.

After we got the Bravinders settled (sort of) in a nice
apartment, we had them over for dinner, along with Dr. Ellison
and his wife, Ruth. What a nice group of congenial people. We
were all pretty tired though, the Bravinders from their long trip,
and we from having been at the airport from 12:30 until after
4:00 p.m. All the planes had been late taking off and coming in.
We might as well set up camp there.

We spent two more hours there again yesterday waiting for the
new group of thirty-five PCVs to come in — also late, of course.
Tomorrow we go out *again*, to greet the new U.S. Ambassador and
family. Then next Friday we go out to the airport *again* to meet
the Beaver with Don and Mike on it. No doubt someone will come
in or go out in between. Thank goodness it's only ten miles out
there. The airport is much busier than usual now because so many
planes from all over are coming here to refuel for the Zambia oil
airlift. Because of UDI in Rhodesia, no planes, trains or trucks are
going through that country. A big plane from Ireland was there
yesterday, carrying a load of oil tanks. At least there is a lot to
watch at the airport now.

There were about eight or ten PCVs on the plane coming in

from Dar Es Salaam yesterday, having been on vacation in various parts of East Africa. Will invited them all over for pancakes on Sunday morning. We ended up with fourteen for pancakes and had a great time. We are going to change our "pancake morning" from Saturdays to Sundays because we'll have more time to relax. Stores and offices are closed on Sundays. We listened to records, drank coffee and heard all about Madagascar, which a group of the PCVs had just visited. It sounded so interesting that we went over to their house later to see all the things they'd brought back.

Friday we went to a beautiful tea plantation at the base of Mlanje Mountain to put Cheena in a kennel while she is in heat. Yes, I misjudged *again*. Mlanje is about an hour's drive from here. The mountain is 10,000 feet high, overlooking tea estates, pineapple crops, and banana groves. Everything was green and gorgeous. Tea estates are breathtakingly beautiful. We came back with a trunk loaded with ripe, fresh pineapples.

I'd taken a PCV out there with me. He told me on the way that he was a biology major in college and was now doing a study on snakes during vacation with a professor from the University of Malawi. I told him we still had that "harmless green tree snake" in our freezer, if he would like to have it. He said that they were interested in all kinds and took it with him.

Later that evening he and the professor (from Stanford, yet — is *everybody* from California?) came over to show us our snake in a jar of preservative and to inform us that our 43-inch "harmless green tree snake" is a boomslang! A very venomous snake. Oh, swell. This is the one that had been in the tree with the kids' tree house and had dropped down almost on Friday's head. Now I *really* wonder where its family is.

We're having a man from the Department of East African Studies at Syracuse University over for dinner tonight, so I must go shop. I'm also going to a shower this afternoon for a PCV couple who are getting married on Friday. My days seem to fill up.

Along with the happy news of Will's new appointment — (every silver lining has its cloud??) — we have our first diagnosed case of malaria in the family. Rick has been awfully sick for three days, and today we got the diagnosis. He's feeling better now, but it is malaria. You say "malaria" here, and it's not much worse than saying "flu" or "cold." Rick happened to be a likely candidate, as he has had three bouts of tonsillitis in six weeks, so his resistance was down.

We all take the oral prophylactic suppressant, but if your resistance is down, it doesn't necessarily suppress it. Also, if a person is taking the prophylactic chloroquine, the malaria doesn't always show up in blood tests. This makes it hard to diagnose. Already the shots of chloroquine have helped, and his temperature has gone down from 104° to 99.4°. Now that we recognize the symptoms and know that the blood test doesn't always tell all, we are pretty sure that I had malaria last March when I was so sick. The miraculous rally you make with the whopping doses of chloroquine is more or less the proof of the pudding.

Will just found out that the African Peace Corps Directors' Conference is in March in Nairobi, and we will all go!! We wish it were in West Africa so we could see that area, but won't really complain. The whole family will go, and we'll see other parts of East Africa at the same time. Whoopee!

Right now though, I feel so sorry for Will. He has (I counted last night) nine concurrent crises going on — seven of which he has to face today. They're all serious things and big decisions, such as whether to send home some PCVs who have goofed up on a few things; and two female PCVs who need to go home for psychiatric reasons; plus several other even more serious problems. This has really been a week of crises. It seems that a whole lot of things have come to a head at the same time — and unfortunately Will has to sort them all out. However, as Director now, I guess that's what he gets paid for.

On a happier note — we put Don and Mike on the train Friday morning to go on the first leg of their trip up to Karonga to stay with the PCVs. The train was a sight to see. It has a steam engine, vintage 1890, we'd guess. It takes twelve hours to go the hundred fifty miles to the lake. I was happy to see that PCVs Fritz and Emily Sparks were going to be on that same train, but I didn't let on, either to them or to the boys, about my secret relief.

Then, that night, the boys were to board the Ilala for the three-day trip up to Karonga. They were really excited. Will and I can't wait to hear about the whole trip when we pick them up at the airport here next Friday.

Our house in Blantyre.

The Family, 1966.
L-R: Mike, Scott, Will, Rick, Don, Jane.
Dogs: Bambo and Cheena.
Presidential flag in background.

L-R: Don, Mike, Scott. Rick's first day of school (1967) with Cheena.

Our house staff, Mas, Phillip, and Friday.

Mas and wife with Janie & Saidi.

Janie & Jane.

Will & Maluwa.

Mike & Alipo in dugout canoe.

Don & the pangolin, "Gloria Thing."

Bill Goat with
Jennie Bravinder and Rick.

Rick & Scott and friends
with our duiker.

Rick & Friday with Bill and
Two-and-Six, ready for school.

PCV Mack McKinnon & Don carrying
some of Mack's hospital equipment into
Nguludi Mission hospital.

Rick, Jane, & Don at
Nguludi orphanage.

Sister Mary Joy. 1965.

Jane with children at
Nguludi orphanage.

Mike & Don presenting athletic equipment from Davis, CA to HHI secondary school.

Will's parents at PCV Bill Luke's primary school.

PCV Ruth Nighswander
and pet monkey.

Rick with PCV Mike Hill.

Mike McCone & Will with two priests in Msiku Hills.

In Ngorongoro Crater. 1966.

Safari camp near Lake Manyara. Lotter boys with Mrs. Falk (L), Mr. Falk (Center), & Steve the guide (R).

Mike with bike.

Ujeni inspecting Jane's hair
for fleas.

Malawi village boy. Painting by Jane Lotter.

Adventures for Don and Mike

Friday, January 14, 1966

We picked up Don and Mike at the airport today at 12:35. They had a marvelous time! They loved the whole thing, even the slow twelve-hour train ride. They occupied themselves, they said, by hanging out the door, shooting their slingshots. (Oh, swell. Glad I wasn't there.) For the three days on the Ilala, they ate at the captain's table and said he was really nice to them. All this was on their own — but I'm still glad that Fritz and Emily, the Peace Corps couple, were on this same trip.

The boat arrived in Chitipa, near Karonga, just before dark, and Tom Popp and Ken Rich, the two PCVs, were there to meet them. What nice guys to invite the boys to do this. Karonga is pretty primitive, with no electricity, only a few stores, and a school. It is surrounded by small villages. Near the place where Tom and Ken live, a bridge had washed out, so they had to carry their stuff on their heads and wade across a hundred-foot-wide stream — shining their flashlights to watch out for crocodiles! Now how's that for a pretty good start on an adventure for a twelve- and thirteen-year-old?

Tom and Ken are very popular in their village. They were wonderful to the boys and are such good examples for them. The village people loved meeting Don and Mike, because they rarely get to see white children. Mike's bright blue eyes probably fascinated them as well — a phenomenon we had discovered when far out in the bush, where the people don't see many fair-skinned people or blue eyes.

The highlight of the visit was going out on a hippo hunt, if you can imagine! A hippo had been coming into some of the villages and eating their gardens, so the people organized a hunt. How would you like to look out your window and see a hippo eating your vegetables and petunias? They tracked him for miles, but didn't find him. Don and Mike said it was pretty exciting — because they never knew when this thing might come crashing out of the eight-foot-tall reeds they were tramping through.

We just found out that hippos kill more humans than any other land animal in Africa. I'm sure glad I didn't know that they were going to go on a hippo hunt until they were home safe.

They went on twenty-mile bicycle rides out to other villages, saw tribal dancing, and in general had an unforgettable time. All this was topped off by getting to fly home today in the little single-engine six-passenger plane, the Beaver. It's about a six-hour flight and low enough that you can see everything below. What an adventure for a couple of pipsqueak American kids.

We are all going to a reception this afternoon at 4:00 for two of our PCVs who are getting married. An American friend from down our road and two PCVs and I got together yesterday to do the cake. The other lady baked the large, three-layered rectangular cake, and then the four of us iced and decorated it. It looks just beautiful (if we do say so!); however, it has to travel about thirty minutes on a bumpy road to the reception. We're crossing our fingers.

Pancakes Unlimited

Monday, January 17, 1966

Now, about our Sunday Morning Pancakes. It is absolutely the best way to be able to feed any number of people. We just always keep well-stocked with flour, sugar, eggs, milk, etc., and it doesn't matter how many hungry people appear at our door. Any PCVs and friends in town at the time are invited, and we have had anywhere from one or two to fourteen or fifteen — or at least we did until this last Sunday. We'd often joked, "What would we do if thirty showed up some time — ha ha?" Well, *thirty-four* showed up yesterday!

It was just one of those things: school vacation and the start of a conference here, so there were an unusual number of PCVs in town. I didn't realize how many were here until we were halfway through, since I was out in the kitchen with my spatula and griddle, or I no doubt would have fainted. The gals pitched in and helped me in the kitchen, while some others helped Mas do the dishes in the back and reset the table for the next shifts.

We kept the coffee pots going so those who were not eating were drinking coffee and playing records or reading magazines (Will's mother sends us practically every magazine in print) in the living room. Some were out in front shooting baskets. Everyone seemed to be having a good time, in spite of having to wait. Our living room and dining room adjoin and are cheery and roomy, so it really is fine for large groups.

Just when we'd fed all but the last three people, our wonderful trusty electric griddle that bakes twelve pancakes at once went *off*. We thought it had burned out, like my electric frying pan has. Oh, no. With plans for draping the front door on Sunday mornings with black crêpe paper and holding memorial services for our "Sunday Morning Pancakes," we struggled on with frying pans and other things for the last eaters. Awful. Later I discovered, with immense relief and joy, that someone had accidentally tripped the transformer switch. The griddle was fine! What a relief. Our Sunday morning tradition can carry on.

[We just recently found out that THE GRIDDLE still lives. It came home to the U.S. with a subsequent Peace Corps staff person. After thirty-five years, I wonder if it still works?]

Yesterday during all the pancake adventures, Rick was crying and sick and Scott was *madly* celebrating his ninth birthday. I had the birthday party to look forward to later that afternoon. Let me say — I would rather *any day* feed thirty-four guests breakfast than have a birthday party for seven little boys around nine years old! The morning went fast, but I thought the afternoon would *never end.*

One scene that struck me very funny in the afternoon was the U.S. Ambassador's little boy, Tarpley Jones, arriving at the party in his chauffeur-driven black limousine. In fact, the Ambassador himself was sitting in the back seat with his son when they arrived. What a contrast between this sleek, shiny black car with its distinguished-looking passenger, and our ancient, battered little old Peugeot parked beside it, with the very *un*-distinguished-looking, perspiring, bedraggled (also ancient and battered) mother of this house — stumbling out over dogs, boys, and toys!

The chicken business is still thriving, and I am the boys' biggest customer. This is supposed to be the off-season for laying, but they are still getting a dozen a day. One week, though, the boys over-sold, or over-promised. I went out to the chicken house and there was Mike — with eleven eggs in a carton for a lady who'd ordered a dozen — sitting by the chicken coop, pleading with the hens to please lay one more!

And I never thought I'd see the day that I couldn't finish baking something until a hen laid another egg, either.

The boys are still on "holiday" until January 24. I can hardly wait. School holidays are *very* long here. At least for mothers.

Sweatshirts, Sandals, Beards?

Tuesday, January 18, 1966

We have been especially eager to get a letter off to everyone because of that *awful* article which has come out in many U.S. newspapers about the Peace Corps in Malawi. A few of the papers we've seen are the *San Francisco Chronicle, New York Herald Tribune, Washington Post,* and a San Diego paper — plus some South African papers.

You can imagine our surprise and horror when we saw the first one! It talked about bearded Peace Corps Volunteers in Malawi, dressed in sweatshirts and sandals, living with African girls, making the Prime Minister angry by being involved with the rebels, and "causing crises"!

First: yes, we did have some problems, but they were grossly exaggerated in these papers. Second: these events were *not* supposed to be publicly released. What did happen: As I mentioned earlier, Dr. Banda was very upset at Peace Corps here because a PCV allegedly had become involved politically with the rebels. Enraged at Peace Corps, he demanded that the PCV be sent home immediately or face imprisonment. This *was* a crisis for Peace Corps.

So that you'll understand what this "rebel" thing is about: not long before we came to Malawi, some of the Malawi Cabinet Ministers had become unhappy with Dr. Banda and wanted to replace him as Prime Minister. Dr. Banda found out about it and "sacked" them. Then they and their followers tried to depose him. Subsequently Dr. Banda had the ex-Ministers sent out of the country, but their followers continued the struggle and became known as "the rebels." Dr. Banda rules with a heavy hand and will tolerate no dissent. At any rate, it is absolutely against Peace Corps policy for PCVs to become involved in the politics of the host country, and Dr. Banda's staff alleged that our PCV had violated this policy.

Shortly after that, Dr. Banda called a meeting with American officials, presumably about something else, to which Will unsuspectingly went. At the time he was the Acting Peace Corps Director. At this meeting, without any warning, Dr. Banda suddenly tossed this bombshell in Will's lap: he said he didn't want any more U.S. Peace Corps teachers, especially and particularly "politically immature" ones!

His Minister of Education, John Msonthi, then spoke up and added all the bit about how the PCVs should dress more neatly. At that meeting, however, *no one* ever did mention "sweatshirts, sandals, beards, etc." that had come out in the newspaper accounts. Someone simply got carried away writing up this story. Also Msonthi stated that the PCVs were "too familiar with the Africans," and Dr. Banda added that he thought the Peace Corps-African relationship should be that of "the doctor to the patient and the teacher to the student." Hmm. Certainly sounds like the old colonialist line to me.

Incidentally, Msonthi, who has always had a funny attitude towards Peace Corps, has just been sacked as Minister of Education. As far as Dr. Banda's feelings of how Peace Corps-African relationships should be — this is a matter for concern, as it is not really in keeping with Peace Corps philosophy.

It seems it is a matter of trying to hit some middle road. Some PCVs have admittedly carried their relationships a little too far. The vast majority, however, could not be accused of improprieties. The sweatshirts, sandals, and beards, and the over-familiarity are in the great minority, so the whole thing is blown totally out of proportion. The "living with African girls" is the most damaging one. It shows how one case a couple of years ago can spoil things for all of us in the present time. Most Peace Corps Volunteers do a superb job.

Now, however, even though the threat is still hanging over our heads, the situation is looking up. Will flew and drove all over the country talking to all the PCVs, and then reported back to Dr. Banda that everyone was really going to try to do a good job. Dr. Banda accepted it well, and, so far, things are looking better. There still is a lot of tension, and sometimes we feel as if we're walking on eggs, but we think it will work out OK. It never was as bad as the newspapers had it, although serious enough, and we'll probably never know how it all got out. Now we pray that nobody else goofs up.

In my own *totally* unbiased opinion, Will did a phenomenal job as Acting Peace Corps Director during all of these trying circumstances and certainly deserved the appointment as Director. If Peace Corps had sent someone new out from Washington to be Director, they and Sargent Shriver would have heard a few thousand words from one J. Lotter — and oh, boy — that would have knocked them to their knees!

The-Right-Side-of-the-Couch

Friday, January 21, 1966

As I write this, I am blushing. I can't believe what I just did. But first, you have to know the embarrassing lead-up to today's *new* embarrassing story. A social success I am *not*.

The preface to the thing that just happened today occurred months ago. We hadn't been here very long when we were invited to a reception at the home of the U.S. Deputy Chief of Mission, honoring the U.S. Ambassador and his wife. Somehow I hadn't yet gotten around to reading the little protocol booklet, referred to as "The Black Book," that the State Department gives out. So, right from the beginning of the party I was not exactly a model of social success. But ignorance was bliss — at least for a while.

First, we drove up among the black limousines in the huge green Peace Corps pickup truck. Our own car, although it wouldn't have looked any better, had a dead battery. But when the doorman opened the truck door for me, I got the giggles because this truck is so high off the ground that I couldn't get out in my tight skirt. Will had to come around and actually lift me out. That was only the beginning.

[Here I need to interject a word about this "tight skirt." Before we'd left California, the American Embassy had sent us a list of suggested clothes I should bring. Especially interesting (and, to me quite hilarious) was that they said that since Malawi was fairly informal, all I would need were: "a long formal, a short formal, and three cocktail dresses." Hilarious because I did not own a single one of the aforementioned. I would just have to make one dress that would do for all the five. Luckily, straight, simple sheath dresses were in style, and easy to make, too. However, I ran out of time, so my dear friend Pat Allen, who absolutely hates to sew, made me a beautiful black brocade sheath which would be my "long formal–short formal–three cocktail dresses" — hereafter and to this day referred to as my "L-F-S-F-3-C-D." I wore it to every formal party and still have this labor of love — if only to look at, long since having outgrown it.]

When we got inside the house, the Ambassador and his wife had not yet arrived. After a while I was sitting very engrossed in a conversation, when I noticed that everyone was standing up. I thought that was odd — but I managed to swallow my hors d'oeuvres and grapple with my drink and get to my feet, too, no doubt with puzzlement written all over my face. If I'd just read

The Black Book, I'd have known that everyone stands when the Ambassador and his wife enter a room.

And, if I'd just read The Black Book, I wouldn't have done the other thing I did. One thing you never, never do — ever — is sit on *the-right-side-of-the-couch.* That is reserved always for the Ambassador or his wife. When we had arrived, there must have been at least twenty vacant seats, but where did I sit?? Of course — you guessed it. A fellow American lady had then kindly tried to rescue me by whispering, "Let's get up and circulate around." I was kind of tired, and that idea didn't appeal to me, so I said, "No thanks," and *sat.* Oh, boy. I didn't know enough yet to appreciate what that American lady was trying to do for me. So the Ambassador's wife then had to look around for a chair, finally selecting the one on *my* right. What else could she do? But still I was oblivious.

Next, of all things, they placed me right next to the Ambassador at the dinner table. Not having read The Black Book, even the honor of being seated beside the Ambassador was lost on me. Furthermore, I called him "Mr. Gilstrap," not "Mr. Ambassador." I followed this by actually sticking my hand in his cup of coffee and spilling it when coffee was offered to us on a tray. I *do* know that was not cool (so to speak) and at this I did know to be embarrassed and *was* embarrassed — but — I didn't giggle. That, at least, was a feather in my cap. The only one. There were a few other minor faux pas that I knew of, like calling people by the wrong names, but I actually lived a few happy weeks before I read The Black Book and found out *all* the other things I'd done.

Now, about today's adventure. The new Ambassador's wife, Mrs. Jones, called me yesterday and invited me to come to coffee this morning. She was having a few of "the girls" over. It turned out to be a "select" group of the wives of the six American department heads. When I walked in, Mrs. Jones was out of the room. Being in a small informal group of women I knew well, I wasn't thinking "Black Book." Chatting with the other women, I simply didn't think and sat on *the-right-side-of-the-couch!* Now I ask you — where was my head? And today had been my big chance to start all over since we have a new Ambassador and wife.

Once again involved in conversation, I didn't see Mrs. Jones enter the room until she was right in front of me and shaking my hand — so I hadn't even stood up (duhh). As she climbed over my feet to get to the middle of the couch, she said, "Excuse me, dear, while I reach here behind you (to my right) for my cup of coffee."

I said, "Oh, this was your se — *seatttt!!*" The light had dawned — no, flashed — I gasped, clapped my hand over my mouth and exclaimed, "Oh nooo — I did it again!"

At this, one of my friends, whose husband is actually Protocol Officer in the Embassy, burst out laughing, as she knew my terrible tale of the other incident. Well, I couldn't believe that I'd done this again. Incredible. Luckily, Mrs. Jones is a very nice and quite informal person. When I apologized she said she doesn't pay much attention to these "protocol" things and thought it was funny. I guess now that Will is Peace Corps Director I can just make my usual faux pas in more select company.

* * *

Saturday a.m.

Rick is finally over his bout with malaria after five days of fairly high temperatures. Scott also got sick on Tuesday and is somewhat better today. Don't know if he had malaria or a throat infection or both. At least with malaria symptoms (he, too, had 104º) you can give the massive doses of chloroquine just in case, without any harm if it's not malaria. So this is what the doctor did, and Scott's blood test was negative too. Lee says he gets about thirty cases a *month* of malaria among PCVs and has only seen a total of two having a positive blood test for it. At the time of testing, apparently, your fever has to be at a peak. I don't know why they even bother with that test.

My present disease is called Kiditis. Terrible, dread disease found only among mothers. Symptoms are most frequently noticed during school vacations when all the kids are underfoot and especially when the other resident adult (father) is out of town. Acute symptoms occur when some of the children are ill and the mother is confined to four walls with *all* of the children at home. Symptoms become even more acute when it rains. Symptoms: waking up in the morning and wishing it were time to go to bed again; increasingly apoplectic reactions with each whining complaint, "there's nothing to doooo..."; louder and louder bad words from mother as she stumbles over wall-to-wall toys; even worse language when the dogs come racing through with all eight muddy feet.

And most embarrassing — when an adult (at this stage an adult is anyone over the age of thirteen) appears at the door, perhaps only to ask a simple question, the mother has the almost uncontrollable urge to grab the person bodily and drag this poor hapless individual into the house — to have coffee and a chat. Doesn't matter who it is, if he or she just speaks English. This is the *acutely* acute stage, when Mother has to get *out* for a while.

* * *

Sunday —

Well, I guess I made up for my lack of "adults" to talk to today. Remember I said our record for our Sunday pancakes was thirty-four? Well, guess how many we had today? Forty-one. And if you count the Lotter family too, that makes forty-seven! Now I'm almost afraid to think of the next one — although we all had a wonderful time.

Two Dirty Birds

February 8, 1966

Well, of all things — Rick and Scott both got well, and then I came down with whatever it was. To put it mildly, I was quite aggravated by this, since Will and I had planned to go to a health conference for five days up at the lake and to leave the kids at home. I had been very excited about it and had been afraid that the kids wouldn't be well enough for us to leave them here. The day before we were to leave, they were fine. Then *I* woke up that morning with a 102° fever. Mad?? *Furious!*

I was so determined to go that I took a mess of pills, a thermos of water to take them with, a pillow to lie down on, and *went*. We drove up to the lake, and I had one whole seat to lie down on, so it wasn't so bad. The next day I was really sick, but I would have been worse off at home with kids, animals, phone, etc. There were eight doctors at the conference, so I certainly didn't lack good care.

We had a beautiful little room right on the beach with a gorgeous view of the lake, and a cool breeze that blew in all day. Everyone was so nice to me. We'd gone up on Friday, and by Sunday night I could stagger in to the dining room for dinner, and was fine on Monday. Will had to leave Monday morning, and the conference would not conclude until Thursday, but I could stay on and relax. My time was *my very own* — a new and lovely experience and especially therapeutic for a harassed mother.

I love the PCVs in the health project, many of whom I've gotten to know well, so I had fun with them. I sat in on a lot of the discussion groups and listened to many of the doctors speak. Eighteen Malawian medical assistants of the PCVs attended the conference. These are the people who will take over the program after this Peace Corps health group leaves. Most of them had never been to the lake, or stayed in a hotel, or eaten in a big dining room, so just having them there added a lot to the meetings.

I learned so much fascinating information. The Peace Corps Health Project has eleven hundred tuberculosis patients throughout Malawi under treatment now. All this has been done by thirty-six PCVs in about one-and-a-half years of work. You can imagine how many people they have examined in addition to that number. One of the biggest problems they encounter is in setting up a card file system for patients, especially since many people seem to move about from village to village, often even changing their names. It's practically impossible to trace some of them and keep them on medication.

Several PCVs did a village-by-village research project on the death rate among children and came up with a 40% death rate by the age of fifteen. The largest proportion of deaths was among children under four years of age. Three doctors flew out from North Carolina (home base of this project), and a Dr. Castle, a well-known and charming Englishman, flew out from London and was a wonderful and fascinating speaker. The Conference was great for me. I came home tan and peeling but happy, in spite of having been sick. It sure cured my kiditis.

Mike came home yesterday all red in the face, sweaty, and excited. He's in standard seven, which is in the high school now. He'd gone out for the high school rugby team — the younger team, which is standard seven up through form two (grades seven through ten). He made the position he wanted, which is fullback. He is thrilled and loves it. He seems to enjoy high school, and he and Don go off on their bikes at 6:45 every morning for school. There are about five miles of hills for them to ride on their way. Mike grumbles some about this, but Don doesn't seem to mind.

[Now the above sentence strikes me very funny because Mike practically lives on his bicycle and has done many bike races and triathlons.]

I heard an interesting conversation the other day. Rick and Saidi (Mas's little boy, age three-and-a-half) had been playing in the yard all morning, and Rick wanted Saidi to come into the house and play in his room. Rick stood on the back porch and shouted in Chinyanja, "Saidi — pitani ku nyumba!" (Come to the house).

Saidi, who still wanted to play out in back with their trikes shouted, "No, Rick — C'mon!" How about that? Rick shouting in Chinyanja and Saidi answering in English.

I want you to know that Saturday our family was invited to lunch at one of the Embassy homes with the new Ambassador and family — and I *did not sit on the-right-side-of-the-couch.* I didn't even stick my hand in the Ambassador's coffee. In fact, unless I find something else in The Book, I don't think I made a single faux pas. It really was nice, and was just the couple who gave the luncheon and the Jones family and ours. The two Jones boys are Scott's and Rick's ages, so they had fun. Then, Sunday, Mrs. Jones called and asked if Scott and Rick could play over there and have lunch. They are awfully nice and don't put on the dog at all. Such a switch from some other ambassadors.

The Joneses were going to send the boys home with the chauffeur, but we were going over that way anyway, so we picked them up (much to Scott's disappointment). When we got there, Ambassador Jones was out in old shorts puttering around in the yard, and Mrs. Jones had on an old pair of faded jeans. A welcome sight. I love their relaxed and casual approach. And, needless to say, Scott and Rick had a ball in that mansion with all kinds of toys and playthings.

We are really impressed with Ambassador Jones. He's seems a sensible man and very interested in everything. He has already gone out into a village and eaten nsima and is traveling all over, seeing the country. Bet other ambassadors never even tasted nsima, the local food staple. He sincerely wants to help the Malawians and has a lot of ideas. He loves to go to the African market with Mrs. Jones and help shop. An unusual sight amongst the foreign service.

Will is still working very hard and has been doing the work of two or more staff people since the first part of October. No Deputy in sight, as yet. At present there are several big matters to be decided, seven or eight crises to be handled, and medical evacuations to be made. There have been some staff problems that Will has had to iron out.

Now staff morale is good, but you'll never believe it — he actually had to terminate and send home a young Peace Corps Volunteer staff doctor, a married man with a wife and two children. (This is no one I've mentioned before in any of my letters.) We both lost sleep over this one (a rare thing for Will), while he was grappling with the decision. It was the hardest thing Will has had to do yet, but it seemed the only thing to do under the circumstances. The whole staff was behind him on the decision, and Washington, DC sent complete concurrence. Guess this is one of the bitter pills that comes with being Director.

Lots of letters came yesterday. *Never* think that anything you write to us is too dull compared to the life we are leading (as some of you have mentioned). We love hearing about things at home. I really don't expect you to write that you went on a hippo hunt or that you shot a leopard in your bedroom. I sit down in a comfortable chair with a cup of coffee to read your letters and read some parts out loud to Will and to the kids. Everything you write is greatly appreciated and enjoyed.

Did I tell you about our two dirty birds? One day I saw the cutest bird cage for sale on the street. Great bargain — so I bought the cage, and then, of course, had to find some birds to put in it. A Malawian boy brought me two supposedly "talking birds" for the cage. We were quite excited. However, these birds turned out to be too big for the cute cage, so we had to go get a bigger cage.

This cage is big enough, but not very "cute." Then we found out these birds are swamp birds and would eat only raw fish. Worse, they like their fish sort of ripe (translate: "rotten"), and they like to kind of fling it around the cage all day. They are truly "doity boids." Now we can hardly walk on the porch without holding our noses. *And* they don't even talk. They have to *go*. We've had them about a month now, and I think today is the day we'll go find some lovely swamp for the doity boids to go back to. Think I'll plant geraniums in the cute bird cage.

Village Health Clinic

February 18, 1966

Will is still holding down the jobs of about three people and running around like mad. A lot of the crises that popped up all at once have more or less been worked out. A man from the Washington staff, who was out here for about ten days, says it looks as if we won't get a deputy for about three months now. So it appears that Will's load won't be lightened for awhile. He seems to be holding up OK but although he's only forty-one, I think I notice a bit more gray on top.

I had the good fortune last week to spend one of the most interesting days I've had here yet. Dr. Peck, head of the Peace Corps health project (tuberculosis eradication), and two PCVs invited me to go out to a village with them to see the new well-baby and nutrition clinic they are setting up. They had chosen this particular village because it was a large one, had a successful dispensary, a small maternity clinic with about twelve beds, and a friendly and cooperative Chief (about the best kind of help you can get). One of the PC health project's African medical assistants lived there and could give lots of help.

We left at 7:30 a.m. and didn't get back until 5:20 p.m., many hours of this spent bumping in a jeep over the roughest roads I've bounced on yet in this country. The roads are really awful now in the rainy season. When we arrived in the village, there were already about a hundred mothers lined up outside with their babies, waiting to have them weighed and examined. They plan to examine and weigh each baby and then have the mothers and babies suffering the most extreme cases of malnutrition stay for a month or so. They will learn how to feed the baby nutritious foods, and also the basic rudiments of hygiene.

Malnutrition is the biggest health problem here. The main diet is maize (corn), with very little else. They grind this up and make a mush out of it, called "nsima," and eat it with their fingers. The adults eat it with "ndiwo" (any kind of sauce), which can make it quite tasty and nutritious. Either chicken or fish makes it especially good, or often the sauce is made only from vegetables. This is breakfast, lunch, and dinner. Children usually get it plain, with little nutritional value at all. Since there are many vegetables that grow well in this soil and climate, it's a matter of helping the people understand the nutritional value and how to use them. Peanuts ("ground nuts") also grow well, and are plentiful and cheap, as well as high in protein.

Some cultural beliefs (Dr. Peck corrected me when I said "superstitions") need to be broken down. A very common one is that eggs cause sterility and thus are never given to girls; also that eggs cause a crooked spine and backache. The PCVs have asked the principal people in the village to help them with teaching, and have taught some African girls and women who have had some home economics training to lead discussion groups and cooking classes. By careful guidance they hope to have Africans teaching Africans and have them carry on with the project.

When we got to the village, we could see that there was lots to do with all these people waiting. Eager to help, I asked Dr. Peck what I could do.

"Well, you can either weigh babies or help the midwife."

He was probably kidding, but I didn't give him a chance to retract his statement, and took him right up on helping the midwife. (I already get to weigh babies a lot.) He did get permission for me to watch a delivery right then. Such an experience and one that I'd never had before.

It was a small, clean delivery room just off the end of the maternity ward. There were two midwives, a minimum of equipment, and no fuss or bother. No anesthetic or medication, and not a sound from the mother. As soon as the baby was born, they got the mother right off the table and she walked right to her bed. Just like that.

And there *I* sat, all goose bumpy and misty-eyed, just watching (and not helping!) the entire birth. The baby was as pink and light as our babies, which is always a surprise to me. I guess I was the only one who was excited about the whole thing. Even the mother didn't look much at the baby (it was a girl — was this why?), and the whole thing didn't seem like any big deal — except to me.

Before I had a chance to really recover from the excitement of that, Dr. Peck said that the Chief wanted us to come to his house for tea. I'd never met a chief before, much less been in one's house. His house was large and of whitewashed mud with a tin roof. It was very neat and clean. He spoke no English, so the medical assistant went with us to interpret. Dr. Peck explained to the Chief, through the interpreter, what the project was all about, and he was very interested and cooperative. He was quite a dignified-looking old gentleman, a very strong chief, according to the Malawians there, and apparently of Moslem faith, as he had on the white skull cap and long robes of green cotton often worn by Muslims.

Later we went back to the clinic, and Dr. Peck examined babies while I helped the PCVs weigh and chart them. These babies are so cute and responsive. The only unfortunate thing was that my white face just *terrified* many of the babies, more so than at the well-baby clinic in Blantyre, because out in the villages so many of them have never seen a white face before. It makes me feel terrible to see this happy little baby on the scale, smiling and laughing until I lean over to get a better look and smile back. One look at me and about nine out of ten babies really wail. It's giving me a complex!

After we finished the clinic, the Malawian medical assistant told us he had lunch ready for us at his house. We had a delicious lunch with chicken and rice, string beans, tomatoes, and lots of other good things. On the way home Dr. Peck's medical assistant was very nice about answering my many questions about things like the tribal markings on the women's faces, the little amulets around the babies' necks, the different kinds of beads around the babies' waists. They all have different meanings. My — I learned so much in that one day — and there is so much more to learn.

For two weeks now I haven't been able to get to the orphanage because of the rains. The road gets impassable (and impossible!) with the mud. This morning I tried again and got stuck in the mud about halfway out there. It just turns into a sea of goo. We skidded around and finally were stuck with the wheels just spinning. This really scared poor Rick, who was crying in the back seat. But, as always, Malawi children appeared from out of the bushes and tall maize, as if by magic. Again, as always, they giggled and laughed and were eager to help. Together they all managed to push the car until we were turned around and could head back for home. We gave them a shilling and they went squishing back into the bushes, with mud up to their knees, laughing happily. Such a typical African scene. But I hated to miss my day out there at Nguludi.

Last week little Noah left us. I just can't imagine the orphanage without him. His father, who turned up out of the blue, had been working in South Africa, and had money to pay for Noah's two-year stay in the orphanage. This happens every once in a while. A father will suddenly appear, usually when the child is about two and could be cared for by the father. The sisters never charge money — but if the father can pay some to the Mission to help out, he is encouraged to do this.

Noah's father had never known what had happened to Noah until he found a sister of his dead wife, who told him where Noah was. He was overjoyed to find his son. For us though, it's such a shock and so sad when we don't get to say goodbye. We know this can happen, but are never really prepared.

Noah is two, just learning to talk, and such a character. He had everyone wrapped around his little finger. He just adored our Rick and got so that he would run all the way out to our car when he saw us coming. He was a little devil as well, and the last time the sisters took him to mass with them, when the priest was leaving the pulpit — Noah said (loud and clear) — "Coka!" (pronounced "choka" and meaning a rather rude "get out of here!"). Imagine! It is so strange not having Noah with us anymore.

Speaking of babies, our little baby Janie, Mas's almost-four-month-old, is just darling and doing so well. She weighs nearly fourteen pounds now and looks exactly like her four-year-old big brother, Saidi. Such a blessing.

Lassim

February 22, 1966

Honestly — it's 6:10 p.m., and at exactly 5:45 I was walking down the hill from the Coxes' house, having gone up there to play their piano (fun!), and it was beautiful out. Rick and I were admiring the sunset, and there were a few scattered clouds off in the distance, but none overhead. Now, less than a half hour later, it is pouring buckets and absolutely black out. It's amazing to see how fast storms come up here. We had gone up to the top of the driveway to watch it come racing in, and people were running up the hill, trying to beat it. You should hear it on our tin roof — like hundreds of fire hoses turned on full blast.

The electricity is off, no doubt because of the storm, and I'm typing by candlelight. We find that it's very lucky to live right next door to the Prime Minister, because if our electricity goes off and we hear his generators immediately go on — then we know that the electricity is off all over. When it goes off in our house and we don't hear his generators, then we know to check all our own fuses. Very handy.

We have had a sad experience. There is a Malawian boy, Lassim, who has been a friend of our boys ever since we've been here and has come over to play several times a week. I think he's around eleven or twelve, and he has always seemed like a really nice kid. His family is very poor, so we've given him shoes and shirts and other things over time. Well, apparently he started taking other items from our house quite a long time ago — and then kept taking more and more. A lot of it we never even missed. So he just took more, probably figuring that the supply was endless.

The other day Don couldn't find his shoes and looked all over for them. Lassim had been here, and Don said he suspected that Lassim had taken his shoes. I was just furious that he would even *think* such a thing. So he decided to ride his bike out towards Lassim's village — and lo and behold — there was Lassim — wearing Don's shoes, Don's shirt, Scott's shorts, Scott's wristwatch (which I'd accused Scott of carelessly losing at school) and carrying one of our TWA flight bags with who-knows-what inside. Lassim immediately ran when he saw Don and got away. So Don went to Lassim's house and found the whole place filled with Lotter belongings that we had *not* given him.

Unfortunately, there was so much stolen stuff that we felt we did have to report it to the police. The police confiscated a lot of our things from Lassim's house, and later we got back both Don's and Mike's transistor radios, five pairs of shoes, shirts, shorts, books, etc. He had sold Scott's watch before they caught him, however.

The whole thing just seems so sad to me. The boys are mad, and I guess I don't blame them because their trust was betrayed — but I can understand how it happened. We have so much (didn't even miss some of it), and Lassim has absolutely nothing. He lives in abject poverty in a miserable hovel with a mother who doesn't seem to care about him at all. He has no father and no one to guide him. I'm not trying to justify his stealing, but I do sort of understand. Rather than having bitter feelings, I'm thinking it seems a rather sad commentary on the state of much of this world.

The police caught Lassim the next day and brought him and his mother both to the police station for questioning. We think he has been sent to some sort of reform school. I hope he'll get some help. I feel just awful about it.

Hate to end a letter on such a sad note. So now here are some little tidbits I always forget to put in: Did you know that the stars are upside-down here? We can still pick out the Big Dipper, but can't find any others. And did you know that when water goes down the drain it swirls in the opposite direction than it does in the other half of the world?

That's all the "did you knows," but I also have a funny. A while ago I was bargaining with a boy on the street for a musical instrument which appealed to me. The base is a gourd, hollow, with a design painted on it. It has a stick across the top and pegs on either end with wire strings attached. Crude, but I really liked it and was thinking of buying it. Then a Malawi man leaned over and whispered to me,

"These strings were found by Jesus Christ."

Boy, that did it! Of course I bought it.

Preparing for Safari

Tuesday, March 1, 1966

"How would you like to take a little drive to Nairobi?" Will casually asked yesterday at lunch.

"A little drive?" I asked, laughing into my soup. "Sure," I said flippantly. "Fine. This afternoon? It's only about two thousand miles over terrible roads, and this is the rainy season. We might make it in a month or two."

"I'm serious," he said.

"You're kidding," I said.

He wasn't. My God. *Drive* all the way up through Malawi, Tanzania, and into the middle of Kenya — with four little kids, yet? I'd married an idiot.

Nevertheless, somehow here we are, actually immersed in our plans for this big trip. We leave in less than two weeks to *drive* to Nairobi. If you will look on your map, you will see that it *is* something like two thousand miles.

First we have to drive all the way north through Malawi, then from the northern part of Malawi we'll go the whole length of Tanzania (formerly Tanganyika) from Mbeya through Dodoma to Arusha, near Mt. Kilimanjaro. From Arusha we hope to take a side trip to the Ngorongoro Crater, Serengeti National Park, Lake Manyara, and a few other places. Getting to the Serengeti plains might be difficult now because it is the rainy season. From there on up into Kenya to Nairobi. All this part of northern Tanzania and southern Kenya is inhabited by the Masai — really interesting and colorful people.

The African Peace Corps Directors' conference in Nairobi starts on March 24. Of course the Peace Corps would pay for Will to fly there, but Will has decided that if we drive, it would be an opportunity for all of us to go. We're buying a second-hand Jeep, a '63 Willys with four-wheel drive. It's being fixed up now and is supposed to be ready this Friday. We're going to sell our little blue Peugeot, we hope. We figure that the money we save by not flying will compensate for any (or maybe *some?*) of the discomforts of driving all that distance with four little kids and all our gear crowded into one Jeep. Well, put it this way — we can't afford to go any other way, and it will be an *adventure*. We'll certainly see the country.

We should make it to Arusha in four days, and then we'll take a breather. There are "rest houses" spaced just about a day's drive apart along the way. We'll have our sleeping bags and camp gear along also. We have to carry our own "petrol," drinking water, and food, but there are cooking facilities at the rest houses. It will take some careful planning on my part.

We had a good laugh Sunday at breakfast when the PCVs were here for pancakes and we were telling them about the upcoming trip. We know that there will be long stretches, whole days in fact, of nothing to see. Dirt road almost all the way, no towns, no stores, no other cars, etc. I said, "Oh well, I'm prepared. I have a little book entitled '838 Ways to Amuse a Child,' and we'll just go through the whole thing."

I got it out then, and someone opened it up and said, "Ah yes, here we have soap carving – and, oh good – plaster of Paris crafts!"

"Well, there's a chapter on travel," I said.

"Ah yes, of course: 'Count the out-of-state licenses.' Let's change that to 'Try to see a car.' Then there is an automobile bingo game where you 'Look for a red barn' (red barn??) – or 'Two birds on a telephone wire' – (telephone wire?). Then, 'When you arrive at the motel'– (Motel?)!"

It was a hysterical morning.

* * *

Saturday, March 5

A very nice American lady from down our hill, Mary Jean McMullen, gave me suggestions on foods to take on safari. Beef jerky was one of them. She said they always make jerky for trips here, and that they always buy all their meat at the Limbe market early on Saturday mornings. So this morning I did something I've sort of wanted to do – or at least thought I *should* do but have dragged my feet about – I bought meat at the open market in Limbe.

Having seen the meat in the Blantyre open African market with flies crawling all over it, I wasn't very enthusiastic about the idea. However, since Mary Jean offered to go with me and show me how to pick out the good meat, I decided to give it a try. My missionary friend, Lois, was interested too, so the three of us went.

We got there at 6:00 a.m., and I was surprised to see how clean and organized the Limbe market is, and also how many other Europeans were shopping there (all white people are called "Europeans" here). Being early in the morning, it was nice and cool, and there were no flies yet – a blessing – and, to my surprise, we had a wonderful time.

That early in the morning you can get all the choice cuts of meat, and I couldn't get over how good it looked. It's all, even filet, either two shillings or "two and six" (two shillings and six pence) a pound. This is twenty-eight cents to thirty-four cents a pound (American). I got a sixteen-pound rump roast for the jerky for what would be $5.60. We also got chambo, lots of vegetables, and with our whole week's shopping done were back home by 7:30 a.m. I plan to do this every week now.

This afternoon Mary Jean is going to come up and show me how to cut up the meat for jerky. You cut it very thin, lay it on racks or cookie sheets, salt it well, and then put it in the oven at 225° for eight hours. It's just supposed to dry. This is all new to me, for sure. I imagine our kitchen will look like a jerky factory for a few days now. The boys really love jerky and are all very interested in this whole process.

I may not have time to write more letters before we leave on the big safari. Lots to do to prepare for this. We plan to return around April 7. And we are looking forward with great excitement to Grandma Lotter's visit after we get back! March and April are beautiful months here. The rains come and go, with sunshine in between. Everything is green and flourishing.

The kids will be on "holiday" then, so we will have more time to show her around. We hope she'll stay a few weeks, at least. Counting this safari holiday, the boys will have a total of seven weeks of vacation!

Safari

Bouncing along a rutted and pot-holed main "highway" in Tanzania in our second-hand Willys Jeep crammed with four kids, all their paraphernalia, sleeping bags, camping gear, food, drinking water, and extra "petrol," I did ponder the mental status of both of us in launching this expedition. As the Jeep sputtered through a rushing stream, with water up to the floorboards and rain pelting down, my worst predictions were confirmed. This is idiotic.

Further north into Tanzania, however, while watching monkeys and racing herds of zebra, I had to admit, "Well, actually this *is* kind of exciting." Excitement was winning out over the craziness of this whole venture.

It really *was* an adventure from beginning to end, and one we wouldn't trade — even with some of the misadventures included. Only the first five or six days actually went as planned, and for the next three weeks *nothing* went as planned. *We* had plans, but the problem was just that the Jeep had *other* plans.

We had figured on making it in five days from Malawi to Nairobi. If we were lucky, maybe we could make it in four. And if we were *really* lucky, we could make it each day to a rest house and wouldn't have to camp. The rest houses are wonderfully convenient. Not only do they have beds and cooking facilities, but although you carry your own food, often there is even a cook to prepare it for you.

We usually had very long drives to make it to the next rest house, some days driving fourteen to sixteen hours, but we didn't have much choice, and we did make it each day to a place to stay. You can only average about 35 mph, as the roads are so bad. Of the 2,100 miles we drove, there were not more than a hundred fifty or two hundred miles of paved road.

From Arusha, in Tanzania, we took a two-day side trip to the Ngorongoro Crater, the Olduvai Gorge, and into the Serengeti Plains. It was a perfect two days and we saw so much wild game it would take pages to describe it all.

The Ngorongoro Crater, a natural game preserve, is an incredible place. It's an extinct volcano high above the Serengeti Plains, with sides dropping down a thousand feet into the crater, which is fifteen miles across. First, you go up the mountain to the rim of the crater, where you hire a required guide to go down into the crater with you. You are allowed to go down only if you have a four-wheel-drive vehicle, which we did. Then you can drive down into the crater, the floor of which is full of wild game.

Wildebeeste and zebra were the most plentiful, and we saw almost all other game except elephant in that one fifteen-mile area. The adventure of the day was having two enormous rhinos charge the Jeep. We had driven to within about forty feet of these two rhinos, when they suddenly snorted and came at us with their heads lowered. Our guide said, "Stay" — but Will thought he said, "Start" — and we took off across the field with these two rhinos huffing and puffing on our tail at 35 mph! Rick and Scott were in the very back, looking out the back window of the Jeep, with these two monsters only two feet from them — and were absolutely scared spitless. We finally outran the rhinos, and then the guide calmly said that they would have stopped if we had not moved.

So now nothing would do but that Will had to see for himself if they really would stop. No one else was that curious, and Scott and Rick were by this time lying on the floor of the Jeep with their eyes covered, but "Fearless Freddy" (as Don and Mike began to call their father) *had* to see. We circled around and stopped, and sure enough, here they came, looking and sounding like a couple of locomotives — head-on to the front of the Jeep — terrifying. But they *did* actually stop, just about twelve inches from the front bumper. Ol' Freddy loved it and tried it several more times. Scott and Rick spent the rest of the day on the Jeep floor — and don't be surprised when you see my gray hair.

Later, our friend Bob Poole in Nairobi told us a hair-raising story about taking a group of new PCVs out in a big Carryall to one of the game parks and doing this same thing — repeating the same "they always stop" — and one of them *didn't!* It gored the side of the vehicle, nearly capsizing it, and I can only imagine how these new PCVs felt.

The only time I was more scared than that was when we were driving up the side of the crater to come back out, on a very steep and winding road, and Will had to stop the Jeep to put it into four-wheel drive — with the precipice only inches from our rear wheels — and Don said, "Mom, do you realize that every time Dad puts the Jeep in four-wheel drive he goes *backwards* two feet first??" Ulp. We all held our breath while Will wrestled with the gears, and finally the Jeep lurched forward.

From Ngorongoro we went down the mountain to the Olduvai Gorge where the famous archeologists, Dr. Louis Leakey and his wife, Mary, found the earliest known human, Zinjanthropus Man. On the way there, I read aloud to the boys and Will from *National Geographic* magazine about this, which made it all that much more interesting when we were shown around the diggings. The Leakeys were not there, but their enthusiastic helpers were.

We were in time to see the huge migrations in the Serengeti Plains. Thousands and thousands of wildebeeste and zebra, enormous herds of them, all on the move. As far as our eyes could see were these huge moving herds. Such a sight. We also saw several prides of lion and chased a flock of enormous ostriches, which are riotously funny to watch running at high speed.

Zebra and wildebeeste play games with vehicles and run alongside in herds — then their "game" is to veer ahead suddenly and plunge across the road just in front of the car, each one seeming to be daring the one behind to make it. The boys loved it, and though we came close, luckily we never hit one. Another favorite animal of ours was the little Thomson gazelle, of which there were multitudes, twitching their little tails and leaping and cavorting around.

We wished we could have stayed there longer. While seeing all this I was reading the book, "*Serengeti Shall Not Die*" by Bernard Grzimek. Grzimek and his son did years of study of the migrations of the herds in Serengeti and Ngorongoro. Now he is the curator of the Frankfurt Zoo. It's so interesting and such fun to be reading a book about the very place you're visiting.

We'd long since given up on our handbook, "838 Ways To Amuse A Child," given to me to preserve my sanity on the long stretches of nothingness. The boys found their own amusement in keeping a running argument on who was scared and who wasn't scared when the rhinos charged the Jeep in Ngorongoro Crater (no one wasn't), and making lists of all the wild animals we'd seen. Scott industriously kept a tally of how many vehicles we saw (about one or two per hour).

When things got a little dull, the atmosphere could be livened up considerably by an elbow placed strategically in a brother's ribs, or a likewise planted foot or hand in someone else's "place" in the Jeep. Usually, just in the nick of time, saving sanity (mine) and heading off multiple homicides, there would be something exciting, like a family of monkeys crossing the road.

About this time I sent my parents a postcard. It was the head of a ferocious-looking lion with its mouth wide open in an obvious roar, and I wrote, "This is Jane in the front seat of the Jeep — 'talking' to her sons in the back seats."

Coming down the escarpment from the ridge of the Ngorongoro Crater, however, was anything but boring. The road was steep and curvy, with sheer cliffs dropping off to one side. I sighed in relief when we finally got down to level ground and said, "Whew! I'm sure glad that escarpment is behind us now." We were now about a hundred miles from Arusha in Tanzania, with two whole days yet to make it to Nairobi for the Peace Corps Directors' Conference. We would make it for sure — and were congratulating ourselves on how well things had actually gone.

Too many sighs too soon, however.

Still in a self-congratulatory glow, Will picked up speed a little now that we were on a flat, though bumpy, dirt road. "Picking up speed" meant going maybe 40 or 45 mph. Suddenly — after an especially hard bump and without any warning, the Jeep careened wildly off the road to the left, totally out of control. We bounced crazily into a field, narrowly missing a surprised little Masai boy herding cattle, and hit two ditches before crashing to a halt, nose down in the third one.

With the impact of the crash, our load sailed off the top of the Jeep, Scott was hurled headfirst from the very back to the floor of the front seat, and Don and Mike landed behind the front seat, covered with all the loose debris not anchored down in the back. Thanks to seat belts in the front seat (the only ones there are in the Jeep) Rick, Will, and I were saved from a trip through the windshield.

We sat in shocked disbelief for a few seconds until Will was able to ask shakily, "Is everybody all right??" Scott, regaining his breath, began to wail, which was a good sign, and we all seemed to be alive. If this had happened only a few minutes before on that mountain — I shuddered thinking of it. Scott was only bruised, skinned up and scared, and we all had bumps and bruises, but miraculously, we were OK.

Shaking and weak-kneed, we extricated ourselves and began to observe the damage. As if by magic, we were almost instantly surrounded by Masai tribesmen, no doubt curious as to why we were sitting there in their cow pasture. Had we not had some experience in talking to Masai before this, and therefore known that they were friendly, and that the spears they carried were to fight lions, not people, we could have been scared to death. Tall and lean, dressed in their rust-colored togas, they rested on their spears and watched us, talking excitedly among themselves.

Finding no broken bones, we treated our minor cuts and bruises, tried to calm everyone down, and then began to pick up the debris. When Will started to examine the Jeep's inner and under workings for some explanation for its sudden inexplicable behavior, he found, to our horror, that the mainspring had snapped, and this had caused the steering and brakes to go out. Then we came to the sickening realization that we really *were* stuck.

It was nearly five o'clock, and we knew we didn't have much daylight left. If we were going to get help, we were going to have to move fast. When darkness falls in Africa, it does just that. It falls, much like a window shade being suddenly pulled, and the earth is plunged into chilly darkness. We had not seen another vehicle in an hour, and the nearest garage, nearest *anything* that could be of any help actually, was in Arusha, a hundred miles away.

Some of the Masai helped Will pick up and reattach our car-top carrier, which had cleverly managed to land right side up about thirty feet away, and in which, thoughtfully, our one precious bottle of wine had not broken. Then, by a combination of a little (*very* little) Swahili, a little English, and a lot of sign language, Will was able to communicate that he needed to get to a short wave radio or police somewhere for help. Understanding, two of them nodded and indicated that they would take him with them.

Telling the boys and me to stay with the Jeep and to lock ourselves in when it got dark, that there was plenty of food and water until he could get back, he kissed us all good-bye. We all had strange feelings in the pits of our stomachs as Will left us and walked down the dirt road, flanked on either side by these tall, spear-carrying Masai. We watched silently until a bend in the road hid them from sight. The rest of the Masai then disappeared, as magically as they had appeared earlier.

I looked at my forlorn little crew, then at our jumbled and disheveled-looking Jeep, and all sorts of thoughts went through my head. Here I was, all alone in the middle of Africa with my four little boys and a wrecked Jeep, and no idea when we would see Will again. It would too soon be dark, and we had no strong and able husband and brave father to take charge of the situation.

Then the strangest thing happened. My feelings of fear were changing to a feeling of intense relief and gratitude that we were all *alive* and unhurt. I had an almost uncontrollable impulse to leap up and laugh and dance with joy! However, I managed to resist this temptation, knowing that the boys would be reduced to utter terror thinking that not only had their father left them stranded in the middle of Africa, but now their mother was freaking out.

Instead, I jumped to my feet and said, cheerily and with as much confidence as I could fake and muster, "OK — let's straighten out this mess and get ready to camp for the night!" Sudden action broke the spell, and we began the task of righting the strewn assortment of gear, spilled food, crayons, apple cores, games — all the dreadful accumulation of traveling with kids.

"Do you think there are lions out there, Mom?" asked Scott, summoning up his utmost nine-year-old bravado and brandishing the machete he'd carried all this way for just such an emergency.

"Yeah," answered helpful Don, "and it's almost dark and that's when they come."

"Probably hyenas too," added equally helpful Mike, "and hyenas can chomp off a man's arm in one chomp and — "

Before my two "brave" twelve- and thirteen-year-olds could catch my glaring "knock-it-off" look, four-year-old Rick was crying and asking, "Are we ever going to see Daddy again?"

This very question had been sneakily trying to invade my thoughts too, but I managed to answer, "Of course. You saw he was in good hands." Four pairs of eyes looked at me dubiously.

Another half hour passed. The only vehicle that had gone by had been a lorry full of Africans who spoke no English and were going in the wrong direction, and I'd gestured them on by. Then we saw a Land Rover coming in the distance, and I ran out to flag them down. When I saw white faces inside, I hoped someone spoke English, remembering all the non-English-speaking people we'd seen up at the Ngorongoro Crater, where this Land Rover no doubt had come from. When they slowed down, I ran out and asked anxiously, "Does anyone speak English?"

From within came a man's voice and these unforgettable words, "Ah sho' do hope so, honey!" Good heavens, was this really the middle of Africa?

The southern drawl came from a jolly, balding, elderly man, who, with his wife, was being driven on a photographic safari by a young British guide and hunter named Steve Smith. Steve introduced us to Mr. and Mrs. Falk, quickly sized up the situation, and, trying to beat the darkness, managed to back the Jeep up out of the ditch, give us some Cokes, told us to wait until they could come back for us, that they would hurry ahead and find Will to be sure that he got some help — and off they went. Just like that.

Darkness fell just as they drove off, and I had to admit that it was a comforting thought to know that I might be spared the responsibility of pretending to be brave while spending the night in the African bush alone with my four little boys.

In less than an hour our rescuers were back, and we were overjoyed to see that Will was with them! The Masai had, in fact, escorted him about four miles down the road to a place that had a government radio shack. Although the sole operator in charge was very sympathetic, rules had prevented him from using the radio for anything but government business. While Will had been standing there wondering what to do next, Steve and friends had driven up. What a welcome sight for Will to behold — and to hear *English* being spoken.

Between them, they had decided that the best plan would be

for Will to go back and stay with the Jeep, as it couldn't be left unguarded, and that the children and I should stay with Steve and the Falks at their camp until Will could come for us. Maybe Will would be able to flag down a vehicle that could tow the Jeep to a little village where he could pay someone to watch it while he hitchhiked into Arusha for help.

This seemed a rather nebulous plan to me, but feeling pretty helpless and not being able to think of anything better, I listened as Steve drew a map and tried to explain to Will how to find the camp, which was apparently quite a distance away. Telling me then to bring just our sleeping bags and a tent, Steve crowded the four boys and me and our gear into his little short-wheel-base Land Rover, meant for four or five people, certainly not eight people plus any gear. Now I wondered how *Will* felt as we drove off and left *him* alone to cope with the Jeep and the African night!

"Won't the cook be surprised when we bring five people back to camp for dinner?" laughed Mrs. Falk, as we sped through the darkness.

"Oh, please don't worry him about us," I said. "Just a bowl of soup would be fine. We're just grateful to have a safe place to stay." After an hour and a half of driving, the last few miles following tire tracks through the bush, we spotted a big campfire in the distance.

Mr. Falk, pointing out that this was the camp, said, "Jane honey, Ah just bet that y'all could use a nice cold gin and tonic about now?" Jane honey sho' could.

Having been told that it was just a small camp for the three of them near Lake Manyara, we were surprised to see six or more tents in a grove of huge trees and what looked like quite a few people milling about. Thinking I'd misunderstood Steve, I said, "But I thought you said the camp was just for the three of you."

"Oh, it is," said Steve. "Those men are the cooks and helpers."

As we climbed out of the Land Rover, Steve spoke in Swahili to some of the men, who quickly brought camp chairs for us to sit by the blazing campfire. Within a few minutes someone handed me a cold drink, and my disbelieving ears thought they heard the clink of ice cubes. Incredulous, I peered into my gin and tonic, and sure enough, there they were — *ice cubes* in the middle of the African bush. It slowly dawned on me that this was another world we'd been taken to. A world we'd read about and seen in movies, and certainly one we never dreamed we'd ever experience.

The boys were being shown around the camp by Steve, while Mr. and Mrs. Falk and I sat by the fire with our drinks and watched the men putting up our tent. After a few minutes, Don and Mike came back to the fire and excitedly whispered into my ear, "Mom! This is just like in the movies. It's a real honest-to-goodness *safari camp!*"

Before this had time to sink into my already whirling head, the cook appeared and, with a slight bow, said apologetically that dinner for the adults would be a little late, but the children would be served in about fifteen minutes.

"Mom!" Scott whispered, "there are *ten* men working here and there's a dining tent and a shower tent and a toilet tent and the shower has hot water and there's a refrigerator — " and he was off again on the run. I marveled at how much information kids can gather in a short time. My poor brain was having a difficult time processing all that my boys were feeding into my ears.

The children's five-course dinner was followed by the adults' seven-course miracle, including delicious homemade soup, filet mignon, fresh-baked bread from a fifteen-foot-long charcoal fire pit, crêpes suzette, and three kinds of wine — all served by green-gowned men with red fezzes on their heads and with white napkins over their arms. I had to pinch myself. Was this real??

After dinner we sat much too late around the campfire, unable to tear ourselves away from listening to Steve's endless stories of his ten years as a guide and hunter and also of his career as an animal handler for the filming of many movies. We could hear the shrill calls of bush babies (like small monkeys) in the trees over our heads and some strange thrashing and grunting sounds in the nearby stream.

"Oh, that's just hippos in the water hole," Steve said. This, of course, calmed us immediately. (!) "Last night a herd of elephant came right past our camp," he said, and the boys' eyes widened even farther. Even as exhausted as we were, I wondered if any of my little family would sleep that night.

When I was finally able to extricate the boys from Steve (or Steve from the boys) and drag them off to our tent, we discovered that in our haste and confusion we'd brought only four sleeping bags instead of five. I was willing to bet that one who wouldn't sleep well would be a mother who would have to share a mummy-type sleeping bag with a squirmy four-year-old.

We'd also forgotten a flashlight, which made me wonder where my head was when I'd brought my knitting but had forgotten my sleeping bag and flashlight. Could we scare away a lion or an elephant with knitting needles? Oh well, Steve had assured us that if we were frightened of anything, all we needed to do was shout and he would hear us, as his tent was right next to ours. Then he reminded us that he did have a gun, just in case. This was reassuring, but I still wished that I at least had a flashlight.

The only one to fall asleep the first hour was Rick. The other three boys were busy whispering and listening to all the jungle sounds of the African night. "Didja hear that?" and "What was that?" and "Just think! Parts of *Hatari* were filmed right here" — and "John Wayne actually camped right here." Finally their voices ran down and I was almost drifting off to sleep, when Rick woke up and began to thrash and twirl in our little cocoon.

"What do you think Daddy's doing now?" he asked, setting me to wondering and worrying all over again. For a brief time I'd almost forgotten the reason for our being here, caught up like another kid in the excitement of this safari camp, all of Steve's stories, and the incredible sounds outside. How *was* Will, I wondered? Was our Jeep really badly damaged? How could we get it to Arusha? And even if we could, could they fix it there? I cringed at the idea that we'd driven all this way to "save money" and so that the whole family could go. At this point I bet Will was wondering why he hadn't just flown to Nairobi by himself, all paid for by Peace Corps, like any *normal* Peace Corps director would have done.

I couldn't stop thinking about that awful escarpment, with its sheer cliffs that we could so easily have gone over — no one would even have known — so now I was *really* wide awake again. Well, I told myself, the important thing is that we're all alive and unhurt. Nothing else really mattered. Not even wild animals, I thought, sitting up to peer out into the darkness through the little net window over my head. I looked more closely at that flimsy net and began to wonder how much protection it would be if a lion or a leopard put a paw (or tooth?) to it. And then elephants... ? As the night wore on, the tent seemed thinner and flimsier by the minute and the animal sounds louder and closer, compelling me to sit up and look out more frequently. Although I imagined plenty, I never did actually see anything, and it was nearly dawn when I finally slipped into a fitful sleep.

The boys were up with the sun, eager to investigate the camp in daylight and to ensnare Steve once again for more stories. Hearing voices and sounds of activity outside and drawn by the unbelievable smell of coffee and bacon cooking, Rick and I unzipped our tent and stepped out on the dewy grass. What a beautiful scene greeted us.

The tents were all nestled in a grove of tall trees so they could stay cool in the shade. The nearby stream was hidden by undergrowth, but we could still hear the unmistakable sounds of the hippos munching and could see many animal tracks leading to the water. High mountains in the near distance and plains close by and this lovely stream — what a perfect place for observing and photographing wildlife. What a perfect place just to *be*. Now we could see why they had chosen such a remote spot for their camp.

Mr. and Mrs. Falk were already having their morning coffee and cheerily greeted their newly extended family. Again I thanked them profusely for rescuing us and again I said I couldn't believe our good luck in being here. They were such a lovely couple, retired and fulfilling a lifetime dream of going on an African safari. They were from Newport News, Virginia, and I will never forget them. But now — what an adjustment for them to bring five people, especially four busy little boys, into their (formerly) peaceful camp. How generous of them.

Steve, after asking how we'd slept, commented that it had certainly been a "quiet night." Quiet night? Slept?

"Who slept?" I asked. I confessed that it wasn't just the crowd in my sleeping bag and the worry about Will and the Jeep that kept me awake, but that I was quite certain I'd heard animals lurking about outside our tent with menu plans which included delicious little boys.

Steve laughed and said, "I'm quite certain that the only animals lurking about your tent last night were tiny bush babies and some night birds, and to my knowledge these little blokes don't usually dine on small chaps."

After a huge, delicious breakfast, the day flew by, each hour adding to the delirium of the boys. With more stories from Steve, who had, for instance, helped on the filming of *Born Free*, which was just due to come out. "Now when you see the lion cub playing with the tire — that's this tire right here on my Rover," and "When you see the lion doing this or that, the way we did that scene was...." And, "In the filming of *Hatari*, John Wayne sat right there in the crotch of that tree."

There was also much discussion and close scrutiny of Steve's gun, the only one in camp, and only for emergency use. Then, after Steve had taken us out in his Land Rover to look for lion (didn't find any), and chased a herd of giraffe, pointing out all the different birds and other wildlife, we each secretly began to hope that Will might not be able to come for us for days.

How had what started out to be such a terrible ordeal just the day before led to this extraordinary and unforgettable experience? With guilt feelings, I realized I'd again forgotten to worry about Will.

Late in the afternoon our hopes for staying longer were dashed when we saw a pickup truck with "US Peace Corps" on the side coming into camp. Its driver was not Will, however, but one who had been sent by Will to retrieve us. Our well-meaning but dubiously received messenger brought us the good news that Will and the Jeep were being helped by a good Samaritan truck driver, and that he was in fine hands. The disappointing news was that this Peace Corps man was to take us now to Arusha.

Saying goodbye to the Falks and Steve and all the helpers enabled us to stretch out the time a little, all the while trying to convince my sons that, "No, I really don't think the Falks wanted to adopt any little boys," and that "Yes, I'm sorry Daddy is just a teacher instead of an African Game Guide, but perhaps you will be able to be happy again someday." And we reluctantly waved goodbye and left this unbelievable paradise.

Our guilt feelings about our only sporadic worries about Will turned out to have been unnecessary. While we were enjoying the comforts and excitement of the safari camp, he was having his *own* lucky adventures. He had waited in the Jeep for a vehicle to pass for only about an hour when he saw a good-sized truck approaching. Flagging it down, he couldn't believe his good luck. The driver, a man from the Seychelles Islands, as it turned out, not only spoke perfect English, but lived in Arusha and was, of all things, a truck *mechanic!* His three Tanzanian companions were also mechanics, and all four were eager to help.

Somehow in the darkness, they managed to tie and wire the mainspring together enough that it could be driven, slowly, five miles down the road to a little store. In Africa there are many little stores where you would least expect to see one, which sell basic things like bars of soap, bags of sugar or salt, and almost always Coca-Cola. This mechanic knew the store owner and arranged for him to watch the Jeep for Will while they drove into Arusha for parts.

The next morning this remarkable man, having purchased the necessary parts for the Jeep, picked Will up at the hotel where he'd spent what was left of the night, drove him all the way back the hundred miles to the Jeep, worked hours doing the necessary repairs, then followed Will and Jeep back to Arusha to be sure he made it all right. After all this, Will had to hide some money for him under a plate in his house, because, other than for the actual Jeep parts, he had refused to take any money for all his time and labor.

We finally made it to Nairobi only one day late for Will's conference. Three days later, we happily chanced to run into Steve and the Falks in Nairobi. We were very excited to see them again.

"Guess what happened that very night you left the camp?!"

they said. It seems they'd all gone to bed early (probably exhausted after having to survive the time with all of us), and about eleven p.m. Steve awoke with the feeling that something was in his tent. Knowing the tent zipper was broken, therefore the flap loose, he cautiously opened his eyes, and there — standing by the foot of the bed — was a large lioness!

He could hardly believe his eyes. Gingerly trying to reach his revolver beside the bed, he accidentally bumped his tilly lamp, which fell with a loud crash. This sudden noise, maybe as effective as the report of a revolver would have been, startled the lioness into backing out. However, directly behind her was a huge male, who was also startled and *ROARED!* Then they were joined by *five* other lions, who all added to the roaring din before running off into the darkness.

All the help was up immediately, lighting all the lanterns and stoking up the fire, hoping to discourage the visitors from returning. The cook's tent, also with a broken zipper, had been entered by one of the lions too, scaring the poor man out of his wits. Steve said that in ten years of being a guide he had never had this happen before and couldn't even account for it. Mr. and Mrs. Falk said that before all the roaring they'd felt their tent being slapped by something and were scared to death. They'd broken camp the next day and come into Nairobi.

"Wow!" I said. "Well, all I can say is that if this had happened the night before, you would have had a corpse who'd died of fright at the first roar, and four little orphans on your hands!"

Safari (continued)
Amboseli

April 6, 1966

Although we had finally made it to Nairobi, and Will had only missed one day of the conference, the Jeep needed more repairs and parts than we had anticipated. After waiting for parts in Nairobi for two weeks, we finally had to leave it in a garage there and plan to fly home ($$$$). We are hoping that someone will be going to Nairobi on vacation and can drive it back to Malawi for us. So much for those plans to "save money by driving" to the conference.

It had been a Friday when Will found out that we would have to leave the Jeep and fly home. There went the budget. Then we found out we couldn't get on a plane for Malawi until the next *Wednesday*. Luckily, since we were staying with our Peace Corps friends, Bob and Lee Poole and family (not sure how lucky for them, but great for us) at least we didn't have to pay hotel expenses. So, making the best of things, Will rented a Ford Thames van (more budget) so we could go camping in Amboseli Game Park from Saturday to Monday night. This experience was also fraught with adventures.

We were all so excited about this idea of going to Amboseli, which is at the base of Mount Kilimanjaro, that we immediately went into a frenzy of packing and getting ready. Saturday morning we tied the tent and all our gear on the top of the van, said good-bye (for the three days) to the Pooles — only to find out that we had a dead battery! I think at this point the Pooles thought they'd *never* get rid of us.

This was the second rented vehicle in Nairobi that had done this to us. We got a push out of their driveway and managed to drive it to town to the rental place, where they gave us a new bus. Of course, this meant exchanging all the gear, retying on top, redoing everything. After so many experiences like this, you begin to wonder whether you're going to get *anywhere*.

Amboseli couldn't have been more beautiful. With snow-capped Mount Kilimanjaro in the background, it almost seemed unreal. First we checked at the little rustic lodge there to find out where we could camp. There was no real "campground" as such, but they told us about a place in a grove of trees about two miles away where people sometimes camp. They even said they would send a lorry with firewood to us in a few hours. So off we went, watching all the way for wild game. There were no other cars or people at all, and we saw a giraffe off in the distance. Already we were excited.

We found the spot and right away noticed elephant droppings around — unmistakable — and knew this would probably not be an uninteresting venture. After we set up our little tent in amongst the trees and got our camp all organized, we decided to drive around for a little while to see what wild game we could find. Bonanza! We saw, and were even able to photograph, rhinos and giraffes with a backdrop of Mount Kilimanjaro. It would be pretty hard to find a more dramatic setting.

When we returned to our little camp, we found that it had been taken over by some visitors — a whole pack of baboons was there waiting for us. Luckily, they couldn't get into the tent, and we hadn't left anything outside. They were so interesting and cute that we sat in the van and just watched them —and they us. There were several mothers with little babies clinging to their backs. After a while, when we opened the van doors to get out, they all ambled away, looking back over their shoulders at these intruders in their territory.

When the lorry with the firewood came, we immediately built a big campfire. After we cooked our dinner on it, we all sat by the fire listening to the wonderful, strange African night sounds. When the boys were bedded down in the tent, Will and I were sitting by the campfire, pinching ourselves and trying to believe that this was all true. All of a sudden, Scott leaped out of his sleeping bag, screaming bloody murder, and our dreamy euphoria abruptly ended. Something had bitten or stung him on the upper inside of his thigh. We jumped up and pulled off his shorts — and a big scorpion fell out! It had stung him twice, which was terribly painful. He was howling up a storm and also was scared — and so were we.

What should we do?? We had no idea whether scorpion stings were dangerous and deadly poisonous, or just temporarily painful and would go away. The only thing I could think to give him was benedryl (antihistamine), which we had in the Peace Corps medical kit, and which we had given for the bee stings in Zomba. We also put some kind of soothing salve on it, but poor Scott kept on crying with the pain. Finally Will decided to drive up to the lodge to ask what to do. People there said that although scorpion stings are very painful, they are not actually dangerous and are much like bad bee stings. It took quite a while, but Scott finally calmed down, aided considerably by a cup of hot chocolate.

However — then no one, but *no one* — was going to have *any* part of getting into *any* sleeping bag. So now this entailed taking every sleeping bag out of the tent, turning it inside out, shaking, inspecting with flashlights, peering into every corner of the whole tent — a process taking hours, I swear. Gradually the boys calmed down and Scott went from dramatic wailing to moans and loud sniffles.

Thinking that I'd better put more mosquito repellent on four-year-old Rick because he had a lot of bites on his stomach and back, I went into the tent and said, "Rick, honey, get up and let's take off your tee shirt so I can put repellent on your tummy and back." I then pulled up his tee shirt — and out flipped a huge hairy *spider!* At this, I totally lost it — screaming and dancing a mad insane jig (spiders have this strange effect on me) — so, needless to say, all the boys shot out of their sleeping bags.

Now *everybody* was all unglued again. Will smashed the spider, commenting on what a big help I was, just when we'd finally gotten everyone calmed down. Oh, dear.

Eventually, all but Don reluctantly agreed to get back into their sleeping bags in the tent. Don was having none of it. He was not even going to set *foot* in that tent and announced that he would sleep on a seat of the van. Will obligingly backed the van up to the tent flap so that Don would be in close proximity to us, while Don was righteously informing us that he "actually would be really helping us out" by being able to see out the van windows and therefore could let us know if he saw anything. Yeah. Uh huh.

Once we were all in our sleeping bags, Will and I tried to act very calm and talk softly, commenting on things like how pretty the night birds sounded and what fun we were going to have the next day going out looking for animals, when suddenly there was a very loud, *very* close-by, scream of a large cat. It was the kind of sound that makes the hair on the back of your neck go all prickly. It was probably a leopard or cheetah, not as deep and rumbly as a lion's roar — followed immediately by another large cat scream. Right in our camp!

Don pounded on the van window, saying, "Dad! Did'ja hear that?" (Was he kidding?) Rick, in the middle of Will's and my sleeping bag with us, stiffened like a little board, his eyes huge. I was covered with goose bumps and felt as if *all* my hair was standing on end. We were almost afraid to breathe. Whatever it was did it three more times over the next half hour or so. By this time I think everyone was planning on joining Don in the van. Tent walls are so thin — just one claw or tooth could — but I made myself stop thinking and tried to resume breathing.

After what seemed like hours, whatever animal it was went away, and all was quiet. Then, just when most of us were finally drifting off to sleep — away off in the distance we heard the most

African sound of all — an elephant trumpeting! The perfect finishing touch.

The rest of that three-day stay was not as dramatic as that first night (thank goodness), and we had a great time and saw lots of game. After we got back to the Pooles' house in Nairobi, Bob Poole told us a story about camping there in that very spot one time. Just when he'd broken camp and packed his stuff in his Land Rover, some elephants came into camp. Unfortunately, he noticed then that he'd left his shaving kit on a log. However, there was always an elephant between him and the kit. He waited. And waited. Every time he started to get out to try to retrieve it, the elephant flapped its ears, looked menacing, and moved toward him — so he'd get back in the Land Rover. He finally just had to leave his kit there — it's best not to argue with an elephant. We decided that we preferred baboons.

[Speaking of elephants and the Poole family, Joyce Poole, Bob and Lee's middle child, is now a biologist and conservationist and one of the foremost elephant authorities in the world. When we knew the Pooles in Kenya, Joyce was about eight years old. She has remained in Africa almost all of her life, studying and protecting elephants. She spent fourteen years in Amboseli National Park and in the early 1990s headed Kenya's elephant conservation and management program. Her two 1997 books, Coming of Age With Elephants: A Memoir *and* Elephants *are well known throughout the world. National Geographic TV has produced a documentary on Joyce and her elephants.]*

Old Purple Face

Friday, April 8, 1966

Hooray — we made it to Nairobi *and* back! We're back in Blantyre again, but it was like an obstacle course getting home. We flew in from Nairobi yesterday about noon, and right up to the moment we walked down the steps from the plane, I wondered if we were going to make it. This is only because every step of the way there had been some stumbling block. It had really become a comedy of errors — but we finally made it.

On Tuesday after our camping trip in Amboseli we were faced with the challenge of packing and figuring out which things we'd be able to take on the plane, weighing them, and deciding how to leave all the rest with the Jeep. If you can imagine *driving* somewhere on a long trip with four kids and all our camping gear (tent, sleeping bags, pillows, footlocker, Coleman lantern, stove, boots) and then having to fly all this stuff back home? We had brought along only two suitcases and had all the rest of the katundu just sort of "loose" in the Jeep. We borrowed some big canvas bags from the Pooles and stuffed them with things like our pillows, which we knew we'd need, and as much else as we could fit. Then we hoped we'd find someone to drive the Jeep and all our junk back to Malawi whenever the Jeep was ready.

Wednesday morning we really had to hustle to get to the airport and were weighing and removing things right up to the last moment. What a job. Lee Poole even got her car all ready in case we had our usual dead battery or other catastrophe. We had to go to the bank to change our Kenya money and pick up something at the American Embassy, but finally made it on time to the airport. Whew. I was a nervous wreck.

Will rushed up to the ticket counter with our six tickets and passports in hand, and I collapsed on the nearest bench, puffing and panting. Then I heard, even over the din of the crowd — "*WHAATTT???*" (I would type it louder if I could) — and I looked over and saw a purple-faced Will, pounding the counter. The flight had been canceled. And they had not called to let us know. It was so unbelievable that I went into an immediate fit of uncontrollable hysterical laughter.

When the airlines actually put us up that night at the Ambassador Hotel, we had the added fun of calling the Pooles to tell them that we weren't leaving after all — and the boys did somehow manage to keep their last and only clean clothes clean for another twenty-four hours.

But this is not the end of this story, if you can believe that. We got to the airport on time the next morning, and after much weighing and juggling found that we were actually ten pounds *under* the weight limit. Then, while heaving sighs of relief, we were stopped and told that our carry-ons had to be weighed — and they were *loaded*. We'd never had this happen before. So, of course, now we were overweight. Somehow, though, Will talked them out of making us pay. Good thing they didn't actually weigh mine with my precious two pounds of mayonnaise, which you can't get in Malawi.

This is *still* not the end of this saga. Will had specifically asked that we have six seats together and had been assured that, of course, we would. So when we went to board and they checked off our names — they had listed only *four* Lotters. Well, you should have seen and heard Old Purple Face then! He demanded the Manager, the President, and I was surprised he didn't demand God Himself — and certainly got people scurrying around (while Helpful Mother again fell into fits of giggles). It was just too much. They found that someone had written LOTTER four times and TOTTER two times and finally guessed that they were all us. We did get six seats together. At this point I was quite sure that the plane would burst into flames or at least have a flat tire or something. But miracle of miracles, we *got* here!

We got here at noon and found that June Stewart had brought over a beautiful lunch for us, and I can't even begin to say how much we appreciated it. Then we had to get ready to give a cocktail party here that night at 5:30 for the Peace Corps Washington African Division Head. We made it, somehow, even squeezing in having to do the shopping for a four-day weekend when all the stores were going to be closed. Amazing what you can do if you really have to. Old Purple Face was even able to pull off being a gracious and calm (sort of) host.

This morning while I was trying to write this letter, eleven different PCVs dropped by for coffee — one, two, or three at a time. They all wanted to know how our trip was, and it was fun to tell them. It's been exciting to read all our accumulated mail, too. The cocktail party last night went off very well, and now we're having this man from Washington in for dinner tonight, so I have to get busy.

The biggest family news of all now is that Will's mother wrote to say that she *is* coming this month. Probably around April 23, we think. We're so excited!!

Grandma's Coming!

Wednesday, April 20, 1966

Will's mother is coming Saturday! The trip will take her five days. She goes from San Francisco to New York, then London-Nairobi-Blantyre. At 69 and traveling alone, she may be pretty tired. We're so sorry we couldn't talk Will's dad into coming. He's pretty much of a homebody and doesn't want to leave his garden and numerous hobbies. We don't know how long Mom will stay, but we hope it will be at least three weeks. Poor thing, though, has to share a bedroom with nine-year-old Scott and four-year-old Rick. Hope this won't lessen her desire to stay longer.

It has been a challenge to get that room ready, I must say. It's a nice big room, with Scott and Rick's bunk beds on one side. We moved one of those big portable monstrosity closets they have here into the middle of the room for a divider so that Mom will have some semblance of privacy. We were able to borrow a very good bed for her, so we think it will work out fine. The real challenge was getting Scott to clean up all his "nests" in all the corners. He makes little nests containing all sorts of small treasures. He has always done this. I made new curtains for the room, which actually looks fairly presentable now, at least for the moment.

A few days ago I found out through an invitation that came in the *mail* that ..."The U.S. Peace Corps Director and his wife" (I guess that must be me) are giving a reception for people to meet all the African headmasters in Malawi who are here in Blantyre for a school conference. Will knew about it and simply forgot to tell *me*. Now really — !

Luckily, however, since it's an "official" Peace Corps event, it will be catered and in a rented hall, not here at our house. But I still would have kind of liked to have *known* about it. What if someone had come up to me on the street and said, "I'm coming to your party"— "Party? What party?"

The party is tonight, and the Peace Corps secretaries have arranged it all, even borrowing the U.S. Embassy waiters and bartenders. The secretaries, Sheila and Sue, had to do the invitations and make all the arrangements while we were away (this was Will's "excuse" for not remembering to tell me), and I've certainly never given a party that I had less to do with. All I have to do is arrange the flowers this afternoon and *try* to memorize the names of one hundred seventy-five guests — and they are not names like Smith or Jones — names like Honorable Minister

Mr. Nyasulu, Mr. H.C.A. Mwonyongo from Mchinje, Mr. and Mrs. Makuwila, Sir Martin and Lady Roseveare. Oh my.

Will and I went to visit some PCVs up-country in a little village Saturday morning and came back extra inspired by Peace Corps Volunteers. Nancy and Duane Laursen are a wonderful young couple who are both teachers. They have been here about six months. They live in typical Malawian housing — outhouse, outside separate cooking room with a wood stove, no running water. This last problem necessitates having to have water carried a mile to them, followed by having to filter and boil it. Nancy, who says she never really learned to cook before, made the most amazing and delicious cinnamon rolls for our breakfast — on that wood stove. I was impressed.

They are the only white people for miles around. Nancy has fixed up their little house so cleverly, with bright curtains and cushions of Malawi fabrics, travel posters, and other cheery touches. Duane has built a wonderful porch swing out of all native materials. They've put up a tetherball pole for all the kids around and have built a badminton and basketball court. They both teach in the upper primary school there, and, needless to say, all the Malawians just love them. I wish everyone at home in the U.S. could see what they are doing. Such good role models for Peace Corps.

We just got some of our slides back from our trip, and there are some sensational (*we* think) ones. So, be prepared to sit through 20,000 slides when we get back. And 15,000 of these will be of lions. Will likes lions. We haven't got the elephant ones back yet, but the ones of the rhinos charging the Jeep are very interesting — all blurrrr — but the photographer (first initial W) was *not* nervous or anything. Noooo —

Surprise!

Monday, April 25, 1966

Saturday was the *big day* that Grandma Lotter was coming, and we all went out to the airport. We were so excited when the plane came in, we were waving and shouting from the outdoor balcony where everyone waits. Grandma got off the plane, and we were jumping up and down and waving from above as she walked across the tarmac. Then I heard one of the kids yell, *"There's Pamp!!!"* What a surprise! Honestly, we couldn't believe our eyes. Will's dad had actually come to Africa.

They were really pretty sneaky about it — having Will's dad come out of the plane about twenty people after Grandma. He came grinning up the stairs, and we hadn't even seen him get off the plane. It hadn't occurred to us to look at anyone else after Grandma got off, so we were just overcome by surprise and excitement!

It's so much fun when anyone's family comes out to Malawi to visit because not only their own family here gets excited, but all the other Americans as well. There were some missionary friends there at the airport to greet a new missionary family who had been on the same plane, and I think they were almost as excited as we were to see Will's folks. Some of the wives rushed up and hugged Will's mom and said how exciting it was to see a grandmother from home. (Now, I hope some other grandparents who are reading this will become inspired to come and see for themselves — as we keep suggesting!)

About sixteen PCVs came for pancakes yesterday, and the folks really enjoyed talking to them. Grandma even found a PCV from Texas who knew a girl she knows quite well. Big state — small world. Luckily there is an empty bunk in Don's room, so Pamp is rooming now with Don. We took both grandparents downtown today and have been taking them sightseeing. We're hoping to combine Will's business with pleasure and take them up to the lake soon. It's so much fun having them here.

We accidentally gave Grandma her first case of culture shock last night at dinner, though. We have these two pet chameleons which we had been carrying around the house to show people how they eat flies. Their names are Willie Mays and Yogi Berra (because they catch flies). This is pretty sensational to watch, as they have coiled-up tongues the length of their bodies. Willie and Yogi have bodies about four inches long, not counting the tails, and you take them on your index finger up to a window where there are usually flies — and wait. Their eyes swivel independently, but when they see a fly the two eyes focus together and zero in on it, and zap! — the four-inch unfurled tongue darts out to get it. Wonderful and unusual entertainment for guests.

Sometime during the day, however, I had put one of them in the bouquet of flowers on the dining room table, as they like it there. But I forgot all about him. So there we were, eating our dinner, when this "monster," all beautifully chartreuse to match the leaves of the flowers, came walking out of the bouquet and right straight across Grandma's plate! To say the very least, Grandma was startled. It's a good thing she has such a good sense of humor. She chalked it up to African-type experiences that "sure wouldn't happen in Alameda, California!"

* * *

Wednesday

The other grandparents had sent a box of goodies for the boys with Will's folks. Pamp says to tell those other grandparents that the bubble gum has been in constant use since ten minutes after coming into the house, and that we have sat in it, stepped in it (previously chewed, of course), and had it stuck to the bottoms of cups. Have you ever seen what happens when you put a cup of hot chocolate down on a piece of chewed gum? Jaws have been in *constant* motion since Saturday. Not that we don't appreciate making the grandchildren happy — but I did have to make a new law that all gum chewing is to be done outside or in the solitude of one's own bedroom, *if* no one else is in there. Funny, I thought I noticed some grandparents smile and nod heads just slightly when I pronounced the new rule. Isn't that odd?

Of all things and of all times, Will has just been smitten with a whopping case of malaria. He is so *mad* — however, too weak even to complain. I called the Peace Corps office and asked his secretary if she had any use for a two-hundred-pound wet noodle, but Sue suggested that I just keep it. He came home at noon yesterday looking like something dredged up from the bottom of somewhere. His temperature went up to 103.6°, and we had to get the doctor last night. I think it will be a few days before he's up and around.

Although Will's dad has been here only five days, already our tape recorder is working, the door handles throughout the whole house work properly for the first time, new vegetables are planted in the garden, the hose is being fixed, and the iron is repaired. Pamp hasn't had a pair of pliers, screwdriver or trowel out of his hands since he arrived.

I took Will's mom out to Nguludi Mission with me yesterday, and it was so much fun to show her around. She loved seeing all the babies in the orphanage and meeting all the sisters. The Mother Superior from Rome is visiting right now, and mom had an interesting conversation with her.

[I had invited Grandma to add a note on the end of my letter to my parents and I'm including it here, as it's interesting to read her first impressions]:

"Just a short report — the trip was long, but intensely interesting. It was wonderful to see the whole family at the airport. The boys look fine; Scott is so tall (rather thin); Ricky has grown and talks so well now; Don has become a teenager with all the usual symptoms; Mike is a firm champion of dogs and they follow him around constantly. Such fun to be with them.

The shopping is an experience! All these black boys besieging the driver of a car with vegetables, fruits, handicrafts, things made of skins, or just begging. The women intrigue me: they wear bright colors, always have a baby riding in a sling on their backs, and baskets or boxes with huge loads on their heads. When they sit, they sit on the ground. The Hindu women have beautiful outfits. This is like an international pageant all day long. You would find it quite a change from California.

Greetings to all. Gladys Lotter."

Happy Mother's Day

May 2, 1966

[To my mom in California]

Dear Mom,

Happy Mother's Day! At this time I'm just hoping that this will by some fluke get there before Mother's Day.

Most people in their right minds upon re-reading what they have just typed, would, after looking at the above *[where I'd made no less than ten typos which I simply left there]* turn in their Typing Badge, but I really hate to turn in two badges in one day. I am *so* ready for those boys to go back to school, that I've just turned in my Mother's Badge today. And right before Mother's Day, too. "Shame" (as the British here say).

Anyway, Happy Mother's Day! And do you realize that this Mother's Day will be a *real* celebration here? The very next day I'm firing off a twenty-one-gun salute — next door Prime Minister or no next door Prime Minister. SCHOOL WILL FINALLY RESUME THAT MONDAY! So that will be my *real* Mother's Day. All this jazz about togetherness is just swell, I guess — but for seven whole weeks??? Oh boy. How it ever happened that our kids lucked out so, with three weeks off *before* school was out and then four weeks of real, honest-to-goodness vacation after that, I don't know. And here there isn't any nice recreation program or Little League to send them off to, either. In fact, this house just happens to have the dubious honor of being the unofficial Teen Center of Blantyre. Furthermore, there is not a Beach Boys record that I can't now whistle and sing all the way through by heart.

If this is trying for mothers, just think how it is for visiting grandmothers and grandfathers. Somehow we'd had the idea that it would be "so nice" for Will's folks to be here during school vacation so they'd have more time with the kids. What ever possessed us? (I'm sure they are wondering too.) Actually we'd thought we'd be able to go more places during vacation, but Will forgot and came down with malaria and messed up all our plans. He's fine now, though tired, but is so far behind at the office that he can't catch up.

In desperation (my theory), Will's folks are going to fly to Salisbury Thursday and thence to Victoria Falls and will come back on Monday, just in time for the Back-To-School Celebration for Mothers. And Grandmothers. And Grandfathers. And Fathers. And little brothers. And neighbors. And probably Prime Ministers, now that I think of it.

Actually, although it's not calm and unconfusing here (the understatement of 1966), I think they've enjoyed themselves so far. The Falls is a "must," and this seemed a good opportunity to take advantage of the time. We've been having all sorts of jaunts here and there, and we love to have someone to show around. Pamp doesn't always want to go, but this has all sorts of fringe benefits for us Lotters, because he likes to stay around and fix doorknobs, faucets, and other recalcitrant or malfunctioning inanimate objects. Mom just loves to go and see it all and gets such a kick out of everything and everyone. She doesn't miss a thing.

We went to a village really out in the boonies the other day to a special program that some PCVs had organized. The villagers were so thrilled that Will had "brought his Very Own Mother From America," that they had us sit in seats of honor. These were large purple pillows on the Chief's porch in front of everyone. They presented Will with a cake that one of the women had baked, did dances, and sang songs. It was a thrill for all of us, and Will's mom just thoroughly enjoyed it. It was a high point for the whole family.

[That event was something that Mom Lotter talked and chuckled about right up to her dying day, it meant so much to her. Sitting on those purple pillows on the Chief's porch and hearing, "The Peace Corps Director's Very Own Mother came all the way from America…." She just loved it.]

Anyway, Happy Mother's Day, Mom Baker. Your present will be late. I'm knitting like mad on your sweater and hope that Will's mom can carry it home to you. Much safer than mailing it. It will be the most traveled sweater in captivity. I knitted on it all through Malawi, Tanzania, and Kenya and it was scared by lions, leopards, elephants, and rhinos. Now it will travel by sea and through Europe. If only it could talk!

Why Will Got Sick

May 10, 1966

Yesterday was quite a day. First — THE BIG KIDS WENT BACK TO SCHOOL! Wahooooo. Then we survived Ricky's birthday party. Much excitement for one day. Actually, the kids at the birthday party were awfully good, although one big nine-year-old brother (initial S) had in mind that he was going to run-the-whole-show, finally having to be gently banished from the scene. The Big Organizer. He'd helped with other parties and had done such a good job decorating, organizing games and all, but I think the praise sort of went to his head, and he was really going to *do* this party. My.

After the party, coffee with the other mothers and cleaning up the debris, I didn't realize how tired I was until I phoned to give a message to Dr. Ellison about something. I must have been sort of incoherent because Lee said, "Jane, have you been drinking?"

"No," I said. "But I just got through with a five-year-old's birthday party."

"Oh," he said, "that's it — you *need* a drink!"

Speaking of which, when Will was sick in bed with his malaria and his folks had been here three days, I went into the bedroom and found him laughing hysterically and thought he was delirious. He said, "Shut the door and I'll tell you why I'm sick." I couldn't imagine what he was going to say, and he said, "I just figured out why I'm sick. I haven't had a drink for *three days!*" Honestly. Since Will's folks don't drink, we'd decided we would pass on it while they are here.

However, about a week later when he was well, he came home really exhausted after an especially bad day at the office. He'd had to terminate a PCV who was a good friend, and it was just awful. He really needed a little pick-me-up, and ventured to ask his folks if they would like a small glass of sherry before dinner — and they actually did have one. So now we occasionally have a glass of wine. Not often, and only one, however.

Our Jeep came back from Nairobi, and were we ever glad to see it *and* the PCVs who drove it! I was so afraid that they might have some trouble with it and have a terrible trip, but all went fine. Because I'm so fond of the two PCVs who drove it, I was especially worried. One, Alice, is a grandmother and PCV secretary. She stayed in our house while we were away and took care of all our animals. Bernie, the other PCV, is a health worker about twenty-four years old and a very nice guy. Alice was so excited about this trip and especially pleased that Bernie wanted her to go along. She is such a good sport — rides on the backs of motorcycles, goes everywhere. They had a great time, the Jeep is intact and only needs some minor repairs now, we *hope*, as it has cost us a small fortune.

Will thinks we can get up to the lake next week for a few days. We really want his folks to be able to see it, and Will does have to go up that way to visit some PCVs, so this will be our chance. We'll take Rick with us, farm Scott out with friends, and leave Don and Mike here with Mas and Phillip.

We had an earthquake last Friday morning at 4:45 a.m. Really a big shaker with a huge roar. Our tin roof rumbled like crazy. We jumped up to get all the kids away from windows. It seemed to last quite a long time. Don was sleeping out on the front porch and had awakened right away. He said he was more frightened by an African lady who was walking down the hill with a load of vegetables on her head and a baby on her back. He said she stood in the street and screamed and screamed. It must seem like the end of the world to people who don't know about earthquakes. They don't happen often here, maybe once a year or so. This one was a good one. Someone said six on the Richter scale and centered in Mozambique.

I have another "Grandma Funny." The other day I took Mom to the beauty parlor. When Scott came home for lunch after Grandma had had her hair done, he noticed her hair (which looked very nice) right away. He said, "Grandma, did you go to the beauty parlor?"

"Yes, I did," said Grandma. "Do I look beautiful?"

"Well," said Scott, "You look — uh — *better*." Mom got a big charge out of that. She has such a good sense of humor.

We had a distinguished guest here for lunch yesterday. Mal Whitfield, the U.S. gold medal Olympic track star, came down from Nairobi, where he works with the U.S. Information Service as Youth and Sports Director. He goes on tour and gives sports clinics for schools and groups. He is really a nice person and does a wonderful job. He'd spoken at the high school in the morning, and both Don and Mike were there. In fact, the "two best athletes" from each form were chosen to participate, and Mike was selected from his grade. He was so pleased (as was his father). The boys said that Mal was so good that he got a standing ovation from the students. Don and Mike were thrilled to have him here for lunch afterwards, and hadn't minded at all saying to their classmates, "Well, he's coming to our house for lunch today."

Mal had given twenty clinics in the last nine days and was

pretty tired but still exuded enthusiasm. He was giving a clinic in the stadium in the afternoon, so I went to watch him. For "someone even older than Daddy" (to quote Mike), he certainly is in terrific shape. He's forty-three and still something to watch. American stock went way up around here.

We have added another animal to our menagerie, but just lost four. I found a cute baby rabbit for sale on the street and brought her home to live with our four guinea pigs — only to find out that the guinea pigs had been someone's dinner last night. We feel just terrible because they were so cute. A dog apparently dug under the fence of the cage and got them. So poor little Lulu Kalulu ("Kalulu" is Chinyanja for rabbit) has to live alone.

Grandparents Leave

May 28, 1966

Will's folks just left last Saturday. I surely didn't get many letters written for those five weeks. Between taking the folks places and people dropping in here to say hello to them, I didn't have time to write. The time went by fast though, and we really did a lot and had lots of fun. Now, Pamp may not entirely agree, I'm afraid. I think he missed his own California garden, and he needs to be busy every minute. There was only so much he could fix around here, and when he didn't want to go places with Mom and me (shopping, to the orphanage, for instance) I think sometimes it was kind of a drag for him. But he did enjoy the bigger trips we took.

On the other hand, Mom and I had a ball. She is so easygoing, and nothing seemed to bother her — boys and dogs racing through the house, chameleons crawling across her dinner plate, even teen-agers' constant Beach Boys records blaring (and *she* a classical pianist and piano teacher!). She was interested in everything and went everywhere with me. She didn't even mind sitting in the car waiting for me when I had to do too many errands. She thoroughly enjoyed seeing everything and loved watching the scene go by. Upon my return to the car, she would give me a full description of all the fascinating things she had observed. I'm sure I couldn't have a nicer mother-in-law. She's so easy to have around.

I have another "Grandma story." One day at lunch I was trying to lay down the law to one of the boys, saying, "No, you cannot do that (something totally unreasonable) today." I got many "why's?" and "but's" in answer, and finally just a silent scowl.

After a few moments of silence, Grandma turned to him and said, "It's difficult raising parents, isn't it?"

We took the folks up to the lake, and they just loved it. It's so incredibly beautiful there. We also took them to a very special ceremony up-country, about a three-and-a-half-hour drive from here, but well worth it. It was for an Ngoni Chief who was to become the Paramount Chief of about 150,000 Ngoni people. This only happens about every forty years and was spectacular. What an opportunity! We went up the day before and spent the night with missionary friends there. In the morning there were thousands of people, many of whom had been walking for days to come to this ceremony. We were among only a few whites there and were given places of honor on the Chief's front porch (but no purple pillows) to watch the dancing. It was truly wonderful.

The Ngoni dancers are the most colorful in Malawi and give me goose bumps to watch. Many of the men are the old "warriors" who wear skirts made of strips of animal fur of all sorts; wide, beaded waist bands and arm bands in intricate patterns; feather headdresses; and bells around their ankles. They carry wooden "head knockers" (these are polished sticks of wood with round knobs on the ends), which they shake as they dance. They dance and chant just to the beat of the many drums. It's very dramatic, and they do this all day and all night.

When I mentioned to this missionary wife that it would surely be something to have one of those outfits to take home, she said that her husband had been able to get one. Then she signaled down to her husband, Paul, who is fluent in Chinyanja. He was able to bargain with one of the men and says he will be able to get one for us. The man wants to dance in it for the rest of the week first, so Paul will get it down to Blantyre to us later. Now won't you all be surprised when Will gets off the plane in San Francisco with his skin skirt and feathers?

Lotter Zoo

Guess what we got yesterday? We finally got our monkey. Also, Ricky at long last got the baby goat he's been wanting. At the same time we were given another chicken. All of this wouldn't be so remarkable except that we were given all these animals down at Port Herald *[now called Nsanje]*, which is a three-and-a-half-hour drive from Blantyre. Or it is supposed to be. Now *that* was a trip.

Will was going down to Port Herald in a big Carryall to see the PCVs, spend two nights, and bring back the trunks and crates of some PCVs who are leaving. So Rick and I decided to go along. We left in an afternoon, spent the two nights there visiting, and planned to be back by noon the third day. We knew we were getting the monkey and possibly the baby goat, but the chicken was a last-minute special gift from a Malawian family in Port Herald.

The ensuing trip should have been on film. To begin with, we were absolutely loaded down with trunks and boxes and all kinds of stuff. It was hot and dusty. Then you add a monkey frantically trying to push the lid of her cage up; a two-week-old goat refusing to stay in his box or *in* anything — climbing all over the whole inside of the Carryall and up on top of all the piles of luggage, or sitting on my lap; and a squawking chicken, who, even though her feet were tied together, managed to keep flapping up out of her box.

All of this was insane enough — and then, of all things — out in the middle of nowhere we had *a flat tire.* Making it all even worse, Will couldn't get the idiot spare tire off. It was locked on, and there was no key. So Will had to leave all of us there beside the road and hitchhike five sweaty miles into Chikwawa, the nearest village, to phone the Peace Corps office to ask how you blanketyblank get the blanketyblank spare tire off. He was simply delighted to hear that the key was, in fact, *there* in Blantyre in the Peace Corps office (x*!!**x#!) They helpfully suggested trying a crowbar. Then, of course, he had to hitchhike back to us. He did find a tire iron though, and with lots of prying, swearing, sweating, and more swearing, he finally got it off and, dripping with sweat, got the tire changed. He was not happy, to put it mildly.

I wasn't too happy either, having waited in the hot sun for an hour with a hungry baby goat who had finished all his bottles, a frantic monkey, a squawking hen, and a tired, hot and fussy five-year-old human. There was no shade anywhere in sight. It was beastly hot and also getting later and later.

I was worried because we were to have a VIP from Washington come for dinner, and I hadn't even shopped yet. The afternoon was further complicated by the fact that I was supposed to play in a tennis foursome at 4:00 p.m. unless I could find a substitute. Now it was already 2:00 p.m. and our "plan" had been to be home by noon. Oh boy. We finally got home at three, filthy, hot, tired, hungry, and thirsty. All *six* of us.

We got the animals all settled in cages and trees, and I hurriedly phoned around but couldn't find a tennis sub. I sent Phillip walking to town to shop for dinner, took a bath (we have no shower), washed my hair, played tennis at 4:00, and came breathlessly in the door just five minutes ahead of Will and guest. But, amazingly, and best of all — good old Mas and Phillip had done the whole dinner themselves, had the table all set, and it was perfect. Chambo and chips (French fries), fresh vegetables and all. This man said he's never had such fish. Whew. I absolutely collapsed when he left. What a day.

Back to the farm — I don't know which is cuter — the monkey, whose name is "Ujeni" (oo-jenny), which means sort of "whatchamacallit" or "thingamajig" in Chinyanja; or the goat, whose name is "Two-And-Six," because that's how much the PCV paid for him (two shillings and six pence, which is about twenty cents). The goat is about the size and coloring of the baby duiker we had, about a foot tall. He follows Ricky wherever he goes, and when Rick runs, Two-and-Six gets so excited that he leaps in the air and comes down on all four feet and then springs back up and twists his whole body around. Honestly, it is the cutest thing. He has his own "house" in the backyard, but much prefers coming into ours if anyone should happen to leave a door open. Right now he's under the table here, licking Ricky's toes. He drinks about four bottles of milk a day, which, luckily, Rick likes to give him.

Ujeni is a vervet monkey, gray with a black face and a white tummy. She's not very big, about twelve or fourteen inches inches from head to start of tail, which is very long. Around her waist she has a leather collar which is attached to a long chain in the huge avocado tree. This gives her lots of room to move around and to swing from her chain. We're going to put a wooden box up there for her to sleep in (on end, the top like a roof).

She's the friendliest monkey we've ever seen. Joe, the PCV, had owned her for two years. She loves to climb on the boys' shoulders and look down their shirts, in their pockets, in their hair for "fleas," and even down into their socks. She has no front teeth (luckily) so if she does bite, it's more like a pinch, which doesn't break the skin. She did do that to me when I was holding her and one of the dogs scared her. She also likes to snatch things, like my hair clip or a pen out of a pocket, and scamper up to the top of the tree. People with eyeglasses will have to watch out.

Most of the PCVs down at Port Herald have monkeys or baboons for pets. While we were there, Rick accidentally bothered one of the baboons when it was eating, and the baboon bit him on the chest. Luckily Rick had a shirt on, so it didn't do much harm, other than scaring him half to death. It didn't break the skin and was more like a hard pinch, but it made a sort of blood blister. Now, I ask you — how many little boys do you know who can display a baboon bite??

Ma Kettle

June 9, 1966

We're having so much fun with our various new "family members"! Ujeni, the monkey, is a constant sideshow. She now has her upended box-house in the avocado tree so she can sit inside if she wants, but can still see what's going on below. The boys put little candies in their shirt pockets and climb part way up the tree to play with her. She comes right down to them, sits on their shoulders, gets the goodies out of their pockets, and does her usual, very thorough inspection, especially in their hair.

Right now, out the window I can see Rick and Saidi, Mas's four-year-old, playing under Ujeni's tree with Two-and-Six (goat). Ujeni is swinging back and forth on her chain, just out of reach of Cheena (dog) who is looking up at her with a very perplexed look on her face. Ujeni swings down and makes lunges at Cheena, obviously teasing her, while making faces and noises (like "nyahh nyahh") and then scampers back up the tree. What a monkey she is.

We had Friday "build" a tree to put right outside our dining room window. He took a tree limb with a fork in it for a perch and "planted" it so she can look in at us — but more importantly, so we can look out at her. She's better to watch than television, which doesn't exist here anyway. She jumps from the perch to the burglar bars over the windows (all the houses here have black wrought iron grills on the windows, called "burglar bars") and peers in and makes faces. It's very funny. So we chain her there when we eat. Wonderful when we have company. She eats almost anything and especially loves bananas. She's quite an addition to our family.

At last we have a new staff man in the Peace Corps office. He arrived last Saturday when all the staff was up at a conference at the Lake. Phyllis Bravinder and I went out to the airport to pick him up and then found ourselves feeling that we should entertain him all weekend until Will and Keith and the rest got home. He's a very nice, quiet man, who is alone here until his wife comes. What a scene to throw him into on his first days in Malawi! I'm not sure whether he likes (or *did* like) kids and/or animals, but I think by the time he had breakfast, lunch, and dinner here on Sunday in this zoo, the poor guy's head was spinning. He will undoubtedly choose to remain childless and petless for life now.

About a week and a half ago, we had around fifty people in for a farewell party for the Health Group PCVs who have finished their tour and are leaving. Then the next morning, Sunday, all the staff put on a breakfast for them here. There were fifty-seven of us, counting staff kids! We put up extra card tables and TV trays, in addition to our big table, and fed them all in shifts. Besides pancakes, this time we had Bacon à la Will, Scrambled Eggs à la Gary Stewart, with pancake and waitress duties handled by June Stewart, Phyllis Bravinder, and me. It was lots of fun, and we'll really miss all that group.

I'm looking out again at Rick and Saidi, and they are so cute together — one so black and one so blond. They play together all day. I can see them chatting away, and since Saidi doesn't speak English, it must be in Chinyanja, which Rick is learning surprisingly well. Someday I'd like to sneak out there with a tape recorder. Now they're doing something with the hose and a box — oh oh, probably giving the goat a bath.

The other day I was cooking, or trying to, with Bambo and Cheena (our two very large dogs), the cat, and the baby goat all in the kitchen with me. The baby goat likes to sleep on the top of the warm transformer in the kitchen, so he, of all of them, did sort of belong in there. I thought, "all I need now to look like Ma Kettle, is a couple of chickens in the kitchen, too," when in came Ricky carrying our new chicken, which suddenly jumped out of his arms and ran clucking around the kitchen! What timing.

["Ma Kettle" was the well-known comic strip hillbilly wife, who was always surrounded in her kitchen by barnyard animals and was my family's favorite comic strip when I was growing up.]

This poor little chicken is a social outcast in the chicken house, and we feel so sorry for her. She is the little brown one we were just given down at Port Herald, and the other chickens, all white, peck her unmercifully and have pulled out all the feathers on her back. An obvious blatant case of racial discrimination in the chicken house. We've had to put the poor little thing in the guinea pig cage by herself.

The reason this chicken is *alone* in the guinea pig cage is that the most recent occupant, Lulu Kalulu (rabbit) sadly didn't survive. She was so cute but probably too young to be away from her mother. We had put Lulu in the guinea pig cage after someone ate all the guinea pigs for dinner one night. And Yogi Berra (chameleon) has disappeared, but Willie Mays (chameleon) is doing fine and now shares his cage on the window sill in the dining room with a cute little white mouse. There *had* been two cute little white mice, but one got out one night, to the delight of our cat, who had a delicious dessert — unfortunately under Scott's bed in the middle of the night, complete with all the ghastly sound effects. The seventeen chickens, no, now eighteen, are fine, as are the two dogs, cat, monkey and goat. So now you are up-to-date on the family.

Oh yes, by the way, Will, Don, Mike, Scott, and Rick are okay, too.

Trying to visit the Lotters

CARTOON BY PHIL DURAND.

A Different Culture

June 14, 1966

I just got back from a trip with Will. We left Friday noon and got back Monday about four. We flew up to Mzuzu in the Beaver, picked up a Land Rover, and drove to Nkata Bay for a teachers' conference. Nkata Bay is so beautiful, as is the Rest House there. The Rest House is up on a hill with a lovely view of the lake, has a big screened khonde (porch) with comfortable chairs to relax in. It truly is a *rest* house and it was wonderful to be able to sit around and talk with all the PCVs.

On Sunday after the conference, we drove to a school really far out in the bush to visit two lonesome PCVs and spend the night with them. Of all the posts I've been to, this was the most remote and the least civilized and developed. No electricity (most PCVs don't have it), no running water or even sinks to carry water to, and an outside "chim" (toilet) which had neither seat nor door, just a hole in a brick floor. It did have walls and a thatch roof, thank goodness.

All of that is not unusual for PCVs, but their house is very old and gloomily dark inside, with few windows and very high dark ceilings. Depressing. Although they are awfully nice and we like them a lot, these two guys seem to have no imagination or incentive to fix up and cheer the place a bit. Even their food was pretty dull, as they have a cook who doesn't seem to have any imagination (or cooking skills) either.

I told Will that I wished he could leave me there for a few days to shape the place (and the cook) up. A few bright local fabrics to hang on the walls and a little spice and variety in their rice and peanut butter existence could make such a difference. We took them a bottle of bourbon.

[Now, reading this, I'm wondering about our judgment on this – we probably sent them straight into alcoholism.]

We also took four steaks, which the cook totally ruined, and a whole pound of butter.

[Swell – not only alcoholism but clogged arteries – but we didn't know much about all that then.]

At least I think we did cheer them up quite a bit. They are both really good teachers doing a great job, and are well liked by

all the Malawians. They don't seem to know why they are
depressed. My heart bled for them because they are so nice. I hope
things get better for them.

All the boys and animals were fine when we got back. Rick had
stayed with the Stewarts, Scott stayed with our missionary friends,
the Coxes, and Don and Mike were fine here with Mas and Phillip.
That crazy goat just loves me and has not been away from my heels
since we came back. The first minute I sat down he jumped up on
my lap. What am I going to do when he gets bigger? Guests are
certainly startled when this little goat comes into the house and
either jumps up on the coffee table, lamp table, or me. The other
day he got up on the back of the couch and ate most of South
Africa off of our Africa map on the wall. But he's so cute. He
really thinks he is a dog, with all the household privileges of the
other dogs.

Will has been invited to give a Peace Corps Termination
Conference in Ethiopia in July, and I might be going with him!
There are a few details to work out first. Actually five — initials
D, M, S, and R, plus M followed by O-N-E-Y. The Peace Corps pays
Will's way and expenses, of course, but I would be on my own. Will
did make a plane reservation for me, in case we can work it all out.

The Bravinders were PCVs in Ethiopia and loved it, and they
are encouraging me to go (as if I *need* encouragement). Also, when
else would we both be able to go on a trip to Ethiopia for the price
of one fare? Nina Rusk, Peace Corps staff in Ethiopia and cousin of
U.S. Secretary of State Dean Rusk, was the one who invited Will to
come to give the conference. We're waiting to hear from her about
accommodations for me. Hope we can avoid a big hotel bill.

I had such a scare last weekend when Will was away. At 5:25 in
the morning, Phillip came knocking on my bedroom window and
said that something was wrong with his baby. I got right up and
had them bring him straight into the house and immediately saw
that he was in a coma, or semi-coma. From what they said I could
tell that he had had convulsions.

I got dressed quickly and rushed them at top speed (23 mph in
my speedy Peugeot) to Queen Elizabeth Hospital. However, I wasn't
happy with the treatment there — there was no doctor on duty, just
a medical assistant who didn't seem too interested. Besides, I
doubted his capability. So we got back in the car and rushed (at 23
mph) all the way out to Nguludi Mission to the sisters there. They
were wonderful, of course, and decided to keep Delia, the mother,
and the baby there for the rest of the day.

In the late afternoon I went back out there to the Mission, and
the baby seemed to be OK. They don't know what it is or was. No

fever or anything. Now today he's sick again, and Phillip says he took him to an African doctor (witch doctor, I'm sure, because he rubbed something black on the baby's body "to make him well"). Phillip says that "white people's medicine won't do any good for African babies." So what can I do?

I'm really worried about him because he has these seizures without being sick first. No fever or anything. Epilepsy?? My dilemma is that if I do take him to a white doctor and something bad happens — then it's my fault. But if I don't do anything and something bad happens, just think how I'll feel. Quandary. This is life in a different culture, for sure.

Addis Ababa

July 14, 1966
Addis Ababa, Ethiopia

As you can see, I did get to come with Will to Ethiopia. We arrived here last Saturday, and what a fascinating place this is! Another world. I know, I know — I keep saying this about every new country we visit, and I'll probably say it a lot more times yet, but so far this is the most other-worldly we've seen. It doesn't seem like Africa. It seems more like an Arabic country. Of course we've never *been* to an Arabic country, but the flowing robes; the very different Amharic language and writing; the half-covered faces of the women; mysterious-sounding music; and donkeys, sheep, and goats everywhere — all contribute to this very different feel.

The people are very handsome, with sort of bronze-colored skin, and rather chiseled-type features, which look more Semitic than negroid. The women, who are beautiful, wear lovely white, long dresses of a hand-woven gauzy fabric with a colored border at the bottom. They usually have another sort of shawl of the same fabric over their heads. I think these are called "shamas." Many cover their faces. The men wear shamas of a heavier white fabric, kind of draped over them, over pants that look sort of like jodhpurs. We just love seeing it all.

Addis is certainly a city of contrasts. Very beautiful, modern buildings on wide streets intersect with little, narrow, cobbled streets lined with very old adobe or mud houses. Pedestrians are often goats or sheep and sometimes cows. It's strange to come out of a lovely, modern hotel and find a cow munching grass a few feet away. The elevation here is 8,400 feet, and the air is cool and crisp. It's the rainy season, with rain every afternoon, but the mornings are nice. It's a big city, about 500,000 people, pretty, hilly, with lots of trees. Lots of monuments and other interesting things. We are hoping to see Haile Selassie's palace today because Will has some time off.

We stayed in a beautiful hotel the first two nights and then the Peace Corps Director, Dave Berlew, kindly invited us to stay with their family. A break for me, since Peace Corps is not paying my expenses — so we were happy to accept. They are very nice people who have four little children, a huge house, cook, nanny, and houseman. With all this help it's easier to feel that we're not putting them out too much.

Will is working hard at the conference, which runs from July 10 to 16. Termination Conferences are held at the end of the

PCVs' two-year commitments. They all must attend one of these before going home to the States. They assess the successes and failures of their projects, make recommendations for the future, and evaluate their experiences. These conferences are conducted by a Peace Corps staff person serving in a different country. It's an important process, and Will is enjoying it. We hope to do some sightseeing afterwards. Will returns home ahead of me, on July 20, and I "have" to stay in Nairobi for three extra days, in order to get the excursion rate, which saves us forty pounds ($120). Gary and June Stewart have just been transferred from Malawi to Kenya, so I'll probably stay with them in Nairobi. That will be a treat.

Now about our "details" (D, M, S, & R at home in Blantyre) and how I actually got to come on this trip: Don and Mike are boarding at the high school for two weeks. St. Andrews is part boarding school and part daily attendance school. This should be an interesting new experience for them. Scott and Rick are home with a really nice missionary teacher who has *offered* to stay in the house and take care of them and the menagerie. I still can't believe I'm here — especially since Scott woke up the day we were leaving with a temp of 101.6°. Does it ever fail? However, we decided that it was just a reaction to a typhoid shot he had been given the day before. Our plane didn't leave until late afternoon, so we had time to be sure he was OK.

On July 6, before we left on our trip to Ethiopia, Malawi became a Republic. There were huge celebrations, with flags and decorations everywhere. Our neighbor, formerly Prime Minister Dr. Hastings Kamuzu Banda, is now *President* Hastings Kamuzu Banda. Consequently, we live next door to the Presidential Palace! There were dignitaries from all over the world and the usual huge excitement with such celebrations.

In the midst of all those festivities, packing, food shopping for the weeks we weren't going to be here, labeling all Don's and Mike's uniforms, underwear, socks, etc. for boarding school, we found ourselves supposedly having Ambassador Gondwe, the Malawi Ambassador to the United States, in for dinner the night before we left. I say "supposedly" because after I knocked myself out fixing a delicious dinner (complete with linen tablecloth and candles), he didn't come! He was to come at 6:00 p.m., and we waited and waited, knowing full well about "African time" (which means *not* on time). He did, however, call at 7:00 to say that he was sorry that he couldn't make it. He is really a very nice guy, and I guess he couldn't help it — but that didn't make me any less mad. It was about a six-hour setback for me in an already tight schedule. Well, c'est la vie, I guess.

We're Back

Tuesday, July 26, 1966

Here we are — home again and relieved that the boys are happy and well. I always have the feeling that I can't completely enthuse about a trip until I see the kids and find out that all was well while we were gone. So, since all *was* well — our trip to Ethiopia was just great.

We were in Addis Ababa for eight days for the conference, and, although Will was busy almost the whole time, he did have some time off to see most of Addis. Mrs. Berlew, the Peace Corps Director's wife, with whom I spent most of my time, since we were staying with them, was really nice and took me all over to sightsee. Will and I did, however, get to see Haile Selassie's palace together and meet his lions. We were wined and dined a lot and really enjoyed ourselves.

We'd hoped to have a couple of days after the conference to go to some of the outlying provinces, but found that we had to fly right out to Nairobi the next morning. This was the only flight out of Addis that Will could get in order to make his Nairobi-Blantyre connection, even though we would have to be two more days waiting in Nairobi. We would have loved more time in Ethiopia, but flight schedules pretty much determine our itineraries.

Was there ever a story in our U.S. papers about three lions escaping in a plane over Belgium? Well, these lions belonged to Jane Campbell in Addis, who is on the Peace Corps staff there. She had raised them from cubs. Two were about nine months old, and one was about a month old. We just missed seeing them by one day, as we went to Jane's house for lunch the day after they'd been sent to an estate in England.

That day she'd heard over BBC that they'd gotten out of their cage on the chartered cargo plane and apparently scared the pilot and co-pilot half to death. They made an emergency landing in Brussels where there were men with machine guns and nets, waiting for them. It's a wonder the lions weren't killed. "They were only trying to be friendly," Jane said. She was *very* upset.

That night we had dinner with her. She came late, as she had received a call from her sister in London, who had met the plane with a new cage. The lions were now properly caged, and Jane was relieved. Her sister had said, "Percy, Olaf, and Sheba are just fine and are all having their bottles, and Lord Bath is here to take them to his estate." Jane gave us some darling pictures of the lions to bring back to the kids. Not quite the same as taking our own pictures *with* the lions — darn — but still fun.

Will left Nairobi on Tuesday, and since I couldn't leave until Saturday, I stayed with June and Gary Stewart and their children. We really miss them in Malawi. Needless to say, I had a great time shopping and sightseeing with June, in addition to going with her to house-hunt, as they are in temporary housing. One of the places June and the kids and I went to see was Lake Nakuru. The thousands of flamingos moving about, feeding at the water's edge are an unbelievable sight. As far as I could see, it looked like an undulating, salmon-colored beach.

I got home Saturday afternoon just in time to give an open house after the national track meet. We had lots of people, followed by our usual typical weekend of dinner guests, pancake breakfast guests (twenty), and more dinner guests. I'm *still* trying to catch my breath and get my suitcase unpacked. Glad I had a nice rest because we're sure right back in the usual whirl of things here.

Now I'm Awake!

Joy, joy. A day that I don't have to go running off somewhere. Not that I don't enjoy the things I do when I go "running off," but a day at home once in a while is so nice. Rick is still asleep — oh oh, that did it. It *had* been quiet.

We've had some rather unrestful nights for the last couple of weeks. We had a prowler one night outside our house, and ever since then, every night it seems one of the kids wakes up, sure that he is hearing something. Last night it was Scott who shouted, no doubt in his sleep, and that scared Ricky so much that he had to come sleep with us.

What happened the night the prowler actually came was that Mike, who had already been talking in his sleep a couple of times, said, "Dad! A man just went by my window!"

Mike's room is just off our bedroom. It's a converted screen porch in the front of the house with two sides of draperied windows and is well lit by Dr. Banda's floodlights on the walls bordering our yard. Our dogs are huge, and there are armed guards all over the place next door, so the last place we ever thought there would be a prowler would be here — especially right in the *front* of the house in all the floodlights. Will told Mike he was dreaming and to go back to sleep.

"*Dad!* He went by again!"

Will got up and took a flashlight and looked outside on the front porch and saw nothing, although the dogs did keep barking. As he came back down the hall to the bedroom, all of a sudden Mike yelled in Chinyanja, "Iwe — coka!" (pronounced "ee-way choka"), which is "hey you — get away!" Then a man went running away up the driveway, and the dogs went wild — but didn't go after him! Swell.

This man had come right up to Mike's window where the drapes were pulled aside about a foot at the bottom of his bed and peered in directly at Mike. How Mike ever had the courage to sit up and shout at the man — ! I would have just frozen. We called the police, who said there had been an attempted break-in across the street from us. A man had broken a window and was trying to get in when the people heard him and he ran. He then apparently came across the street and went to the house next door to us, got into their living room, stole all their keys in order to come back another time (they had to have all their locks changed), and then came here.

While waiting for the police at 4:00 a.m., Will and Mike went out with baseball bats and the dogs. They looked up and down the road but never found the man. The police were really surprised that anyone would come here and, of course, so were we. There have been nine burglaries in ten days in our neighborhood.

The day before yesterday Will had asked me to go to a house over in Limbe to see if it was ready for a new staff member to move into the next day. Of all things, the night before, a burglar had broken in and slashed down all the drapes. There wasn't much else to take, as the furniture was too heavy — and the night watchman never heard a thing. Probably asleep in the garage.

There are many burglaries here in Blantyre where there are so many unemployed and really *hungry* people. The volunteers out in the countryside tell us that crime is almost non-existent. Some of them have not locked their houses for two years. Even in the cities where there are burglaries, there are very few personal assaults or crimes of a violent nature, though. Guns are almost unknown, and most of the police don't even carry them.

Sunday night, or rather Monday morning, the phone rang at 2:00 a.m. This is always scary. Will stumbled to the phone.

"Will — are you awake?" (What a question.) "This is Ambassador Jones."

"*NOW* I'm awake!" blurted Will. This struck the Ambassador so funny that he told us later that he's going to put it in his memoirs some day.

The Ambassador said there had been an accident, and Will's heart sank, but it did not involve a Peace Corps person. An American Crossroader had fallen on Mlanje Mountain. American Crossroaders are a group of young volunteers, usually high school age, who go to work in developing countries for a few weeks. The Ambassador told Will they needed our Peace Corps doctor, or someone else "fit" if he wasn't available, to go with a climbing party up the mountain. Will phoned Lee Ellison, our Peace Corps "fit" doctor, who then left at 3:00 a.m. with the hiking party.

It took two days to get the boy down and to the hospital here. He is badly hurt but alive, with a fractured thigh and a concussion, among other things. He had fallen near the top, which is 10,000 feet in elevation. It was quite an operation to get him down. They had to spend the next night in one of the huts up there on the mountain.

We are having a flurry of Peace Corps weddings now. We just went up to Lilongwe to one this last weekend. One of our PCVs who is in the agricultural cooperative group, known as the

"CO-OP group," married a young Dutch woman who is here working with the United Nations. There is to be another wedding of two PCVs this weekend, and soon another PCV will marry a man from Britain. Just a month ago a PCV married a British teacher. Will feels like Old Dad, as he has to give his consent to all of these and has to interview the prospective spouses. Good practice, I guess.

[On the subject of weddings, this seems a good place to interject an interesting story that I never did write home about, unfortunately. For that reason, I don't know the exact dates when this all transpired.]

One day President Banda called Will in, but Will had no clue about why. To his surprise, Dr. Banda told him that he, as Peace Corps Director, must *forbid* a marriage that was planned between an African American PCV and his white British VSO (like Peace Corps in Britain) fiancée. Will was aghast at Dr. Banda's demand, and as much as said so. We knew this couple and knew of their plans to marry, and Will told Dr. Banda that there was no way he could, or would, forbid a PCV to marry, as long as it would not affect his or her work. So Dr. Banda said *he* himself would forbid them to marry in Malawi.

It seems that the parents of the young British woman had actually telephoned President Banda from Britain and demanded that he forbid this interracial marriage. It was incredible. Will explained to Dr. Banda that Peace Corps Volunteers have the right to marry whomever they wish, just as long as they are able to continue doing their work. Dr. Banda was very angry and insistent.

Will was so mad that he told the President that before he would tell this couple they could not marry, he would cable Washington, DC and resign his position as Peace Corps Director and tell them why. (Pretty scary thing for Will to do.) However, there were no more words about this from the President after that day. Will went right away to talk to Roy, the PCV, and tell him what Dr. Banda had said. They really appreciated Will's support, but decided that between Dr. Banda and the parents, it looked as if there would be nothing but trouble if they went ahead and married in Malawi. They decided to wait and were married when they got to New York.

[There is a special happy sequel to this story – one that I just love. About twenty years after all this happened, we went to a big Malawi Peace Corps reunion in Tennessee. There were about one hundred fifty ex-Malawi PCVs and spouses there. Among them were Roy Frazier and his

wife, Jill. We all sat in a huge circle and shared what we have done with our lives since those days, especially the impact Peace Corps had on all of us. When it came to Roy, he surprised Will by thanking him for the way he had stood up to the President about their marrying, and announced that they are still happily married!]

Drat!

My letters seem to be getting further and further apart —
partly because of the fact that our warm weather has started and
we are spending many happy hours at the pool. On the days that
Don and Mike don't have afternoon school, they ride their bikes
directly to the pool and meet us there. It's so nice. (A hard life,
huh?)

Will is now in the States for about two and a half or three
weeks. He's in Washington, DC and also in Syracuse, New York for
the training program for new PCV teachers. We had a card from
him en route, and he was especially enjoying the reactions of the
three Malawian language instructors who were accompanying him
to Syracuse. None had ever been out of Africa. Two had never
been outside of Malawi and had never flown before. You can just
imagine what it was like to see it all through their eyes. Just seeing
Blantyre for the first time, one of them from up-country
commented that he thought Blantyre must be like Johannesburg,
South Africa, which he'd seen in photos. (Blantyre is like Very-
Smalltown USA). I can only imagine what he thought when he saw
the New York skyscrapers.

Wouldn't you know that the second night after Will left we
would have a burglar? Luckily we weren't aware of it while it was
happening, and they didn't get into the house. They did, however,
steal two of our bicycles from the front porch, right under my
open bedroom window. It turned out to be a gang of *eight* escaped
prisoners. The sight of just one burglar would have been enough
to give me a heart attack.

We discovered the bikes were gone in the morning when the
kids went out to go to school. At the same time we realized that
the police were next door at the Gunns' house, where a lot of
things apparently had been stolen from inside the house. Both
Mr. Gunn and Will were gone, and the police think it was a
planned thing. They were real pros and didn't make a sound —
even had a stolen car to transport their newly acquired goods in.
Also, strangely, the dogs didn't bark. The police say these men
are clever at luring dogs away with pieces of meat. I must say, the
Malawi police are on the ball here, as they caught one of the men
and recovered some of the "loot" just two days later.

I'm also quite sure that the police must read every James
Bond book out. That morning after the burglary they came right
over, all looking neat and handsome in their starched uniforms,

and the officer in charge said,

"Good morning! I am Inspector Msombe, and I have just visited the scene of the crime next door."

When I said that two of the children's nice American bicycles were stolen, they all chorused so sympathetically, "Oh, shame."

Later, after they'd recovered Scott's bicycle, I had to go to the police department to make some special arrangements to take it home, as it was supposed to be held for evidence until the trial. I pleaded that Scott really needed it for school. The inspector was very nice and said, "All right," and turned to another policeman and said, "Mrs. Lotter may take the exhibit home now," continuing to study some fingerprint charts with his magnifying glass. I was tempted to say, "Thank you, 007."

Will's new deputy, Jim Kelly, has been so nice to us. He insisted that we have a night watchman while Will is gone, and immediately sent one out when he heard about our burglary. I must say that three hairy nights had gone by before Jim heard about our burglary, though. At least one child (if not I) was getting up several times a night, saying, "I think I hear something" — so it's reassuring to go to bed now and not have to worry. We've been the only American family (in government pay) not to have a watchman, actually, and although the government does pay for them, we haven't felt the need for one before.

I feel sorry for night watchmen, who have to stay up all night and walk around and around the house. This watchman is a character, and the kids just love him. He comes at 7:00 p.m. and stays until 5:00 a.m. He wears a beret, big black boots, a big overcoat (and this is our hot season) with a wide belt into which a claw hammer is tucked. He carries a metal skeleton of an umbrella, which, without the cloth part looks like a spear and is, he says, to "spear the enemy."

When Jim brought him out to meet me, he clicked his heels and saluted me! Last night when a friend came over to visit, he clicked his heels, saluted, and opened the car door for her. She thought she'd come to visit a queen or something. He is a former soldier who fought with the Rhodesian African Rifles in Malaya *[now West Malaysia]* and Singapore during World War II and has lots of tales to tell the boys. We probably won't have the heart to let him go when Will comes back. However, he is so eager to be *sure* I know he's patrolling and doing his job (and not sleeping, as many of them do), that he makes his feet crunch *loudly* on the gravel driveway in front of the house; then, as he walks on the grass, in the back, he coughs and clears his throat — so it's crunch-crunch-crunch-cough-cough-ahem-ahem-ahem all night long. He's not sleeping — but neither am I.

I had such a funny experience today. Since there weren't enough ladies to fill out a tennis tournament (they're always having tennis tournaments here), I said I would enter. It was a "partners drawn" thing where partners' names are drawn out of a hat. My partner turned out to be an older, veddy British man in his sixties, who is a good, but very serious tennis player (neither of which am I). He looks and acts somewhat fearsome on the courts. In fact, one day when we were first here, I was watching him play and he scared me to death by shouting, *"Drat!"* when his partner missed a shot. I swore to myself that I would never play with Mr. Goodban. So, of course — guess who drew *me* for his partner? I was cringing and just waiting to hear him say *"drat!"* when my name came up.

Today was our first match, against another older man and a young Scottish woman who is a friend of mine. This other man has to be the epitome of good sportsmanship, as well as a fine player — "Lovely shot, Jane," and "Oh shame, *just* out a bit" (out ten feet), great encouragement to both his partner *and* me. Such a nice man. He didn't know that I really know that Mr. Goodban is actually sort of nice, at least off the court, and that I understand his cool exterior (understatement), so as we passed by one another at net between games when Mr. Goodban and I were down a set, Mr. Rouse said to me, "Don't let him put you off, Jane — he's just an old grouch!" This struck me so funny that I relaxed a bit and played much better after that.

Amazingly, Mr. Goodban didn't say *"drat"* even once when I blew my shots! We lost — and I was secretly relieved, as I wouldn't have wanted it to progress to the inevitable *"drat"* stage.

"Gloria Thing"

October 12, 1966

We are babysitting the oddest animal. We think it's an armadillo, but it doesn't look like the pictures in the encyclopedia. The African name is "nkhonga," and we are supposed to be very lucky if we have one. It looks sort of like a large artichoke with a hard shell and a tail. Including its long, flat, wide tail, it is about two feet long. It's very shy and curls up in a ball with its tail wrapped around its outside. Its face is so cute, with a long nose and little brown eyes.

The new Peace Corps doctor bought him (her/it?) from a boy on the street and decided that the name of the first person who asked "What's its name?" was going to be the name of "it." And Gloria, the Peace Corps secretary, was the first unwitting asker — so now its name is "Gloria Thing." "Thing" because we don't know what the thing is.

Since the doctor had to go on a trip the next day, he brought Gloria over to the Lotter Zoo to be kept. Of course. So we put her (we say "her" now because of the name Gloria) in the old duiker cage in the backyard that night. Unfortunately it was too dark to inspect the condition of the cage and apparently some of the chicken wire was loose. So, late that night — I was still awake reading — the night watchman (thank goodness for him) rapped on my window.

"Madam, Madam — the thing is out!" he said, excitedly.

"What?" I couldn't imagine what he was talking about.

"The thing in the wire is out!"

At first I couldn't understand what in the world he meant, and thought some wires had fallen down in the yard. I got up, put on my robe and went out. I finally understood when he made imitations of a small animal crawling on the ground. (By "in the wire" he meant "in the wire cage.") We went running out with the "torch" (flashlight here) and saw Gloria making a beeline for the neighbor's yard — not the President's, luckily. Donnie woke up and the two of them went on a chase after her and finally managed to catch her and get her into a box. Then we had to bring her in and lock her in the back porch washroom for the night. We couldn't think where else to put her. So we cleared everything from the floor up onto the sink in there — milk bottles, laundry soap, etc.

Although you would never guess by looking at her, she can climb. After a while we heard crashing and glass breaking. We ran and opened the porch door to look. She had climbed up the smooth straight legs of the table, up over the lip of the table, and then from the table onto the sink, where she proceeded to knock off milk bottles, cans, everything — in the middle of the night, of course. With those little stubby legs, yet, to say nothing of such a cumbersome-looking body! So we had to take everything out of there until the next day when we could fix up her cage.

We had no way of warning Mas and Phillip though, and that's the door they come in each morning. We couldn't leave a note because they can't read — so they were a bit surprised, to say the least, when they came in at 5:30 a.m. and found this strange animal in the washroom. However, by now I think they are getting used to this sort of thing with our family (crazy Americans). At least it wasn't a leopard or lion.

That same day we had a bit of excitement out in front. I heard all this yelling and looked out and saw about twelve Africans throwing rocks and hitting the trees across the street with sticks. Friday and Phillip were right in the middle of it, and I was afraid it was a fight. I ran up the driveway, prepared to defend my loyal workers (I have no idea how) and found out they had seen a very large snake which had gone up in the trees. The dust was flying and they were all shouting and after about ten minutes of this they did knock it down. They all beat on the poor thing as if their very lives depended on it. I was yelling, "That's enough — don't smash the head or we can't identify it!" (Those Americans again.) Finally they stopped, actually with the snake's head still intact, amazingly enough. It was green and fifty-three inches long! I guessed it was a boomslang.

I called the University of Malawi, and a professor of Zoology came out and got it. It was, in fact, a boomslang. I'd guessed right, remembering that "harmless 43-inch green tree snake" we'd killed in our tree. However, a boomslang *is* hard to tell from a green mamba. This last one was actually the first live snake I've seen here, except from the car. Friday has killed about eight in our yard, but I'd never seen them before they were corpses.

I may have mentioned the new little baby we have at the orphanage, Martina, who came to us at six months weighing only five pounds? In that first week she gained a whole pound, and in the following two weeks another pound, so that by the time she was seven months old she was almost seven pounds. She is just adorable and very bright and smily.

Yesterday when I went out to the orphanage though, she was sick and in just two days had lost a whole pound. She is holding her own, and we have our fingers crossed — but you should see her. Her legs are the size of my fingers, and she is seven months old!

She must have amazing stamina, though, as she only weighed three pounds at birth. When her mother died, her father managed to keep her alive in the village, but she got measles at four pounds. The father then took her to another mission hospital to some nuns who nursed her and got her up to five pounds. He then brought her to Nguludi. We all just hover over her and love her because she has put up such a good fight. The nuns moved her from the orphanage over to the hospital (there at Nguludi), where there is someone to watch her day and night. Tonight I heard she is a bit better, though still very sick, and still in the hospital.

We're having two Peace Corps people from Washington for dinner tonight. They are here giving a Peace Corps Termination Conference. We'll have our usual chambo menu. I just bought forty pounds of meat at the African market, which is "aging" in the fridge for five days. I am so proud of myself now that I am doing this meat-buying in the open market. Can you imagine *me*, standing undaunted by fly-covered entrails lying around, and pointing up at huge carcasses of meat hanging in the open-air tin-roofed stall, saying, "Hack here," and "chop there"? They wrap it all up in newspaper, and I put it in my basket, pay a kid to carry it — and off I go. The meat is actually inspected and graded, though, and I only buy meat when it has been freshly slaughtered — and very early in the morning before the heat of the day. A year ago I would have fainted at the very thought of doing this!

Termites, Anyone?

October 26, 1966

Yesterday was our nineteenth wedding anniversary, and by coincidence it happened to be a day that Will and I were supposed to go on a trip, so we were going to combine business with pleasure and celebrate. The German Ambassador had invited us to go up to Lilongwe to a "little concert" given by African students who are using musical instruments donated by the German government. The Ambassador thought we would be especially interested because these students are being instructed by a young woman PCV teacher there.

We decided this would be fun, so we planned to go up in the morning, check in at the old Lilongwe Hotel (which we love), maybe work in a little tennis, go to the late afternoon concert, then have a lovely celebratory dinner in the hotel, spend the night there, and come back the next morning.

Well — so much for these grand plans. Just before leaving for school at 6:30 a.m. yesterday, Don doubled up with a horrible stomachache. When it didn't let up, we thought maybe it could be appendicitis, so we called the Peace Corps doctor. Lee Ellison came right out. He said he really couldn't tell as yet, but to watch him carefully and stay in touch. So there went our trip. Will, of course, had to go ahead and go. *Then*, when it was already too late for me to catch the plane, Don's stomachache let up. Stopped. He felt fine. In fact, he was absolutely fine *all day*. He was feeling perfectly *fit*. So was I — *to be tied!*

I told Don that the least he could do was produce one more excruciating pain during the day (as I passed by the living room and stuck my tongue out at him). Or even a little one would do. Darn kid ate all day and felt swell. Grrrr.

I must say though, that all the boys were awfully cute to me at dinnertime. They knew how disappointed I was, especially since Will has been away so much. So, first Don said he would plan and "do" dinner. They put a chaise lounge out on the front lawn for me and brought me a lovely cold drink. Then Don disappeared into the kitchen, plotting with Mas about dinner, and they all went inside.

When they called me in, I saw that they had put flowers and wine on the table, and had little wrapped-up presents for me. They were so cute. Don had fixed delicious spaghetti all by himself, Mas had made salad, and there were hot rolls. I couldn't stay mad. Later on Will called and said the concert had lasted three-and-a-half hours (!) and was followed by "high tea" (which is almost like a meal), and we wouldn't have wanted that nice cozy dinner at the hotel anyway — so I felt better. It wouldn't have been the way we'd planned (is anything ever?).

We've found out that "Gloria Thing," our long-tailed artichoke, is a pangolin. We found her in an encyclopedia at the same time a letter came from Pat Allen at home, saying that she had found it. It's also known as a "scaly anteater," although it isn't even in the anteater family. Gloria seems to be doing fine, and her repaired cage is on firm concrete so that she can't dig out.

We also have discovered something else about Gloria. Loud noises, like clapping our hands, scare her, and she quickly rolls up into a ball with her big flat tail wrapped tightly around her. We're sure this is to protect her tender underbelly. The benefit of this, for us, is that when she is rolled up we can actually pick her up – *carefully,* as we've heard that a pangolin can "saw" off a dog's leg if it gets near the tail, which has very sharp, saw-like edges on its scales. We make sure that we keep her tail *tight* against her body and don't get our hands in between it and her body. So, if she has to be moved or caught, we clap our hands, and she rolls right up. We hold her *very* tightly and not for long!

We feed her a shovelful of termite larvae every day. The first day that I described to Friday, our gardener, what we needed to feed her — "those fat white worms in the ground that turn into termites," he knew right away and marched out into the back yard, stuck his shovel in just once, and voilà! Feast for Gloria — hundreds of fat, juicy, white wormy-looking larvae. Yum. It's fun and interesting to watch her eat. Her tongue is about twelve inches long, narrow, and bright pink, and she sort of folds it or rolls it like a tube and just slurrrps up the ants. We just dump a pile of the dirt that contains the larvae and ants into her pen and she sticks her tongue all the way into it to get her dinner and doesn't even get her face dirty. Termites, anyone?

I'm afraid Gloria is stealing Ujeni's thunder now, as so many people come around to watch Gloria eat. However, Ujeni is doing her best to put on a show. Yesterday I took my cake pan out to give her some leftover crumbs — and she grabbed the whole pan from my hands and ran to the top of the tree with it. Now how would you explain to dinner guests that the cake would have been ready sooner but a monkey ran with the pan up to the top of a tree — ?

Goats (Kids) Go To School

November 10, 1966

Yesterday was a big day — The Day The Goats Went to School — boarding school, at that. Yes, you read right. All the "kids" except Rick are now in school.

I think I forgot to say that about a month ago we were given another goat (which we needed like a hole in the head) out in a village. I know that it's a great honor to be given a goat, but — ! He's sort of a teen-ager, much bigger than Two-and-Six, very friendly and enthusiastic, and given to butting people cheerily when they're not looking. The boys gave him the very original name of "Bill."

One day the Health Department came around and informed us that "a neighbor" had complained about our goats (now *who* do you suppose?), which are not supposed to be allowed in the city limits. When I pointed out to the inspector that our neighbor *Himself* kept goats, he said, "Well, there are laws for some, and then, you know — heh heh...." The goats would have to go.

This happened just about the time that the two goats, having begun to get a bit out of hand, got loose and ate our entire new lettuce crop. I was furious. So after this incident I was ready to say goodbye to the goats, anyway.

Then we got the bright idea of donating them to Scott's school, St. Andrew's Prep School, which has a Farmer's Club with a whole acre of fenced field where they keep sheep, ducks, a donkey, chickens, and no goat. We talked to Mr. Walker, the Headmaster, who said they would be delighted to have Two-and-Six and Bill, especially because they are so tame and fond of children.

So yesterday — I don't know what got into me — I got out two of Scott's old blue-and white-striped St. Andrews school ties and tied them on Bill and Two-and-Six. What a picture they made. First, I couldn't resist taking them by the Bravinders' house to show Phyllis and Jennie. Then Rick and Friday and I took them, all properly uniformed, to register for school.

We marched right to the Headmaster's office, and I went in and said (with a straight face): "Mr. Walker, I have two new students for you."

This was rather bold of me, as Mr. Walker and I haven't exactly hit it off all that well. Will had even gone to the Peace Corps Halloween party as the "Headmonster" of St. Andrews School, carrying a big stick, and we could only hope he had never heard about that. But Mr. Walker had actually been friendly a few weeks ago for the first time (he smiled), and someone told me that he has a good sense of humor.

Well, Mr. W. was superb! He, also with a perfectly straight face, said, "Well boys, come along with me and we'll find you a classroom!"

Then we went to each of the classrooms on one level. The school is built on different levels of the hillside, with about six classrooms in a row in each building, all with outside corridors. He went to the window of each classroom and made comments such as, "Mr. Couper, I have two new students today. Do you have seats for them in your class? They are properly uniformed and ready to start now...."

About this time some of the kids would have looked out the window and started giggling. I was trying to keep a straight face, but Rick and Friday, who were holding the goats' ropes, could hardly contain their laughter. Mr. Walker, however, was quite wonderful and carried this off at each classroom with great aplomb.

"I imagine these two will do better than some of your students, don't you, Mrs. Barnes?" and "Well, if you don't have a seat for these boys, Mrs. Dale, I think they should trade with two boys I see who are not properly uniformed and have no ties. These new students are properly uniformed."

We finally did put them out in the Farmer's Club, a wonderful place right there on the school grounds. Poor little Two-and-Six, who didn't want me to leave him, hung around my legs and bleated. It was just like leaving a new kindergartner the first day of school! He kept trying to come out the gate after me. He *is* only eight months old. That was sad for me, I must say — in spite of my wrath about the lettuce incident.

My parting words to Mr. Walker were that I expected them to learn to read within a year, and he answered, "Oh, six months, I should say."

Today Scott reports that Two-and-Six already loves it there now and runs to the fence to play with all the other kids (joke, joke). Bill is fairly blasé about it all, but does enjoy the grass and tasty flowers.

I have much to do, as we are giving a "sundowner" (cocktail party) for fifty tomorrow. It's for the Ministry of Education and headmasters of Malawian schools, Peace Corps Staff, and a few American Embassy and British High Commission people. Last year we gave it at a school. Though I think it will be nicer here, it does make me look at our house with "other eyes" and wish I'd covered this chair or fixed up that other one. It is being catered, thank goodness.

The rains have started, so I'll spend less time around the swimming pool rationalizing that I was really only there because Rick was almost ready to swim and therefore we *needed* to be there. Never mind that it was beastly hot. As a result of all this pool time, though, Rick did learn to swim just last week at the Peace Corps Conference at the lake. Amazing what a kid will do with a large and appreciative audience of cheering PCVs! The first swim seems just as exciting to us as the first steps, and it was a big day in Rick's life.

We're Staying!

November 21, 1966

The latest news from this front is that we are going to stay about three months longer than we'd intended. The University just sent word that they would extend Will's leave of absence a bit longer, as requested by Peace Corps Washington.

We are happy and grateful for lots of reasons — aside from the fact that we love it here and hate to leave. Leaving in January, as originally planned for the end of two years here, would not be good timing. Two new groups of PCVs arrive then; Will now finally has a full staff for the first time in more than a year and would love to stay awhile and just savor the new feeling of being able to be *one* man instead of three; we would arrive home in March if we left in January, and this would be mid-semester for the boys and difficult. By leaving in mid-April, we would arrive home sometime in June — in time for summer school for the boys so they could make up some work and find out where they will be placed in school. Also, the weather will be much nicer for travel in May and June.

Don and Mike, however, were horrified at the thought of another semester at St. Andrew's High School. So we think that rather than start them again (and face mutiny) when the new semester starts in January, we'll find tutors and have them tutored in the subjects they will need at home and have missed, such as American history and the new math.

Scott will continue standard three at St. Andrew's Prep School. He had a wonderful teacher this year: a Scotsman with a handlebar mustache, twinkly eyes, and a real interest in and love for children. Rick will start standard one here. The semester ends just past the middle of April, so he will nearly finish. Rick, however, is more excited about getting his school uniform than the actual fact of going to school.

I must confess that the reason I'm getting this letter written is that I'm "grounded" with a bad shoulder and can't drive, because I can't shift the Jeep. It's like driving a Mack truck. Until this happened I never realized what a gadabout I was. Last week I couldn't type or do anything — what a bore, but this week maybe I'll make up for lost time. The shoulder problem has turned out to be calcium deposits, probably caused by bruises last March in our Jeep accident in Tanzania, although it never did hurt until last week. It's slowly getting better with cortisone injections.

The rains are starting, sporadically as yet, but already things are turning green. Our frangipani trees and bougainvillea are masses of blooms. Our avocado tree is so full of avocados it's unbelievable. This, in spite of all the monkey has eaten. It's *her* tree. Friday just brought in a whole basketful this morning, and the tree is still full.

Sadly, our pangolin, Gloria Thing, had to join the many others in the animal graveyard in our backyard last week. We never did actually know its sex, but since its name was Gloria, we just refer to it as "she" or "her." We only had her a month and she had become quite tame. We were surprised to find her dead one morning. We wondered if we should have let her go, but hadn't done so because she had one gimpy leg, and we weren't sure she could fend for herself. We're all in mourning (again).

A couple of months ago Mother Catherine gave the boys a young turkey to raise for Thanksgiving. We've put him in with the chickens, and he's grown a lot. However, we've decided that he won't be on our Thanksgiving table, rationalizing that perhaps he'll be bigger for Christmas. Actually, as you can probably guess, it's that he is too cute. Don't know what we'll do when Christmas comes.

Our Sunday morning pancake breakfasts are still booming. Now they are taking on an international flavor. Yesterday we had about seventeen, only about half of whom were PCVs. Lots of VSOs (British version of Peace Corps: Volunteers in Service Overseas), a French volunteer, and a few other British. They are usually brought here by PCVs to begin with and then we always invite them to come any time. It's really fun.

I'm looking out the window into the back yard and see that there is some friend of Friday's talking to our monkey in the tree. Uh oh — he's wearing glasses. I'm just waiting for Ujeni to snatch his glasses off and run to the top of the tree with them. Her favorite trick. She is so cute, and such a — well — monkey! We all love her. She is up in the tree on her chain and has lots of room to swing and play and tease without getting to the ground. She especially loves Don, and every time he climbs up to see her, she puts her arms around his neck and kisses him. True love.

Kitchen Adventures

November 25, 1966

I'm still full from Thanksgiving dinner last night. We devoured our fourteen-pound *store*-purchased (as opposed to our home-grown) turkey, and had invited four PCVs to help us. Two of the guys have been living on Likoma Island for two years, pretty isolated, and have been eating fish, goat meat, and nsima — so needless to say, they *really* enjoyed it.

Scott had two Thanksgiving dinners, having gone to the U.S. Ambassador's house for a Thanksgiving lunch birthday party for his pal, Tarpley Jones, the Ambassador's son. He was picked up by Ambassador Jones's uniformed chauffeur in the black limousine and then later returned by same. That always tickles me. Old nine-year-old Scott manages to live pretty high on the hog.

As long as we're on the subject of meals — we had an "adventurous" (at least for me) one few weeks ago. We were having some VIPs from Washington here for dinner, but I had to go out for most of the day. So I decided to have a roast and mashed potatoes, which Mas can do quite well by himself. I would only have to do a salad and dessert.

In the morning before I left for the orphanage I got Mas started on a jello salad. He knows how to do this because he's done it before: lemon jello, paw-paw (papaya) balls, canned pineapple chunks, and sliced bananas. When I came home at 1:00 o'clock, I looked in the fridge and there it was. Beautiful. I praised him all over the place. I knew it had taken him hours because he is so careful and conscientious, and I knew that each paw-paw ball was individually perfectly hand-sculpted and each banana slice just *so*. Big double recipe in my 9x12 pan. So that was ready.

Then before I rushed out on my next errand I tried to get a strawberry Bavarian cream done. I was quite excited about this because we rarely get cream and the Kandodo store had it the previous day. For this recipe, first you heat strawberry juice with unflavored gelatin and put it in a bowl in the refrigerator. Then when that partially sets, you fold in whipped cream and crushed strawberries. Very simple.

However, this strawberry gelatin hadn't jelled enough by the time I had to leave again, so I couldn't put it all together. I would only get home just before the guests were to arrive, and it couldn't wait until then. So I carefully explained it to Mas — showed him each bowl — told him there were just three things to put together. 1) You whip the cream in one bowl. 2) The gelatin is in the second bowl, and when the gelatin "sets" in that second bowl, you just fold the whipped cream into that. Then 3) The crushed strawberries are in the third bowl, and you stir them carefully into this mixture. That is the Bavarian cream dessert. I carefully repeated the instructions three times to be sure he understood. Easy. Thought I.

When I came home just before dinner, I hurried out to the kitchen and said, "How did the dessert go, Mas?"

"Fine, Madam." I looked in at it in the fridge and was surprised it looked so big, but I was pleased. However, it didn't seem set yet so I put it in the freezer for awhile to firm up more and again complimented Mas. He looked a bit tired, and I asked him if he'd had a good rest this afternoon. "Well, no, Madam, but it's all right." I didn't have time to pursue it then and let it go.

We sat down to dinner, which looked lovely. Beautiful roast beef, mashed potatoes, fresh string beans. I noticed that the jello salad was not on the table and said, "Mas, would you bring the salad?" Blank look.

"You know — that beautiful jello salad you made this morning." Blanker look. So I said, "The jelly?" (That's what it's called here.) Look of horror. "Well, I'll get it, Mas." I looked in the fridge. No jello. I looked in the cupboard — an empty 9x12" pan. (??) "Uh, Mas, wh-where is your beautiful salad???"

He opened the freezer and pointed to the strawberry bavarian cream. When I looked surprised and a bit perplexed, he said, "But Madam, you said to beat the jelly and add the cream and strawberries...."

Then it dawned on me that Mas had confused the two "jelly" dishes. Of course! Poor guy. I told him it looked just wonderful and would be fine.

However, later I also realized he had used the *hand egg beater* because he's afraid of the electric one. Can you imagine beating up a chunky fruit jello salad by *hand* — pineapple chunks and melon balls in *set* jello? To say nothing of all his morning work of each carefully sculpted paw-paw ball and banana slice and pineapple chunk being ground to goop. No wonder he didn't get a rest — it must have taken him all afternoon to beat it all up! He did say, yes, that Phillip had to hold the bowl for him because it was pretty hard to beat.

But — the dessert was delicious! A new invention. Strawberry-Bavarian-Cream-Fruit-Jello-Salad dessert. Very original, to say the least. Poor Mas. He's so sweet and conscientious and felt awful when he realized it was only the other gelatin he was supposed to beat, not his beautiful salad. We told him it was delicious and that it didn't matter at all.

He tries so hard, and we do just love him, but we keep having these little communication breakdowns. Usually I can figure out where we've gotten off the trolley. In this case, of course, it was having two jellos. My fault.

The other night Will knocked over his glass of water, and I said, "Mas, could you bring a rag?" — and he rushed in with a plate of butter. (???) Then I remembered the time I'd asked for salt and pepper and he'd brought in a roll of aluminum foil, and I'd figured that one out. He calls aluminum foil "silver paper," and "salt and pepper" sort of sounds like "silver paper." So I thought surely I'd figure this one out too. To this day, though, I haven't figured out the connection between the rag and a plate of butter.

A couple of days ago I had to have another cortisone injection in my shoulder and, since the shot is so painful, the doctor decided to give me a small shot of morphine to get me through it and the following few hours. Well! Thirty-six hours later I was still reeling and feeling *horrible*. No pain, I'll admit, and my shoulder felt great — but unfocused eyes, dizzy head, nauseated stomach, ugh — I guess I'm allergic to morphine. I barely could get my pies and salads done for Thanksgiving dinner yesterday (I did them myself this time.) The Peace Corps doctor who had given me the shot felt terrible. It really was a very small dose — guess I'm not cut out for the drug scene.

Small World

Thursday, December 8, 1966

With nothing done for Christmas and our Christmas letter not even finished, I have no business sitting here writing this letter — but as you see, here I am. I *have* to tell you about my fantastic day yesterday.

Will had gone up to the north to Chitipa and Karonga on Monday; there was no flight down Wednesday (yesterday) and some other people needed transportation to go up there, so the Peace Corps chartered a small plane from a new charter service here. There was an extra seat going up and back, and Will suggested that I go along. This way I could see Karonga and have a joyride also.

Two doctors had to go there. One, who is British, is the new Chief Medical Officer for Malawi. He came to pick me up at 5:30 a.m. and is one of the most charming gentlemen I have ever met. He looks like the typical Englishman in the pictures: tall, about fifty-five, longish face, mustache (*always* the mustache), booming voice, and, of course, the great British accent. He has spent all his adult life in medical programs in foreign countries, mostly in the Far East. I made him talk until he was nearly hoarse about all the places he has lived. Nepal is his #1 favorite in the world — and I told him about our almost having been assigned there, and of our interest in that country. So we hit it right off. His most recent post was Bangkok, which he also loved. But he is terribly happy to be back in Africa again. He was so interesting. We hope to see more of him, and since he is a bachelor, it would be nice to have him over for dinner and for the kids to hear his tales.

That was just the beginning of this nice day. The weather, though hot, was beautiful, the plane superb, and the pilot very nice. There were only the three of us for the first leg of the trip. We landed at a little place on the lake called Nkhotakota to pick up Dr. Bill Peck, who is in charge of the Peace Corps health group, and his wife. The landing strip — ha — that's a laugh — this *field* we landed in made my hair stand on end, but we made it. The married PCV couple that the Pecks were visiting are health workers. They live right next to the field, and they all waved as we came over. People came from everywhere to watch this great event. Planes come in there maybe once a month or so, so we were completely surrounded by Africans of all sizes by the time the plane taxied to a stop. I wished I'd had the camera.

The Pecks boarded and we took off, flying along the lake low enough to be able to see fishermen out in their dugout canoes and to pick out many familiar spots. What fun it is to fly so easily, looking down on the hot, dusty roads we have spent so many long hours driving. We made it to Karonga in three hours. It's about four hundred miles in distance and it takes at least two whole days to drive.

The pilot flew us very low over the part of the country called the Nyika Plateau, which is the top of a whole range of mountains about 7,800 feet in elevation. It is almost uninhabited and full of wild game. We were looking for animals but didn't see any. Some people have seen zebra, lots of antelope, and even elephant. It looks like some other world up there and, according to reports, just about is. Two of our PCVs hiked up there last year for five days and found a village where the people said they hadn't seen a white man in many years. They communicated in sign language, gesturing that a very old man was "this high" (indicating that he had been about four years old), the last time a white person visited.

Will and the PCVs were there to greet us at the Karonga airstrip, and we visited both of the female health workers, the married couple who teach, and the single fellow who also teaches. The people love them all. We had lunch with Bob McCreary, the single guy, as he has the least company. He lives in a little African brick house with a grass roof, outdoor kitchen and outdoor "chimbuzi" (toilet) house. He said he was so excited to have us that he felt just the way he would if his parents came to visit. He is such a nice guy. I get all choked up thinking about it. I took some fresh cheese and a big can of chocolate chip cookies (we chop our own chips, by the way) for all the PCVs there. Bob said, "Gosh, real homemade cookies. Now I *really* feel like my Mom came!"

Then, a most amazing experience — one of the volunteers said he wanted us to visit his friends at the "Chinese Camp." There is a team of twelve Chinese men from Taiwan working in Karonga for two years, doing a rice-growing project to teach Malawians how to get better yields. We hiked out there to this little, very primitive camp. We met the leader of the group, a Mr. Ling, who speaks excellent English. He was wonderfully hospitable and had us sit down, then brought out three kinds of scrumptious melons and cut them up for us to eat. Such a treat. Then Mr. Ling said he had been in America at one time.

"Where?" we asked.

"San Francisco for a few days, and then in a place called *Davis*."

Can you imagine??! He was in Davis for a month studying

agronomy, stayed at the University Hotel, and especially remembered Dean Briggs well. He was quite upset when we told him that Fred Briggs had died last year. Can you picture this scene — sitting way out in a remote bush area in a little tin hut under banana trees in Africa, talking to a man from Taiwan about mutual friends in Davis? What a small world.

We also visited one of our Malawian friends there who is now the Government Agent, which is like being a mayor or governor of a district. We had a beautiful trip back and landed before dark, which is a necessity as there are no runway lights at our airport. That was a day to remember.

Christmas 1966

Monday, December 26, 1966
Merry After-Christmas!

Whew. That's all I can say. The five-day foot race that I feel I've been in is over! Christmas was wonderful, with never a dull moment. We broke our family tradition of turkey dinner on Christmas Day and had it instead the night before because of our open house on Christmas Day. I think it would have been so mean to have PCVs here for the open house *smelling* a turkey cooking and not able to eat any because we can't invite everyone.

We invited the new Peace Corps doctor, Dave Clark, and his wife Carol, who are both lots of fun. We also invited Mary Lou Callahan, our new Peace Corps Staff "Lady," which we all jokingly call her because she is our first "lady" staff — and she's all of twenty-four years old.

After we didn't have the heart to kill our turkey for Thanksgiving, rationalizing that he would be bigger for Christmas, he got some kind of fowl (foul) disease and died all of a sudden about two weeks after Thanksgiving. We were just sick about it. He had gotten so big and beautiful, and we had raised him from the age of nine weeks. Well, at least we were spared having to kill him ourselves, much less *eating* him. So we bought a turkey.

With the house all decorated and Christmas carols on the record player, we ate our delicious dinner by candlelight. It was really nice. Our Christmas tree is ten feet tall, a pretty one this year, and it looked very festive with its homemade ornaments. (No, in *spite* of.) However, this tree was unique in that it also had four live chameleons crawling around in it. Bet you don't see many Christmas trees like that at home in the States.

After dinner we decided to go caroling — and what a scene! Dave played his ukulele, Will played his violin, Don drummed a bucket, Mike drummed an African skin drum, Mary Lou, Carol and I "played" combs (you put a piece of waxed paper over a comb and hold the comb up to your lips and hum and it makes a weird sound), and the rest sang. *We* thought we were sensational. *So* sensational that we all piled into our Jeep to go over to Limbe to serenade the rest of the Peace Corps staff, who all live on the same street. We "earned" ourselves refreshments at the Ellisons' — which really may have been the only way they could *stop* us. Such a fun Christmas Eve.

Our Christmas Day open house was great fun. It was a race to the finish line (4:00 p.m.) for me, when people came. It was smaller than last year, about twenty-five, as we are between groups of PCVs right now, and most of those who are still here were traveling. So we were mostly staff. I guess they must have had fun because they didn't leave until after 9:00 p.m.

Ricky provided the main afternoon entertainment with his new bicycle that Santa brought. It's the cutest little blue two-wheeler with white balloon tires, looking sort of like a mini-motorcycle. Rick is ecstatic. It did have side wheels, which Confident Rick wanted *off* right away. He had learned to ride a smaller two-wheeler a couple of weeks before, but this one is bigger and we had some misgivings, as his feet barely reached the ground when he sat on the seat. But — off he went, and the thrills and entertainment began.

While we all held our collective breath, he went furiously pedaling down the driveway, weaving and wobbling like mad — and right straight into the garage door! He and bike were OK (a little surprised, both of them, but not hurt) and we were all in hysterics. Will and I were reminded of when one of the neighbor kids at home was learning to ride his two-wheeler. It was the "keep-pedaling-no-matter-what" school of thought — narrowly missing trees, dogs, parked cars, and wobbling up over curbs, weaving across lawns — with all of us holding our breath, just like yesterday. Rick was great entertainment.

One of the most fun parts of Christmas was giving Mas, Phillip, and Friday their Christmas presents. Last year we had given Mas and Phillip U.S. Timex watches, so we gave Friday one this year. Friday actually danced with joy. We gave Mas and Phillip transistor radios which Will had bought in the States. Neither had a radio, so they were thrilled. We gave their wives money to buy material for new dresses and gave all the children books and toys.

A new group of thirty-four volunteers comes in a few days. Next month a group that was supposed to go to Nigeria arrives. Because of the political situation in Nigeria, they've been transferred to Malawi. They've had to have an extra five weeks of training to learn Chinyanja and to learn about Malawi. After thirteen weeks training for Nigeria, they must be plenty sick of training.

The weather has been hot, with only a little bit of rain so far. Everything is beautiful and green, though. It seems like magic the way the very first rains bring back all the green. It's been pretty muggy, and a good rain would be welcome now. At night it has been so still that we can hear the drums from across the hill on the other side of the ravine. The last few nights they've sounded eerie and somewhat sad, which seems odd because this is such a happy time. During the day small groups of Malawians come around and dance and get pennies and cigarettes and candy, but at night they play this sad beat — rather haunting. Lots of times we hear them at night with wild fast rhythms and singing, and it sounds as if they're having fun, but this has been depressing the last few nights. Odd.

The Great Highway

January 10, 1967

The first week in January we had another wonderful time at the lake. Will had a conference with new PCVs in Lilongwe, a two-hour drive from the lake, and he suggested that I take the kids up to the lake and rent a cabin. He would come up later. Carol Clark went with me, as her (Peace Corps doctor) husband, Dave, was away that week. The boys all like Carol a lot, and we had great fun. We had arranged to rent a very large and comfortable cabin right *on* the beach which only cost one pound ($2.80) a night.

We took Mas with us, which was perfect, as he had never even *seen* the lake before *and* he did all the cooking and laundry. The water was only waist deep for about seventy feet, so there was no worry with kids. The Malawian fishermen put their nets out three times a day right there in front of our cabin. The nets, which are very long, are taken out in dugout canoes about a quarter mile apart, leaving streamers of braided vines on the beach. Then they come back in and pull on the streamers — four or five men and usually Ricky. The net finally comes in right in front of us. It's incredible — the most beautiful fish of all kinds, sizes, and colors. Tropical fish you would pay so much for in the States — and of course, our favorite *chambo*.

We bought chambo in the 4:00 p.m. catch several times. It was still flopping when Mas cleaned it and *good?* Oh boy. It only costs six pence a fish, compared to "one-and-six" (one shilling and six pence, which is about twenty cents) here in Blantyre, and there is no comparison in flavor. Watching the fishing nets go out and come in furnished our entertainment for the whole week.

Will never did get to the lake, though — instead, he and eighteen PCVs got food poisoning and were sick as dogs. Isn't that awful? What a welcome for new volunteers.

The roads are terrible now because of the rains, and *I* (note I said *"I"*) had driven the Jeep all the way up to the lake. I took some of our kids and some PCVs and followed a Peace Corps Carryall carrying the others, so that if anything happened neither vehicle would be stranded alone. On the way up to Lilongwe a car in front of the Carryall had skidded in the mud and overturned, scaring all of us half to death. We all stopped and jumped out. The top was crushed, the windshield had popped out, and none of the people had seat belts on. They turned out to be four French priests, who were all okay. Lucky people. I think maybe they have a special pipeline to the Powers That Be. We took them all in to

Lilongwe and dropped them off at a nearby Catholic mission.

At the end of that wonderful week at the lake, we drove to Lilongwe to meet Will. We divided up our forces, and Will drove our Jeep with Rick, Mike, Mas, and me to go back home. Will had to get back to Blantyre as a new group of thirty PCVs was coming in at noon the next day. The others stayed over in Lilongwe to come back with a Peace Corps driver the next day. As it turned out, we should have stayed, too.

We had left Lilongwe after dinner for the five-hour drive home in darkness. Never a good idea, even in good weather. We started out in a light rain, which soon turned into a heavy storm and a nightmare of skidding all over the road at 25 and 30 mph. Scary. It was so awful that after about an hour and a half we finally had to give up and look for a place to stay the night.

We found a little "hotel" (ha) in Dedza — at this point we were not the least bit choosy — and all I wanted to do was to get *out* of that Jeep and off those horrible roads. After very little sleep we got up at 5:00 a.m. to try to drive on into Blantyre. These roads! Between Dedza and Ncheu, buses and trucks and cars had skidded all over during the night and were stuck everywhere, blocking much of the road. We knew then that we would never have made it over the mountain the night before. We barely made it the next morning. We've never seen it so bad. Heavy rains wreak havoc on unpaved roads. And this is the Main North-South Road, the "Great Highway" of Malawi.

On our way back Will said, "By the way, you do remember we're having a reception this afternoon at five for about fifty-five or sixty people?" In the dim distant past I did seem to have some recollection of Will's saying something about this — and here we were, arriving home with a whole Jeepload of dirty and sandy clothes and people, and all the junk to be unpacked. However, Will's super secretaries, Sue and Sheila, had taken care of the whole thing and arranged to have it catered by the hotel, ordered all the food, drinks, ice and everything. All I did was arrange flowers and hide unpacked suitcases under beds.

This reception was for the group that had been trained for Nigeria and then was transferred here. Their field is environmental health, so there were quite a few people from the Ministry of Health, the American Embassy, and, of course, all the Peace Corps staff. Once again, we made it to our own party just by the skin of our teeth.

Rick's First Day of School (Plus)

Tuesday, January 17, 1967

Today is a big day at our house. Rick started school! The first day of school for any kid is a big and emotional one for mothers, but seeing all these little kids in their new uniforms makes it even more so. They look so very cute.

The little boys wear gray twill shorts and shirts, blue and white striped neckties, gray kneesocks with blue stripes on the top, little royal blue felt caps with the school emblem on the visors, and black shoes. The little girls wear royal blue cotton dresses with white trim around the neck and sleeves, white kneesocks, and gray felt hats. These are standard uniforms all the way through the high school here, with some variations in the ties and hats for the boys. When we took Rick and Scott to school, I got all choked up seeing these proud little standard one kids in their uniforms "just like the big kids" (to quote Rick). Rick has been "practicing" wearing his whole uniform every day since we bought it last week.

* * *

Wednesday

Well, I didn't get very far with this letter, and now I hate to go on because yesterday ended up being a *horrible* day. What started out all cheery and happy (at 5:30 a.m.!) ended up terrible. At the time I left off above, I had to take Donnie to town. I dropped him off at the Peace Corps office, where he was helping with sorting papers and doing errands, then went on to do some happy things like looking at dress patterns and fabrics.

Then, I was backing out of a diagonal parking place on a slight hill, had looked both ways, stopped to let someone by, looked again, and had barely started to move on out, when I felt a "whonk" on the back of the jeep. I looked and, to my horror, saw a bicyclist lying in the street! I can't imagine where he had appeared from, and since I was already three quarters of the way out and had seen no one coming, I couldn't imagine how this bicyclist had not seen me or why he hadn't gone around me.

It turned out that he was really speeding down the hill and apparently looked away and then crashed into me (witnesses say). I jumped out of the car, trembling. He had started to get up, and then quite dramatically sank back on his back with his arms flung over his head behind him. He looked just dreadful. Traffic kept going back and forth, and there I stood over this "body" and no one offered to help me. No one. This was on one of the main streets of Blantyre, and everyone just stood there on the sidewalks and stared. It felt like slow motion. Ages went by while I *alone* was standing in the middle of the street directing cars and buses around this poor guy, saying, "Will *someone* help me???"

At last one of our PCVs chanced by, and was I ever glad to see him! He yelled that he would run and get Will and call the police and ambulance — and went tearing off. All this time the prone fellow appeared half-unconscious, although I couldn't be sure. At least he wasn't dead — or bloody, thank goodness. After a few minutes, which felt like hours, people began to move closer, which at least protected this poor fellow from being hit by another car. Then suddenly it seemed as if hundreds of people crowded around. No one spoke English, and they all just stared. And no one helped me. It was like a nightmare.

Then a worse thing happened. Two British police (white) came. They were portly, older, with trim mustaches, and were terribly nice to me, saying, "It's all right, don't worry, he's all right," — and saying to the Malawian man, "Come on, Bambo, you're okay — get up, get up" — *slapping* his face on both cheeks! This absolutely undid me.

I kept saying, "Oh, don't do that! He may really be hurt. Oh, *please* don't do that!" It was just terrible. They couldn't possibly know whether or not he was hurt internally or had a skull fracture or something.

When they proceeded to move him, I shouted, "Oh no — wait for the ambulance — he might have a broken back or neck or something!" All to no avail.

They kept saying nice things to me, "Now don't worry, Madam, just go sit down," and tried to sit the man up. Then, carelessly and roughly, along with about four Malawian police (who are just as bad with their own, apparently), they hauled him over and literally *dumped* him in the back of the police truck! I couldn't believe it. All of this really upset me more than the actual accident. I kept trying very hard to act calm, however, and thought I was doing fine — until I saw Will and the Peace Corps doctor, Dave Clark, come running down the street — and I burst into tears.

Dave went to the hospital with the man, examined him thoroughly, and luckily found him to be okay. What a relief. He may have been acting pretty dramatic, as we've been told that quite often people do if they get hit by a car here — but how can you be sure? Is there any wonder why so many Africans hate Europeans (whites)? I'm sure he was in shock at the very least.

After all, his head had made a dent in the back of the Jeep, so it at least had to have *hurt*. His bicycle didn't even have a scratch, and later the hospital released the man. But I remained a wreck.

I had to fill out a report saying that I was to blame since he had the right of way, even though I was clearly out and had looked carefully and was barely moving. This report upset me some, since I didn't feel it *was* my fault. Two people have come to me to say that they would be witnesses, that the man simply was not looking. This has happened to Will twice and nothing has come of it, so maybe nothing will happen. Well, the main thing is that the guy is OK.

When Will had his first "encounter" with a man on a bicycle, we had not been here very long. It was a very strange experience. It was while we were still living in the Peace Corps Field Center. One night a bunch of PCVs were telling about an awful thing that had happened to an Italian tea planter out near Cholo. While driving, he had hit a man on a bicycle, and when he got out of his car to help the man, people gathered around, were terribly angry and threw stones at him, injuring him quite seriously. The PCVs were saying that people here say if you hit someone with your vehicle, you should not stop. Will had said, "There's no way I would not stop." A long discussion ensued — and then, unbelievably — it happened to him early that very next morning!

He and Rick had just taken the older boys to school in the Land Rover. They were on a fairly busy road when a man on a bike suddenly came out of a shady path into the road right in front of them. There was no way Will could avoid hitting him. When it happened, in spite of the previous late night discussion, Will said that it never even crossed his mind *not* to stop. The man did, in fact, appear injured. A crowd gathered, but no one would help Will get the man into the back of the Land Rover. The crowd grew larger and they all just stared. Then someone threw a hat at Will, and he thought — "Oh oh — here it comes." However, fortunately, it turned out to be the hat of the injured man. Finally, after Will pleaded in Chinyanja, someone did help him carefully get the man into the back of the Land Rover so he could take him to the hospital. The man was not badly hurt, luckily, but did have to stay in the hospital. Will went to visit him there a couple of times and the Peace Corps bought the man a new bicycle and also gave him some money.

But now back to *my* continuing awful day. I went shakily home after the accident and Dave came over and gave me a light sedative to calm me down. I tried to start thinking positively, and said, "Well, at least Rick will soon be home from school and it will be such fun hearing about his first day because he is so excited." A little after 12:00 here came Rick. I ran out, eagerly asking, "Well, how was it?"

Unbelievable answer — "I *hate* it and I have a *crab* for a teacher and I'm *not* going back!" Stab. We couldn't have been more surprised. We all just about died. He had been so excited and had counted the days and the hours, and practiced wearing his uniform. We were all just stricken.

We all tried to "positive-talk" him out of it. "She's not really crabby. Teachers just have to be strict the first day." At the lunch table Helpful Scott said, "Yeah, she really is a crab!" (And today Scott wonders why his shins are black and blue.) When out of Rick's earshot, I quickly phoned around and found to my relief that this woman is a good teacher, that the kids who have her do like her and that he will probably eventually like her, too.

Later that afternoon Will and I remembered that we had talked with Rick about how there were going to be two standard one teachers who were both really nice. They both happened to be very pretty and also young. He had even met one in town one day with me, a really cute and very friendly American. Although we told him that he might not get Mrs. Castle for his teacher, we assured him that the other one would be equally nice.

As it turned out, unbeknownst to us, there were too many standard one students, so they had to add a third teacher. She is probably a very good teacher, but she is neither young nor pretty, is quite heavyset, and extra strict. To make it worse (in Rick's eyes), when they had arrived at school that morning, all the standard one students were put together in one class. He was happily sitting with his friends, when all of them were assigned to other classes. They were taken out by this cute Mrs. Castle and the other young teacher. A crestfallen Rick had to stay with the "old bag" (Rick's words).

Mulling all this over later, Will also pointed out to me that we had all made such a fuss over how wonderful he looked in his uniform. He modeled it every Sunday morning at our pancake breakfasts, and all the PCVs "oh'd" and "ah'd" over him. So, after all this great admiration, Will said maybe Rick expected the teacher to say, "Gee, Rick, you look *great* in your uniform." Who knows?

Well, it is now 11:40 a.m. Wednesday, the second day of school, and I will post you on what-happened-with-Rick-the-next-day-at-school as soon as I know.

First, I must add another thing that happened just this morning. The Veterinary Department came and hauled away a dying rabid dog from *our* front yard! We had seen this dog earlier and had thought that he was a starving village dog from across the canyon. He had looked so sickly that I had kept our dogs in the house, just in case. I should have called the Veterinary Department, but he wandered away. Anyway I just couldn't face one more crisis, even a slight one, at this point.

Sure enough, someone did call the Vet Department. I hadn't seen that the rabid dog had wandered back into our yard. If I'd seen him again I really would have called. So here came the veterinary truck with the dramatic-looking white-coveralled men with gloves, poles, and a cage. It seemed like a bad and sad movie when they dragged this dog into the cage with a hook on a long pole and took him away. The vets said they were quite sure he was rabid and will let me know. Life is never boring with the Lotters.

4:30 p.m. — *happy day!* Will and Don picked Rick and Scott up at school at noon, and I ran out to greet them with great question marks in my eyes, crossed fingers, and a hopeful look — and saw all smiles. Don, sitting in the back of the Land Rover with thumbs up, was nodding "yes" to me. Whew. Rick jumped out saying, "I *love* school and I *love* my teacher!" Again, whew!

Donnie has been so cute about all this, just as concerned as Will and I are. He is so good to Ricky, taking him places and teaching him things. He takes him swimming and for bike rides and reads to him all the time. He was even up at 5:45 a.m. to help Rick tie his tie and then went along with me to see him go into school. He was just as devastated as we were yesterday, and then so happy for him today. Ricky is really lucky to have such a good big brother.

I just came back from town and shopping, feeling as if everyone was staring at me and saying, "There's that lady that hit the bicyclist." Maybe it wasn't so, but I felt that way.

Oh, honestly. As I said — never a dull moment. The electricity is off so we can't start dinner. We are waiting for the electric company to come. And now I just looked out the window and saw the very top of the avocado tree shaking like mad. Ujeni is loose and clear up at the top! Pause. Hmm. Ujeni is loose *and* the electricity is off. I ran out and checked, and, sure enough, the wires are near the top of the tree. Mas's wife said that when we were gone this afternoon Ujeni got loose and jumped up on the wires and "fire went across" and she jumped, crying, into the tree! Poor little thing.

Now the electric company has come, and the man says our monkey is lucky to be alive; that she apparently grabbed the two wires at the same time and they crossed, causing the fuse to short out immediately. If she had grabbed just one of the wires, she would have been electrocuted! Don climbed up the avocado tree to untangle her chain, which took real balancing skills because she was so excited that he was up there, she kept jumping on his head. She is back on her chain now, and I hope she knows not to do that again.

I wonder what else will happen while I am trying to finish this letter. Well, life is not dull around here, that's for sure.

Black Mamba

This is a true story of miracles. It really should be called "Margaret, Mamba, and Miracles."

Margaret Castro, one of our Peace Corps Volunteers in the Health program for tuberculosis eradication, was riding her motorcycle alone out in the bush about four miles from her health dispensary. Her station and dispensary are in a place called Mwanza, about fifty-four miles from Blantyre. She was riding a brand new Peace Corps motorcycle, so she was being especially careful, going only about five mph on this bad road. This "road" was merely two tracks in the dirt, with tall grass growing in the middle and on both sides. It is probably traveled by one car about once a week.

Margaret had come into the Peace Corps office in Blantyre just the previous day because she was having problems with her old Peace Corps motorcycle. It kept stalling on her, stubbornly refusing to start up again, which necessitated pushing it for long distances. Will had then issued her a brand new one. There she was, happily driving her new motorcycle very cautiously when she saw what she thought was a stick standing up on the left side of the road. As she got closer she suddenly realized that the "stick" was a snake! A *very* large dark one. To her horror, this snake was vertical from the ground, taller than her head and looking down on her! She turned on the speed to try to go past it fast — but it went right along beside her. When she saw that its mouth was open and its neck was arched back, she knew it was going to strike — and that she couldn't get past it.

Incredibly, she had the presence of mind to turn her motorcycle over to the left and into the snake to try to knock it down so that at least it couldn't strike her face or upper body, which she knew could be fatal — while at the same time trying to throw herself off the motorcycle to the right. Not an easy maneuver. However, while doing this she realized that the snake had somehow wrapped itself around her left leg. Miraculously then, the motorcycle fell right on the snake, trapping it and releasing it from her leg so that she could scramble away.

She could see it writhing and hear it thrashing and striking the wheel and everywhere it could reach. Because the snake was so long, for a few horrible seconds she thought there were two of them and wondered how she could ever escape the second one. It was only then that she discovered that the snake had, in fact, struck her on the left shin. It only stung a little at first, but she looked down and saw the dreaded fang marks.

Quickly grabbing her Peace Corps medical kit which she always carried out in the bush, she got out the snakebite kit. It was supposed to have a cutting blade and a suction device to suction out the venom — but there was no cutting blade! She tried to suction the blood without cutting and couldn't get much at all. Then she saw a Malawian man coming across the field and yelled to him for help. To her dismay, when he heard her yell "njoka" (snake) he hesitated in fear. However, because she was fluent in Chinyanja, she was able to convince him that she desperately needed his help. Cautiously he came over and was able to kill the pinned snake with a large rock.

She knew that she immediately needed a tourniquet. Seeing a Malawi woman with the ever-present baby-carrying cloth, she asked for a small strip of the cloth. Wrapping it tightly on her leg above the fang marks, she picked up her motorcycle, said a little prayer of thanks when it started right up, and drove like crazy for the dispensary four miles away — praying all the way that help would be there at her station.

Margaret said that if it had been her old motorcycle, it never would have started up again, as she'd had to push it three miles the last time she had ridden it. Having the new motorcycle was only the first of a series of miracles. She knew that she would probably not have lived had she still had the old one.

Now she was praying all the way to Mwanza that her Malawian medical assistant would be there at the dispensary. He was often out and about in other villages. He was there. That was the second miracle.

The third miracle — and perhaps the most amazing — was that Margaret herself, only the week before, had come into Blantyre to get some snakebite serum for her dispensary because a little boy had been bitten by a mamba and had died. So she had the general serum right there. The medical assistant administered it to her immediately.

At this point they weren't sure the snake had been a black mamba, but thought by her description that it was — and yet she was still alive while everyone knows that black mamba bites kill almost immediately. But to be on the safe side, she would have to be given specific mamba antivenin. Margaret had also been issued a vial of that very type of antivenin, but because it needed to be kept refrigerated, it was in the nearest refrigerator — fourteen miles away.

Then yet another miracle: there happened to be one car there that day. Often there are none. So they sent someone speeding off to get the other serum. When the driver returned with it, the Malawi medical assistant knew exactly what to do, probably saving her life.

Someone was sent to bring back the dead snake for identification, and sure enough, it was a deadly poisonous black mamba — eight feet long! It was later taken to the Malawi Museum, where staff members believe it might be the largest mamba ever seen in Malawi.

At first Margaret didn't have to be hospitalized. They kept her here in Blantyre at Dr. Peck's house. A week later, though, all her joints swelled up, and she looked like a balloon (she said) and was rushed to the hospital. They think that this could have been a reaction to the antivenin, but no one is sure. This swelling went away after a few days and except for the very messy wound itself, which ulcerated and is still draining, she is almost fine now. Snakebites are one of the hardest things to heal, often ulcerating, with the skin continuing to slough off and not healing. Being bitten on the shin, however, where there isn't a lot of fleshy area to carry poisoned blood to other parts of her body was also a very lucky thing.

Of course the news of Margaret and the mamba has spread all over Malawi. Her story and photo with the mamba were in all the Malawi papers. Mamba tales abound. Some people say that the mamba can travel 35 mph with two-thirds of its body elevated vertically, propelled by one-third of its length on the ground. Other wild stories are being bandied about, describing people being chased in a Land Rover with a mamba racing alongside trying to strike the driver in the face — and on and on. We don't really know how fast a black mamba can travel, but we do know that its bite is practically always fatal.

[Our curiosity led us to find out the answers to some of these mamba questions. The black mamba has been clocked at 17 mph – not quite as fast as 35 mph, but fast enough if it's chasing you. It can travel with one-third of its body length elevated, but not two-thirds.]

We all think it is a miracle — Margaret, especially. I went to see her in the hospital and was totally covered with goose bumps while she told me the whole story. Margaret is incredibly lucky. She says that if any of those "miracles," such as the new motorcycle, the newly acquired mamba serum, her medical assistant being there, or the car being available hadn't happened, she would not be alive today.

Margaret is a physically strong and very religious young woman. She says her prayers kept her alive. Will wanted to have her transferred to a less remote station, worrying about her peace of mind, but she would have none of it and wanted to go right back again to Mwanza. One tough lady!

[There is a current very interesting sequel to this Margaret story. In 1995, almost thirty years later, I was with my weekly Spanish conversation group in Davis when the subject of snakes came up. In my stumbling Spanish I was telling the story of Margaret and the mamba, but did not happen to mention Margaret's last name. One of my friends got this funny look on her face and exclaimed (in English, in her excitement), "That was Margaret Castro, and I know that story!" I had never heard what had become of Margaret after Peace Corps. I only knew that she was from Southern California. This friend, Pat Foster, then told us a very interesting story. By this time, even though Pat was very fluent in Spanish, having been a Peace Corps Volunteer nurse in Colombia, we all broke into English so as not to miss any details.

In 1969, after Peace Corps, Pat was working in a community clinic in Southern California which had been set up to serve primarily the Spanish-speaking community. Margaret Castro applied for the position of health educator at this clinic, and her interview with the community board of directors became a great topic of conversation.

The board was largely made up of Spanish-speaking women over sixty. They said that Margaret told them that she felt God had called her to apply for this position because he had saved her from death more than once so that she could come to San Ysidro, near San Diego where her family lived, and serve the poor in this clinic. She then went on to tell about being bitten by a black mamba snake while in the Peace Corps in Malawi, Africa, and almost dying, except for luck and the "grace of God." She had also talked of her years before Peace Corps, working with the poor in India, where she became so ill and lost so much weight that she had almost died. She completely convinced this board that she was sent by God for this job. She said that this job was the reason God had twice let her live and that she was meant to be hired. And so she was.

My friend Pat then got to know Margaret well and said she did an outstanding job. Whatever qualifications Margaret might not have had for this job, if any, she made up for in determination and total commitment.

Pat was especially thrilled to know that I knew Margaret and that the black mamba story was indeed as dramatic as Margaret had described. We could only shake our heads and exclaim at what a small world this is.]

Yes, Madam

Thursday, January 26, 1967

I guess I should have my head examined. Of all times that I don't have time to take on anything else, what with organizing for the trip home, sewing, shopping, etc., I'm starting painting lessons *now*. Crazy, I know. This is something I've wanted to do ever since we've been here, and I'd brought along all my paints and supplies, but I just never got started on my own.

Now I find that my wonderful artist friend, Lois Cox, the missionary wife I've been good friends with all these two years, says she would love to give another friend and me lessons. I'd never dreamed of asking her because she is so busy with five little kids and no household help. I love her art — she's able to capture the bright colorful African feeling of a busy market scene, or the relaxed beauty of a peaceful landscape. Now I'm so mad this wasn't two years ago! Today we are going for our first session — driving out to the bush somewhere. It should be fun.

Will is coming home from up-country today, too. He went up on Monday and is going again next Sunday for a week-long health conference up at the lake. There are three doctors flying out from the States for this conference, so we are going to give a cocktail party for them Saturday and have some of the local doctors, the Minister of Health and several others from the Ministry, the Chief Medical Officer, and all our staff, of course. This one I'm going to do myself with no caterers, but it's only for about twenty-five or thirty people, I think. I was happy to find out that Minister Chibambo and his wife have said they will come. Will is going to be pleased. So often the ministers are invited to things and can't come for one reason or another.

Don and Mike have started their tutoring in math with a Canadian teacher here and just love it — if you can imagine. This man is wonderfully enthusiastic and loves math. He makes it almost like a game for them. Both of them say that in just four days with him they have learned more than in a whole semester at St. Andrews. They go to his house for two hours a day. Next week they start their English, social studies, and geography tutoring with Phyllis Bravinder, who has taught eighth and ninth grades for many years. She is planning to gear a lot of their studies and compositions to the countries we'll be traveling to on our way home. It really sounds good, and they like Phyllis so much.

Also, I'm finally playing tennis again, as my ailing shoulders are both fine. I'm taking lessons to get properly back in shape and going. Will's African tennis partner, Maluwa, is teaching tennis now and doing such a good job. Will has coached him for two years, and has also educated him on the fundamentals of teaching tennis. He teaches *exactly* as Will has always done, and unless I open my eyes, I'd think it was Will on the other side of the net telling me to "follow through" or to "keep your racket on edge." (What? Jane plays tennis with her eyes shut?)

Maluwa is getting over his shyness about correcting a white person now. This must have been terribly hard at first, as it goes against everything Malawians have been taught since childhood. At first he would hardly ever say anything during a lesson except "very good" if it happened to be OK — and nothing at all if it was wrong. Now he has quite a lot of students, and is gaining confidence and beginning to speak out — and in such a sweet way — "good foot work, but you didn't get your racket back quite early enough." He is so nice. Coaching tennis will be a wonderful way for him to earn extra money now.

The other thing Maluwa just can't seem to do though, is to call me Jane, or even Mrs. Lotter. He still calls me "Madam." I guess it's too ingrained. I have a lesson this afternoon, if it doesn't rain. What a nice day for me — painting in the morning and tennis in the afternoon. How very frivolous.

One very hot day last week I was having a lesson from Maluwa. He was hitting the ball from one side of the court to the other, causing me to run back and forth from side to side, and I had gotten hotter and hotter and slower and slower, and more and more clumsy. He still does have some problems with disagreeing with anything I say, and when I just couldn't manage to get to yet another shot, I said, "Oh Maluwa — just like a cow...!"

And he said, "Yes, madam."

Monkey Business

Saturday, February 4, 1967

Such an exciting thing happened yesterday. Will received a cable from Peace Corps Washington asking him if he would be interested in being the Project Training Officer for *Nepal* — starting in July in *Davis*, California! And, if Will is interested, they want him to take an all-expenses-paid three-week visit to Nepal on the way home. If he is *interested?* Ha. Are they kidding?

Will fired off a cable to Washington saying that he is definitely interested, but must have concurrence of the University of California at Davis. If the training is in July and August, it may not conflict with his university duties anyway, so we're waiting now to hear from the university. Imagine — of all the countries Will might have done the training for — to have it be Nepal! Having originally thought we were going to be assigned there, we've been especially interested in Nepal ever since. And to have the training program be in our own hometown of Davis, yet!

This also means that we'll probably have to leave here two weeks or so sooner — which panics me, as it's getting so close — in order to spend that much time in Nepal and still keep our boat reservations from Japan to San Fransciso on the President Wilson on May 24.

My letters from now on may be short and farther apart, as I have so much to do to get ready to leave. My "wardrobe" was all planned for cool January originally, so now I have to add more hot weather clothes, since it will be much hotter in India and Malaysia. I can't buy a single thing here and need cool, drip-dry things for travel. So I'm sewing like crazy.

Our party last week was a success, and Minister Chibambo and his wife actually *did* come and were very nice. There were about thirty people, I'd guess. Scott helped me make little open-faced sandwiches all afternoon and did such a good job. Then all the boys helped pass food and serve drinks. Who needs paid caterers?

Rick still loves school and seems to be doing well. He is reading quite a few words and is very proud of himself. This reminds me — I must go ask Mr. Walker, the headmaster, if the goats have learned to read yet!

We took care of a baby monkey for ten days for Mary Lou Callahan, our new staff "Lady." He is only seven weeks old and is the most adorable little thing. He was in a cage out on the porch a lot of the time, and part of the time in a little box on window sills in the house — until he discovered what fun it was to climb out and leap all over from chair to chair, and up on tables. He's only about six or seven inches tall and loves to be held — so guess who was holding him a lot? He also loved to snatch food off my dinner plate.

One day we put the baby monkey out in the tree with Ujeni. They were so darling together and just loved and hugged each other — but what a mistake that turned out to be! We didn't dare leave the baby out there at night and had a terrible time separating them to bring him inside. Don had to climb up the tree and literally pry him out of Ujeni's arms. The baby cried pathetically, and I had to hold and pet him for hours to calm him down. Ujeni kept anxiously watching the back door for us to bring him out and was all upset. So was I — in fact we all felt guilty and terrible. From then on, we couldn't let them even *see* each other anymore. It was heartbreaking.

Mary Lou just returned last night after her Nairobi meetings and took him back. We had gotten quite attached to the little guy and were sad to have him leave — but we sure learned a lot about monkey business.

From Will

February 19, 1967
(Now this is Will writing)

Because Jane is sewing madly trying to make some dresses for our trip home, I've been given the assignment of bringing you up to date on the latest news from "this side" (term frequently used by Malawians to describe their surroundings). It's Sunday afternoon, and it's the first time in ages that I've had some free time.

I played one set of tennis this morning with Maluwa against Vatteroni (the Malawi champ) and his Italian friend. To our amazement and great satisfaction, Maluwa and I beat The Champ and his partner 6-0, which mainly indicates how much Maluwa has improved in the last six months, as I haven't played much and certainly haven't improved. This afternoon I've been listening to Mozart and reading *Sports Illustrated*. Nice to relax.

This past ten weeks probably take the cake for the "hairiest" period of my two-year tour. It all started around the first of December. We received a "priority" cable from Peace Corps Washington asking if we could take thirty-four volunteers assigned to Nigeria who were unable to go there for political reasons. They had just completed sixteen weeks of training in environmental health and child care at La Jolla, California. In twenty-four hours we dashed around meeting with Ministry of Health officials, President Banda, and our own staff. All the Malawi Government officials, including Dr. Banda, of course, wanted these people. We happily notified Washington that we could take them. However, they would need to have a special Malawi training program first.

I won't go into all the preparations, but briefly, it meant that we had to quickly plan a four-week special training program for them in Puerto Rico, where they had to have intensive language training, plus cultural and sociological studies on Malawi. This meant finding language instructors and sending them to the U.S. in four or five days' time. We also had to find training staff, mainly ex-Malawi volunteers, who knew the country well. On top of this, our staff here had to find about twenty-five posts, including housing, in "bush" areas where these volunteers were to work.

Although the Malawi Government must make the assignments and provide the houses, one of the facts of life is that our staff has to double-check at the site at least two times: first, to make sure there actually is a house, and second, to see whether the people in the community really know that a Peace Corps Volunteer is coming.

One of our Peace Corps doctors and my deputy were assigned

the job of setting up the training in Puerto Rico and planning the program. They did a beautiful job, and the net result is that we have an excellent Environmental Health Program, which I feel is really making a contribution to Malawi's health system.

On top of this, we were expecting thirty new teachers to arrive in Malawi from Syracuse on January 1, just ten days before this Nigeria group would arrive about January 10. For each new group we have to plan a ten-day in-country orientation program, in part so that Malawi Government officials can speak to them before they report to their posts. It was a chaotic time. As if that weren't enough, we also already had two conferences planned for the last two weeks in January for volunteers who had been in Malawi for a year: one for our teachers, and one for our TB volunteers. The final conference ended on February 5.

The first six weeks that volunteers are in their posts are usually busy periods for the staff also, for obvious reasons. If volunteers are going to get "culture shock," they usually get it during the first six weeks. Frequently they also get the "Malawi trots," an inconvenient condition which doesn't help; or they're missing a necessary piece of equipment, such as a bed, or even a schoolroom to teach in. All this means many mad scrambles by our staff, usually from one end of the country to the other.

Fortunately I have a great staff, and the various problems have been solved, with the exception of two cases where the volunteers in question just couldn't make the adjustment and had to be sent home after being in the country only four or five weeks. Incidentally, this is not uncommon worldwide, but it is always a traumatic experience for the volunteer and is not very pleasant for the staff, either. You hate to see someone fail in anything, especially when they have their hearts set on "making it." On the other hand, the satisfying aspect of this entire experience has been seeing the other sixty-two new volunteers making the grade.

Now to family news. Ricky is delighted with school. It is a kick to watch him go off to school with Scott in their school uniforms, caps and all, with book "satchels" on their backs. Don has been real cute, getting up early to help get Ricky ready — especially tying his necktie for him, which has to be just right. Don and Mike are doing wonderfully with their tutors. We think the tutoring is really going to pay off, especially in math.

The latest word on our departure is that we'll probably be leaving Malawi around March 19 or 20. We've decided to go home through the East instead of through Europe. We have reservations on the President Wilson from Japan on May 24. We'll arrive in San Francisco on June 5 and in Davis on June 6. We leave Malawi

April 9 and go to Dar Es Salaam, Nairobi, Bombay, Kathmandu, Calcutta, Sarawak, Hong Kong, and Japan, where we board the ship. Hard to imagine.

Wedding

March 3, 1967

Eek — less than two weeks until we leave. We have just finished all our termination physicals and shots. Time is galloping, and what a lot there is to do. We leave on Sunday, March 19. Our exact itinerary is just now shaping up. Everything has been approved by the university for Will to head up the Peace Corps Nepal training at Davis this summer, after which he'll resume his regular teaching duties. He has to be in Nepal the end of March, as there will be someone there from Washington, DC to discuss the Davis training program. We'll be in Nepal for three-and-a-half weeks. We are so excited.

My sewing machine gave out on me, so I had to quit my sewing, but I had finished most of what I'd planned to do. A dressmaker is doing the rest. There is no such thing as "drip-dry" material here. I made a supposedly "drip-dry dress," and it dripped and it dried — and looked like a piece of crumpled-up tissue paper. What a disappointment. I do *not* want to have to iron on this trip.

* * *

March 14, 1967

I'll only type this as long as it takes my hair to dry in my silly but trusty hair-bonnet dryer. Time is all-important now. As usual, I'm about forty steps behind and running like crazy in all directions. The packers are coming tomorrow! You would never guess what has gone on the last few days. First, Phyllis and Keith Bravinder had their new baby a week ago — a sister for Jennie. She's beautiful. Her name is Sarah. I got to see her right after she was born. Phyllis is doing fine, and I'm so glad I got to see the baby before we leave.

[These two Bravinder girls, who are like daughters to us, have remained close to our family over all of these thirty-four or more years. I try to convince Phyllis that I really am their Mom. We all call one another "framily," which means more than friends but not actual family.]

Then we "did" a wedding. I was "mother of the bride," as well as matron of honor, and Will was "father" and gave away the bride. It was very exciting. Even though it was a bit untimely in our present schedule, we wouldn't have done otherwise for anything.

One of the PCVs who was extending his tour of service for another year went home on leave and decided he wanted to marry the girl he'd gone with for some time. He had to get Will's permission first, though, so he came back after his leave, got permission, and then had Ginny fly out here to marry him. She's a wonderful young woman, and we had them over right away to see what we could do to help with their plans.

Well, in typical male fashion, Jim had it "all figured out." They would be married at his station at Chiradzulu by the Magistrate there, and then they would have a small reception at the home of one of the PCVs. They wanted no "folderol." I timidly ventured the suggestion that maybe they might like a small church wedding with no "folderol" and with the reception later out in Chiradzulu? No. This was just fine. OK. Even though impersonal, it would be fine.

So Ginny was out in the "bush." Although Jim's station is only a half-hour drive from here, there are no stores, no electricity, no phones, and no transportation into town. With only one other female PCV out there, and four helpless (though very sweet) males, she was trying to plan a nice wedding. Poor thing got more and more depressed. Finally, on the Sunday before the next week's wedding, they were at our house and when Jim had gone out of the room, Ginny sat down beside me and said, "Oh, I'm so upset and depressed about this wedding," and was on the verge of tears. Then we talked for hours.

She was afraid they couldn't change any plans because the invitations were already out. I convinced her that it was *her* wedding, and she could jolly well change whatever she wanted if she was not happy with the plan. Then I suggested that Will take them out to see the old Church of St. Michael here in Blantyre. Built in 1888, it is so pretty and historically significant, maybe they could just take a look. Well that did it — and from then on I had fun playing "mother of the bride" and helping with all the plans. What Ginny really needed was someone to just simply say, "OK, look, how about doing it this way?"

They were married at 9:00 a.m. in the old church in Blantyre, with the still-scheduled reception at 11:00 o'clock out at Chiradzulu. Just before the ceremony we found out that they wanted Will to give Ginny away and me to be her witness. We were terribly flattered. It turned out to be a lovely wedding and so much fun for us. They are such great people. Jim has always been one of our favorites. Somehow, I'd gotten the wedding cake baked and decorated the day before. It was then just a matter of safely transporting it out to Chiradzulu, and arranging the flowers and food in time for the reception. It all went off beautifully.

Of course, all this time I was supposed to be working on packing. Sunday morning we had twenty-six for breakfast. Monday night we had twenty for cocktails, and here it is Tuesday. Now there are going-away parties every night, too. Hmmmm. At least not at *our* house. I can see that it's going to be a challenge to actually make it to the plane a week from Sunday.

[Don has reminded me of a unique "cake-carrying" story that seems timely to tell here. When we were packing to leave Malawi, Don's best friend, Danny Judd, baked a cake for us. Danny's family, American missionaries in Malawi, lived about three miles out of town. How would he get the cake to us on his bicycle?

With fourteen-year-old ingenuity, Danny built a little bicycle trailer, much like a wooden box with wheels, to hook onto the back of his bicycle. But would the cake survive the many hills, curves and bumps?

No problem. Here came Danny, pedaling up to our porch pulling his trailer. And, just barely fitting into the trailer, sat his smiling little ten-year-old sister – carefully holding the cake!]

90,000 Pancakes Later — Leaving Africa

March 1967

On March 19, 1967 we left Malawi. Having to say goodbye to Malawi and all our friends was *so* hard! It was also saying goodbye to a whole new meaningful, rewarding, and exciting way of life for me.

I *hate* goodbyes. We'll see a lot of our Peace Corps friends again, but we felt we were really saying a final goodbye to our Malawian friends, Mas, Phillip, Friday, Maluwa, and others. The boys were so worried that Mom would cry and embarrass them in front of everyone at the airport (so was I), that I first fortified myself with two tranquilizers and then warned everyone not to say "goodbye"— just "so long." And for heaven's sakes not to say anything *nice* to me, or I'd simply dissolve. I'd planned to wave my spatula as I left all our friends, but unfortunately forgot to put it in my purse.

When the final call to board came and we had to leave everyone, the great lump came into my throat, but good old Phyllis Bravinder saved the day by saying, "Well, so long — glad to see you go — hope you have a rotten trip," so we could all laugh. I even managed to keep the lump and tears under control until safely out of sight on the plane. The boys were amazed and proud of me. (Thank you, Phyllis!)

We started our trip off with a bang. By the time we got to our first stop, Dar Es Salaam in Tanzania, we'd already lost one suitcase. It had been tagged in Blantyre and we had the stub, but it either went on some other flight or was stolen at the Dar airport. Cables went everywhere hunting for it, but to no avail, and now we have filed insurance on it.

It was Rick's suitcase — and he was the only Lotter with a decent wardrobe. At age five he gets the dirtiest the fastest, so he had many more things than the others and therefore a large suitcase. We each have our own suitcase (no sharing/fighting). However, I did put some extra items in Rick's suitcase, such as two boxes containing some sixty of our best colored slides (sob), my hiking Keds and tennis shoes, a whole bag of new yarn to knit a sweater on the way home, and numerous other things. Needless to say, we are sickest about the slides. Of all of us, however, Rick is the easiest person to find clothes for. Now if *my* suitcase were the one lost after all that frantic last-minute sewing, I would have had a screaming, foot-stamping, very embarrassing tantrum right there in that airport.

[Seventeen months after our return to the States, we had a phone call from the San Francisco Airport saying that a suitcase with our name on it had just come in from Greece. At first we said it must be some mistake, as we'd never been to Greece. Then they described the color and again read the tag. We couldn't believe it. It was the lost suitcase! They delivered it to our house, and in it were the SLIDES, and, of course, all of Rick's long-outgrown clothes. Everything seemed to be there except a bottle of gin (not Rick's). How had this suitcase gone to Greece when we hadn't? Where else had it been? Interesting.]

We loved Dar Es Salaam. The weather was hot but not unbearable, and we enjoyed shopping for Makonde wood carvings which we'd started collecting. However, somehow we always manage to get to know the Peace Corps doctor wherever we go, by having some kind of emergency. When the kids went swimming in the Indian Ocean at a lovely beach, Mike stepped on a sea urchin and got fifty-five spines in his foot! The spines, which have a purple dye in them, go in quite deep and break off when you try to pull them out. The purple dye makes them look really horrible. The Peace Corps doctor said he'd never seen so many sea urchin spines in one foot, and couldn't get any of them out. He said, though, that he "thought" they would eventually dissolve. *I* thought it looked so horrendous that I envisioned immediate amputation, or other such ghastliness.

That night, thankfully, the nice hotel proprietress was so concerned that she asked if we would like to have her private doctor come and take a look. He has had lots of experience with these things. The doctor came over to the hotel that very night. He was a jolly, typical British man: starched shorts, kneesocks, bush jacket, bushy beard, bushy voice, and a "bush" remedy. His "prescription" — put a ripe papaya on it overnight!

With tongues in cheeks, we did as he said, put a slab of very ripe papaya on the bottom of Mike's foot and tied a towel around it to keep it on (and keep it off the bed). Don, sleeping in the same room, said Mike was saying "Ish gish" every time he turned over all night. I didn't sleep much either, with my poor little kid and his ghastly purple foot looming in every nightmare.

We could hardly wait to look at it in the morning and all gathered around for the unwrapping of the papaya gush. To our great surprise, Mike's foot actually *did* look much better and even felt better. Of course, we'll never know whether it would have anyway, or if it actually was the papaya. The spines did not come out and continued to hurt a lot for about a week, giving Mike some trouble walking. However, it's about three weeks later now, and they don't hurt at all, yet still look purple and plenty dramatic. Mike claims they are his most unusual and interesting souvenirs of our trip, eagerly and proudly showing them off to anyone who will look.

After three days in Dar, we flew to Nairobi for three more days. We had planned to stay with our friends, the Pooles, again, as they have two little guest houses out in back of their house, and we had stayed there before. However, little Bobby Poole (Rick's age) had chicken pox — *just* what we needed! Luckily, former Malawi Peace Corps good friends, Gary and June Stewart, live just up the street from the Pooles, so Rick, who is the only one of our family who hasn't had chicken pox yet, stayed there with Don.

Most of our time was spent with Will haunting the airlines about the suitcase, and I shopping for clothes for Rick. The airlines gave us an "emergency" amount of £10 ($28) which did not buy much.

One of the things we, especially the boys, enjoyed seeing was the start of the big East African Safari Race. This is a four-day automobile race which goes some thousands of miles. We packed a picnic dinner with the Pooles, borrowed the Stewarts' Land Rover, and in our two vehicles started out to a spot twenty miles away where we could see them tear by, cross a railroad track, go onto a dirt road, and over a bridge. However, on the way, with usual Lotter luck, we had a blowout in the Stewarts' Land Rover — and there was no spare.

Luckily our two vehicles were traveling together, so there was nothing to do but to go on with the Pooles or we'd miss the race. So, chicken pox or not, we all squeezed into the Pooles' station wagon. Five Pooles and six Lotters! We crossed our fingers, put Rick at one end of the vehicle and Bobby at the other, and told them both not to breathe. The race was exciting, and the boys were overjoyed when one of the ninety-two cars broke down right in front of us, got hurriedly fixed with a part from the car of some innocent (but delighted) bystander, and was off again. It was a memorable day, and so far we see no evidence of chicken pox on Rick. We hope it was worth it.

We left Nairobi with a flourish. The Pooles had left on a vacation, and we were busy all day washing and ironing and packing ("we" — ha!) and were to be picked up at 6:00 p.m. to go to the airport. About four o'clock, Don discovered that someone had gotten into one of the guest houses where we had been staying and had stolen $50 in travelers' checks and £4 (about $10) in Malawi money out of his wallet. A fortune for a kid — all the money he had earned and saved for the trip home: birthday and Christmas money, as well as egg-selling profits. Poor Don was devastated.

Of course, this new crisis necessitated having the police come, much questioning, much time, more confusion added to the usual confusion of packing, cleaning up, cooking and eating dinner, and still being *ready* by 6:00 p.m. Amazingly, we were ready on time and did manage to make the plane. However, we also managed to leave a whole bunch of Will's and my clothes hanging in one of the Pooles' guest rooms. Will's *only* suit, his *only* other pair of slacks. Our luggage was getting lighter and lighter with each stop.

On March 26, 1967, we bade a final and heart-wrenching good-bye to Africa, and flew that night to Bombay, India.

On the Way Home
India

March 27–April 1, 1967
Bombay, New Delhi, Agra, Jaipur

We landed in Bombay at about 4:30 a.m. on March 27. Riding into the city on the airport bus, we saw all the things you read about. It was still dark, but light enough to see people sleeping on the sidewalks all along the way. Cows, considered sacred in India, wander around wherever they please, knowing full well that they are the only things for which the driver of a bus, car, or taxi will put on his brakes.

Even at that hour we were horrified by the wild driving. The only rules for driving seem to be to go as fast as possible, honk all the way, cut in wherever you can (and often where you can't), and pay no heed to silly things like white lines or pedestrians. To each his own. Only cows are safe.

The airlines had made reservations for us at an inexpensive hotel. Since the more desirable rooms were still occupied at that hour, they put us in temporary rooms until noon. However, we later realized that these temporary rooms were, in fact, occupied too — by bedbugs. No one got bites but me, and I was prompted to write a song, to the tune of *Moonlight In Vermont* – "Bedbugs In Bombay." They *love* me, and I itched for five straight days. Not knowing yet about these other occupants, we slept most of the morning. We were later moved to nice air-conditioned rooms with *no* other occupants.

We were awakened by the sounds of "splaatt splaaattt" outside our window. Looking out the window, the boys were convulsed to see a lady on the fourth floor across the street dumping out her garbage onto the sidewalk below! Walking is hazardous because you have to watch not only where you put your feet (cows, you know), but above you, as well.

Bombay has four million people. People everywhere. We were really struck by the incongruity of the miserable poverty and absolute squalor side-by-side with obvious affluence. A lovely modern apartment house or home would have hovels made of cardboard and tin right beside it. The harbor and the beaches were scenic to see, and the kids all had exciting camel rides on one of the beaches.

Easter Sunday, after we had our egg hunt in the hotel room (isn't that amazing — the Easter Bunny even found the boys' room in the hotel in Bombay!), we took an electric train ride out to see a temple. It was a Holy Day, and people were running all around smearing colored powder paint on one another. We thought this was all quite amusing, until a boy came running up in the train station and smeared bright red paint all over the side of Will's face! No one had warned us that someone might get carried away and try to put some on *us*. We were so surprised that before we could recover, he did it again on the other side of Will's face! The boy was about eighteen and didn't seem drunk — just happily carried away, you might say. In his shock, Will grabbed the boy's arm and a policeman came along and escorted the guy away. Will had an awful time getting the paint off, and for several days looked like an old has-been actor who hadn't quite removed all his makeup.

After two days in Bombay, we flew on to New Delhi. It's quite a pretty city, with lots of tree-lined streets and nice homes. The weather was really good to us in India, as it was actually cool. I wore a cardigan the whole time. We found the people very friendly and always anxious to help us find our way.

Traveling in foreign countries for two and a half months with four active boys and a limited pocketbook is an interesting and enlightening experience, to say the least. We started this trip four weeks earlier than originally and *financially* planned, because the Peace Corps had invited Will to go to Nepal. We'd actually planned on going to Nepal, but this was much earlier than we'd anticipated. We already have our boat reservations from Japan to San Francisco for the end of May, and certainly don't want to give them up. Not wanting to give up this opportunity in Nepal, either, we're learning to pinch every penny, rupee, baht, yen, etc., cut all frills, stay in the cheapest places, eat the cheapest food, and still see a lot of the world. Our long trips are, of necessity, by plane, but we use every less-expensive mode of transportation on land — trains, buses, streetcars, subways, rickshaws, horse carts, bicycles, and *feet*. Especially feet. We are having all kinds of memorable and funny experiences that we wouldn't have had if we could actually have *afforded* this long a trip.

The boys are wonderful sports, and we've found that to travel cheaply (to use a term loosely) and lengthily with four children, parents must have four ingredients:

1) a bottle of disinfectant and an old gym sock
2) several clotheslines
3) a jar of peanut butter
4) and most important: a sense of humor!

With these you've got it made.

Our arrival procedure in a new place is always the same: Mom to the "johns" with the disinfectant and old gym sock to scrub off any lurking disease; boys to the peanut butter to stave off constant hunger (which never stops anyway, *anyplace*); Mom to wash the dirty laundry and hang it on our three travel clotheslines to try to dry before our next trip out; and only *then* — off to sightsee. Jane would like it to be known that each and every "loo" on our trail across the world will have been properly disinfected at least once (although it does create a bit of a problem when the sign on the door says "Men"). Also, speaking of hunger — we all abide by strict orders not to leave a single edible item on a table when we exit a restaurant. Pocket everything — rolls, crackers, whatever is legal. Butter and other soft things (within reason) can go in mom's purse. You'd be surprised how good stale rolls taste later when you're starving.

A funny thing happened our first night in Delhi. Somehow the hotel reservations we'd made got mixed up, and we had to find another place to stay. A kind Indian gentleman at the airlines office said he'd help us find another "nice, reasonable" hotel. After some phoning around, he said he'd found us a nice one for only seventy-nine rupees ($10) a night for all six of us. Great — that was much cheaper than the other cheap one would have been.

As we drove up to this "cheap" hotel, we sort of wondered. Then, when we were shown to our rooms, we *really* wondered — they were huge and quite elegant. The manager had already said he'd make special arrangements to have dinner ready when we got downstairs, as it was late and after dinner hours. We couldn't back out now. When we saw the dinner menu and the orchestra playing — oh oh — we *knew* someone had misunderstood something. We felt just like the Hollywood Hillbillies who had gone looking for a Foster's Freeze and had accidentally found themselves in the Ritz. Will then excused himself from the table and went out to, ahem, check on the charges. He came back and said, "Chow down, kids — eat all you can — the honeymoon is over tomorrow morning when we check *out* of here!" It was a "small" mistake of some three hundred rupees. It was not seventy-nine rupees a night, but three hundred and seventy-nine rupees! This was almost *five times* more than our budget allowed. We had a ball while it lasted and then moved to a more "modest" hotel the Peace Corps Director recommended.

We took a three-day tour from New Delhi to Agra and Jaipur. We went first to Agra, about a four-hour pleasant train ride from Delhi, to see the Taj Mahal. It was spectacular. The beautiful white marble and all the intricate inlaid precious stones are something you just have to see to appreciate. With totally accidental scheduling, we were there just after full moon and had the added treat of seeing it again that night by moonlight.

The next day we took a long, hot, dusty bus tour to Jaipur with an English-speaking guide whose English we couldn't understand. Jaipur is one of the oldest cities in India. In addition to four million people, there were camels, horses, goats, dogs, and sheep in the busy streets. Don and Mike each bought an old sword — huge things — which we now have to lug wherever we go. We went through some lovely old palaces there.

Once there, we went on a government tour bus to see the old walled city, Fateh Pur Sikri, and the Red Fort. The three older boys would listen to the guide talk for awhile, and then be off to climb up to the tops of the walls and turrets. We just figured that after awhile if we looked up to the highest point in a fort, we'd see three heads. And, sure enough — each time.

We do have some questionable memories of Ricky happily tootling a toy flute all through the Taj Majal and the long trip by bus, the question being: did that passenger really *accidentally* step on the flute when Rick dropped it?

One thing the boys will probably not forget, rather than the beauty of these old palaces, was the weapons collection in one of them. This collection contained such things as a steel bow and arrow, the "arrow" of which was, instead of a point, a crescent-shaped blade — to shoot and instantly decapitate your enemy! The boys simply cannot understand why we wouldn't let them buy one to take home. Such unreasonable parents.

The other thing they will probably remember is the elephant ride up a hill to and from the Pink Palace on a hilltop in Jaipur. Scott had an upset stomach that day and said he only felt fine while riding the elephant. So now all we have to do whenever Scott gets a stomachache is find an elephant.

On the Way Home
Nepal

April 10, 1967
Kathmandu, Nepal

Finally I've found some time to use my typewriter that we've
carried all this way and which Will has threatened to sell several
times. We are in Kathmandu, Nepal, having arrived here on the
first of April. We will be here about three-and-a-half weeks.

In preparation for Will's being the Peace Corps project
training officer for Nepal at Davis this summer, he is spending
his time out living with PCVs to better know their needs. We're
staying in the Shanker Hotel, which is an old Rana palace, not too
expensive, not too many people, and plenty of room for the kids
to run around. Now I can write more than just a postcard about
our trip so far.

One of the things we had so looked forward to doing in Nepal
was to meet with Willi Unsoeld, who is on the Peace Corps staff
here. In 1963 Willi took a leave from the Peace Corps to climb
Mt. Everest. He became one of the first two Americans to
successfully reach the top. Will had met Willi in Washington, DC
before we left for Malawi and had talked a lot about what a great
guy he is; a fascinating character, to say nothing of how *famous* he
is. After Will met him in 1964, when we thought we were going
to be posted in Nepal, we read with even more interest all the
accounts of the Everest climb, and how Willi had lost nine toes on
that expedition.

We all looked forward so much to meeting him, his wife,
Jolene, and their four kids. Don and Mike are especially eager to
be able to meet such a famous mountain climber. However, as luck
would have it, the Unsoelds were leaving for Hong Kong on holiday
the day after we arrived. Our boys and their four children, who are
about the same ages, did meet one another the night before the
Unsoelds left. A Peace Corps staff family had all the Unsoeld and
Lotter offspring over for dinner while Will and I were unpacking
and getting settled in, and the Unsoeld parents were packing to
leave for holiday. We parents never did get together. What a
disappointment.

Nepal is just as beautiful as we'd heard. The Kathmandu valley
is surrounded by mountains, and on clear days you can see the
snow-capped Himalayas beyond them. Kathmandu is much more
primitive and ancient and seemingly untouched by the modern
world than we'd expected: old winding, narrow streets lined with

ancient three-storied buildings; little shops opening right onto the street without sidewalks; temples everywhere; and crowds of people and cows on the streets.

Except for the bicycles with bells clanging, bicycle-pulled rickshaws, and an occasional car, walking through the bazaar is like going back into the fourteenth century. The shops are so small that there are only a few that you can even go into, which necessitates standing right in the street to negotiate with the shopkeepers.

The old buildings have beautiful, ornate carvings wherever you look: pillars, posts, and window frames — designs everywhere. Cows have the right-of-way, being sacred as well as plentiful; they walk or lie down wherever they please. You *do* have to watch where you put your feet. Chickens seem to find life on the ground too hazardous — you see them wandering around on the rooftops or out on third-story balconies. The streets are so crowded that it's easy to lose one another if you don't watch what you're doing. The other day Will was startled to find himself walking along happily carrying on a conversation with a cow that had usurped my place. Even though the cow may be sacred and special, *I* didn't feel too flattered.

One thing that we really enjoy in Kathmandu is that the people don't seem to pay any attention to us. There are fewer white people than in lots of places we've been, yet the Nepalese seem not even to glance twice at us. You can stop and look in shops, and the shopkeepers don't try to high-pressure you either — it's very refreshing.

Will left on his first trip out to visit PCVs just the morning after we arrived here. He put on a backpack and was flown in a little plane ninety-five miles out in the hills ("hills" they call them, and they are 8,700 feet high!) This little plane is called a "STOL," which stands for "Short Takeoff and Landing." It is said to be able to land on a postage stamp. They circled and landed on a tiny leveled spot on the top of a mountain near a village called Rumjatar.

The headmaster of the school in Rumjatar greeted Will warmly and took him to his house for lunch. The people were very nice to him, but a funny scene ensued. They served a very large bowl of curried rice and vegetables which was delicious, but very *hot* (as in hot peppers). Will's eyes started to water. He tried not to choke and was dying for some cold water — but they served hot tea. He finally finished the bowl and complimented them on how good it was — so they refilled his bowl! He about died, but didn't want to hurt their feelings or seem ungrateful, so, with streaming eyes and nose, bravely carried on and ate it all, said good-bye and started off for Okaldunga to visit the PCV.

To get to Okaldunga, which is on top of a mountain, he had to hike down one side and up the other of all the mountains in between. For the PCV it's an eight-day hike in to Kathmandu. Talk about primitive "Peace Corps image" living — no bed, stove, fridge, running water, bathroom. He sleeps on a straw mat on the floor, eats rice with his hands, drinks tea. About once a week he gets meat, which is either goat, chicken, or buffalo. Sometimes there are eggs. There are plenty of vegetables and some fruit, though.

This PCV is very happy and content and doing a good job. He is a community development worker, a graduate of Harvard Law School, working with the village governments of about forty-four villages. He speaks, reads, and writes Nepali fluently, which is necessary, as very few people know even broken English. Will learned a lot about how the Nepal PCVs have to live and thoroughly enjoyed his five-day stay there. The people were very hospitable and warm.

The kids and I got to fly out in the little plane when Will was to be picked up, so we were able to see that very gorgeous area, too. The flight was exciting because we flew along parallel to the Himalayas and got a fabulous view of Mt. Everest and the other high mountains. We could hardly believe our eyes when we saw where the pilot was going to land — whew — it *looked* like the size of a postage stamp. It was as if they had simply sliced off the top of the steep mountain and called it an airstrip. I guess if you don't make it the first time, you just keep on going and circle back to try it again. But we made it.

We could see Will waiting there for us and waving. The hill people gathered around the plane and stared at us. Maybe they had never seen white children before. Will had acquired a beautiful hand-woven blanket, a marvelous but ominous-looking khukuri knife (the national knife), and a likewise-looking beard.

In order to be there when the plane was to come back to pick him up, he had hiked all the day before, and had arrived in a little village in the evening. He had wandered alone into the village and thought he would just ask someone if he could sleep on their floor. Before he could ask anyone, a young boy met him and said in broken English, "We feel very bad for you. You are all alone. You are very tired. You are carrying your own pack. You must come stay in my home." They were wonderful to him. They gave him rice and tea, some Nepalese beer (thick and whitish, much like Malawi moa), and a room of his own, just big enough to lay out his sleeping bag. About eight people slept in the next room, which wasn't much bigger. Only the young boy spoke any English.

Will said he had to keep pinching himself to be sure this experience was real.

We picked him up on a Thursday, and on Saturday morning he was off again; this time to fly to Pokhara, west of Kathmandu, and then to hike a full day to a Peace Corps post. He's in his element and just loving it. He'll return next Thursday. Then on Saturday he leaves for Davis, California, for the final week of the Nepal PCV training. From Davis he goes to Washington, DC and Virginia for more meetings — and then finally back to meet us here, or possibly in Bangkok — or somewhere? We hope. He'll be gone about ten days or so.

We got a look at the King the other day at a celebration here in Kathmandu. I wonder how many kings we'll ever see? We also went with a Peace Corps staff family to have tea with the monks at a Buddhist Monastery. Betty, the Peace Corps staff wife, teaches English to the monks. Through them she was able to arrange for us to meet the famous nine-year-old boy who is supposed to be the fourth reincarnation of the teacher of the Dalai Lama (the spiritual leader of all the Buddhists in India, Nepal, and Tibet). What an experience for us.

This special little boy was in a room by himself, sitting on a kind of dais. We had been instructed to put the palms of our hands together and bow our heads and give the Nepalese greeting, "Namaste," when we entered. A PCV who is teaching the boy was also there. The boy, who speaks no English, just sat there quietly while we drank our tea. All of a sudden the little boy got the giggles — apparently the PCV had made a face at him and gestured at a vase in the corner. When we asked the PCV what he teaches the boy, he said, "Well, math, science — and don't tell, but in that vase over there are the paper airplanes I just taught him to make!"

The monks in this monastery felt quite relaxed around our group because they have known this Peace Corps family for a long time. Betty rides her horse up a couple of times a week to teach them English. She has no car, and it's too steep for a bike. We were looking around their temple, or chapel, and they were showing us all the offerings for the gods when one of my eagle-eyed kids (Scott) noticed, in a dish of money offerings, what certainly looked like one of those gold-paper-wrapped candy coins. Giggles erupted among our boys, with whispers and pointing at the case. Then, one of the monks wondered what had happened and got down to look at it, too. Betty had to explain to him about the candy "money," and at first a look of astonishment came over his face — and then he laughed and laughed and called in the other monks — and they all roared with laughter. That "rare" coin, which was in a glass case with some very old, valuable gold coins, had apparently been there for years and years. Leave it to Scott to spot it.

Mike came up with a wonderful phrase the other day. We were talking about stomachaches (a fine subject) and about how when I'd had one in Delhi, one of the Peace Corps wives had said, "Oh yes, that's called the Delhi Belly." So now that some of us have had more of the same in Nepal, Mike asked if it shouldn't be called "the Kathmandu-du??"

Don and Mike are going to go to Bangkok on their own for six days. They are tired of "templing with Mom," and I have to admit that there isn't much of interest for teenage boys here. We've watched them operate in a new country, learning the money, ordering food, finding their way around, and looking for inexpensive places to eat, so we succumbed to their pleading to let them go on ahead to our next stop. Could this decision possibly have been aided and abetted by the sheer physical force of Togetherness, of which our family has had *lots* by now? We are *all* happy with this decision. They are going to fly out with Will when he leaves Nepal for the U.S., and he'll get them settled in the Bangkok YMCA, where we already have reservations. Scott and Rick and I will carry on with "templing" and seeing Kathmandu.

Friends at home in California told us to look up an American couple in Kathmandu, Al and Nancy Chandler, both of whom are working here. What a lucky thing for me, because they have been showing me all around. Al is an attorney here with a Syracuse University project which sends people to developing countries to work in government. Nancy, who is an artist, is doing a project right now helping a woman anthropologist collect weavings and art for the Smithsonian. Would you believe that Al and Nancy are from Berkeley and San Francisco and both graduated from Cal *(UC Berkeley)*? Another one of those "small world" happenings.

Nancy speaks Nepali and has become my guide. We have spent whole days together, bicycling miles and miles to see temples and to collect special art pieces, prowling back alleys and going up and down back stairs — what fun I'm having. Scott and Rick usually stay with Peace Corps families while I explore to my heart's content.

Al and Nancy invited us to their wonderful old Nepalese farmhouse out in the countryside to have our very first buffalo burgers! Their house is a typical three-story Nepalese adobe-type house with mud floors, low ceilings, and doorsills you step up over. Interesting house, interesting and delightful people — and interesting and delicious buffalo burgers. What luck to find the Chandlers and have such experiences. I'm learning so much.

On the Way Home
India (continued): Calcutta

April 19, 1967
Calcutta

[Here I had time only to write a short note to our parents in California. Rick and Scott and I were just in Calcutta overnight on the way between Kathmandu, Nepal, and Bangkok, Thailand. I can't help but wonder what the grandparents at home in the U.S. must have thought when they heard all this from Will, who was in California by then.

Here is what I wrote home]:

Would you believe:
    1) Will is in Davis, California?
    2) Don and Mike are in Bangkok, Thailand?
    3) Scott and Rick and I are in Calcutta, India?
It's all true, and we're all fine and having a good time — but isn't it funny? Don and Mike flew with Will from Nepal to Calcutta and then on to Bangkok. I simply wasn't through with Kathmandu yet and didn't want to leave.

Will got the boys settled in at the Bangkok YMCA, an international hostel which was highly recommended to us, where we had reservations later for the whole family. He left money and their passports with the manager to keep in a safe, numbers to call in case of emergency, gave the boys a spiel on how they could save money by doing their own laundry, etc., then took off for the U.S.

I wonder what adventures Don and Mike have had in this week? They are only thirteen and fourteen, but are very able and capable and love to go places on their own. I haven't worried at all. I wonder if I should have? Well, tomorrow we'll find out.

[Now, looking back, I can't imagine letting a thirteen- and fourteen-year-old go to a strange city alone. And in a foreign country? But at the time, it made perfect sense to us.]

On the Way Home
Thailand

April 21, 1967
Bangkok, Thailand

I was so excited to see Don and Mike when Rick, Scott and I got to Bangkok! They looked fine and intact — no visible casts or bandages — and they immediately informed me that they had had a real "blast." I wonder if they even missed me. (Silly mother. Of course not.)

By the time Rick, Scott and I joined them, they had the whole Bangkok bus system figured out, had found a pizza parlor, a milk shake place, and, of all things, a roller rink. They had made lots of Thai friends, had gone on several tours (two all-Thai-speaking ones for Don), and they both had money left. They had, in fact, done their own laundry. On our first meal together in Bangkok, Mom was severely reprimanded and lectured on extravagance when she drank two milk shakes.

Don and Mike nearly knocked me off my feet when we arrived by saying, "Oh, by the way, Mom, Willi and Jolene Unsoeld want you to call them right away at their hotel."

"What? The *Unsoelds* are *here* in Bangkok?" It took me some time to register this bit of information, especially since I had been so disappointed at not having been able to meet them in Nepal. Furthermore, Don and Mike didn't even *know* the Unsoelds. How did this happen? Besides, the Unsoelds were supposedly in Hong Kong, not Bangkok. Then they told me this amazing "small world" story.

Don and Mike had decided to go see the famous Bangkok floating market, a thing all tourists do. This is a huge marketplace on the river, where all the canal boats come in and out with their wares. It is teeming with people, canal boats, fruits, vegetables, flowers, and color. Tourists take canal taxis to observe the scenes of life along the many canals.

So here were Don and Mike in the enormous confusion of crowds of people milling about, when they heard someone call their names. They were surprised because they certainly didn't know anyone in Bangkok. They turned around, and there were the Unsoeld kids whom they had met in Kathmandu! Willi and Jolene were equally astonished because they had never met Don and Mike (and were probably quite shocked that these two boys were there alone in Bangkok). Now, what are the odds of a meeting like that happening in a huge, busy place like the crowded floating market in Bangkok? Or anywhere, for that matter.

The Unsoelds then took Don and Mike with them to see the sights and have some meals together. Willi insisted that they at least *taste* "birds' nest soup" in Bangkok — that it would be part of their "acculturation" to that part of the world. Reluctantly, they did. He also regaled them by constructing a toothpick house on the table in a restaurant, and successfully lighting it without burning down the restaurant. They were mightily impressed, of course.

The next day after I arrived was to be the Unsoelds' last day there in Bangkok, so we spent a wonderful day together seeing sights and walking through beautiful parks. I really enjoyed getting to know them. The older kids hit it off well and plan to write to one another. Jolene told me about the long wait in Kathmandu while Willi was on the ascent of Mount Everest. Knowing that one of the other climbers had died made it especially difficult. And just to think that Willi actually lost nine toes on that climb makes me shudder — I can't even begin to imagine. Wonderful and courageous people I feel privileged to know.

Amazingly, Will actually did find us again after ten days away in the States. He still hasn't decided whom we were happiest to see — him, or his suitcase filled with American goodies we hadn't had in two years (Fritos, Hydrox cookies, licorice — *important* things). We loved Bangkok and the people, as well as the canal boat rides, the colorful floating market, the ornate temples, and the exotic flowers and fruits.

Rick was so excited when Will rejoined us that he was running and tripped and fell — fully clothed and fully submerged — into the fishpond in the lobby of the YMCA. This was followed the very next day by his running full-tilt, head-on into a pillar in the lobby and thereby acquiring the Shiner of the Year. If it was attention that Rick wanted, he certainly got it. For weeks, this dramatic black eye compelled everyone — absolutely *everyone* — everywhere we went, to comment in every language, as it changed from black to purple to blue to green to yellow. Luckily, good-natured Rick thought it was pretty funny, too, and even learned to say in Thai, "I ran into a post!"

On the Way Home
Singapore, Sarawak, Hong Kong

April 25–May 12, 1967

Singapore, next on our route, was to have been just one overnight stop enroute to Kuching, Sarawak. Sarawak is in Malaysia on the island of Borneo. We were going to visit our good Peace Corps friends, the McCones, who had been in Malawi with us. Mike was now Peace Corps staff there. Because of crowded flights out of Singapore, however, our one-night stay became a three-night stay. Since the airlines were not able to get us on a plane right away, they arranged to put us up at a wonderful hotel for the first night. This is referred to as a "necessary layover," luckily for us.

When we found out that they were not going to put us up for another night even though they could not get us on another flight yet, Will went out scouting for a really cheap hotel. He found one. The taxi drivers who took us from the fancy Singapura Hotel to this other one were absolutely *positive* that Will had made a mistake. Maybe he had, but it *was* the actual one Will had found, and indeed it was cheap. And rightfully so. At first I thought that they had simply forgotten to put sheets on the beds. But no — it turned out that they didn't *own* sheets for the beds. Since no one spoke English, it was tricky, but we cleverly found that they had extras of the seersucker bedspreads which could serve as sheets. For only $9.00 a night for the six of us for two nights, we didn't complain, and our budget keeper (W) was very happy.

We finally got on a plane from Singapore and flew to Kuching to spend four delightful, fun-filled days with the McCones. We loved their airy seven-bedroom "house up on stilts." The seven boys had a great time together.

Hong Kong for eight days was next. We stayed on the tenth floor of the International Guest House in Kowloon, completely fascinated with the busy streets and nightlife below — the boys even *more* fascinated with the views into tenth-floor hotel windows across the street — making it necessary to lock up the binoculars. We took junk boat rides around the harbor, went on the Victoria Peak tram ride, went shopping, and always wished we had more money. We celebrated Rick's sixth birthday with lots of *real* ice cream while watching *I Love Lucy* in Chinese on TV!

Because of riots in Hong Kong starting the day before we were to leave, we almost missed our plane to Japan because we couldn't get a taxi (let alone *two*) to the airport for the six of us and our mountain of luggage. Our picture wouldn't be complete here without some description of our luggage. In all, counting our hand luggage (cameras, binoculars, flight bags) we had twenty-one pieces, which we had to count, re-count, and re-re-count all the way. After having that one suitcase lost on the first leg of this trip, we got smart and Organized Our Forces so that each of us was responsible for wearing, carrying, and watching certain pieces. It was a formidable array of motley shapes, sizes, and colors to begin with, tennis rackets and soccer balls among things being bulky to pack, but it got even worse when Don and Mike began collecting swords and daggers in each of the countries we visited. Their four-foot-long Indian swords of heavy silver gave us fits all the way. Then, when three suitcases lost their handles, necessitating their being tied with rope, it was just the finishing "classy" touch we needed. In addition to needing two taxis to get us and all this stuff to and from all the airports and hotels, we had to fight off porters with dollar signs in their eyes.

Will was able to frantically flag down two enterprising private car owners (one with a station wagon) and pay them to drive us to the airport. When we breathlessly arrived just in time for our flight, we were informed that they had already filled up the economy section in which we had reservations. However, there was *no way* Will was going to have us all go back to a hotel and try again. Finally, after witnessing the wrath of Will, Japan Airlines decided they would "have to" put us in First Class.

By this time, the boys had become real connoisseurs of Economy or Tourist class air travel and just exactly what benefits they could expect, or somehow finagle. First Class offered them a brand new travel adventure. We would wager that Japan Air Lines has never had a more appreciative and eagle-eyed group of passengers. No detail went unobserved or undiscussed, from the cloth (real) napkins, silverware (real), to slippers (real) and Mom's and Dad's champagne (real!). It seemed a fitting and wonderful climax for the last flight of our trip.

On the Way Home
Japan

May 22, 1967
Tokyo, Japan

A quiet little Japanese inn on the outskirts of Tokyo (at least it was quiet before we came) has served as a resting place for which we were all ready by this time. One trip to Mount Fuji and one trip on the Bullet Express to Atami were about all we could manage, other than exploring Tokyo and the little neighborhood around the inn. We saved forty dollars by taking an all-Japanese-speaking tour to Mount Fuji, and we saw everything the others saw, besides affording all sorts of entertainment to all the Japanese tourists who were fascinated watching *us*.

The boys have made wonderful friends in the neighborhood, and we all have found favorite little places to eat. But — we never have gotten used to the hot (scalding!) baths, or the toilets with no seats. And we have never been able to convince the boys that they *cannot* wrestle on the nice, soft mats on the floor because elbows and feet could (did) go right *through* shoji screens. But we love the inn and the sweet and friendly couple who run it.

Would you believe that in the whole two and a half months of travel we only lost one of us, and that was only *once*? It was, in fact, me. In Tokyo, in case we got lost, we each always carried a paper with the unpronounceable and unreadable Japanese name of our little obscure inn, and the equally unpronounceable street name, written in both Japanese and English.

I'd gone shopping in downtown Tokyo, and had stayed too late. When I came up out of the subway coming home it was night, and everything looked so different to me that I became disoriented and confused. It was a route we'd taken many times, and though I knew I was supposed to take a streetcar, I didn't know which *direction* to go. I stood there on a street corner for a while. Oh well — no problem — I would just show a taxi driver my little piece of paper with the name and address of the inn, as we'd instructed the boys to do if they got lost. Then I looked in my purse and, with a sinking feeling in my stomach, realized that I had given the boys my last copy of the paper.

All I knew was that the streetcar I should take went past the zoo, the only landmark I knew. I could do it in daylight just fine. After I passed the zoo, I knew to get off the streetcar at a green Coca-Cola sign, and from there I could find the inn. But now it was dark, and I was really lost.

I started looking for someone who spoke English, to ask where the zoo was, so that I could at least go in the right direction. I couldn't find anyone who spoke English at all. Not *one* person. I went in and out of little shops. People were very nice and terribly concerned about me, but could not grasp my problem. The only thing I could do then was try to ask in sign language where the zoo was. (Try that sometime!)

A crowd began to gather while I went through various antics. I just kept saying names of animals, "lions — tigers — elephants," hoping that someone would recognize an animal name. Just short of my desperately going into a gorilla act, jumping up and down, roaring, and clutching imaginary cage bars — someone caught on. Whew. Much happy chattering, nodding of heads and pointing in the direction of the zoo, followed almost immediately by gestures of "No, no…" as I waved goodbye and made off for a streetcar going in that direction. Louder chatter and utmost concern, and much consultation of their wristwatches. Of *course* I knew the zoo was closed at this hour of the night, but how could I explain all *that* in sign language??

I was so relieved to get back to the little inn that I didn't know whether to laugh or to cry. So I did both. And Will and the boys had not even been worried at all. Fine thing!

We have loved our two weeks in Japan, staying in this little all-Japanese inn. We can't communicate and didn't know until too late that it is uncool (literally) to cool down the hot bath with cold water. Even so, they always invite us to bathe first before all the other guests, and are always very nice to us. I think we are their first-ever American guests, and I bet they hope we're their last.

We leave in two days (May 24) to sail home to San Francisco on board the President Wilson. We'll get to San Francisco on June 5.

On the Way Home
On Board Ship

Monday, May 29, 1967
The President Wilson

Guess what? If I don't finish this letter today, I'll finish it tomorrow and it will still be today! We cross the international dateline and get to do May 29 all over again. Wish this could happen once in a while at home when I have too much to do.

This morning when I got out the typewriter for the first time in awhile, I was shocked to find half the keys off, everything out of whack, and several keys actually bent. I know now that my fears that it was being tossed around pretty much were true. This I had guessed because even some of the stitching on the leather case was coming apart. It's taken me an hour and a half this morning to put all the keys back together so that it can type at all. It's a good thing that we have today again tomorrow.

This ship is just *great*! There is only one thing wrong. The food is *too* delicious and *too* plentiful. If I don't muster up some Will power (how funny — I just automatically capitalized "will") by the time we get off this ship, I won't be able to get into any of my clothes. Mike is having this problem too, but can't quite stop consuming all those delicious cinnamon rolls at breakfast. Unfortunately, they put whole baskets of them on the table, and you can eat all you want. Then along comes lunch with all that good American ice cream we haven't had in two years. Will has been exercising his "Will power" and doesn't even go *into* the dining room at lunch time. Don eats two whole entrées every meal, like a hungry cowhand, and never puts on any weight. We'd all lost some weight in India and I, especially, was so pleased. But now — oink oink.

Good grief, it's lunch time already and I'll go into the dining room with all sorts of good intentions to exert willpower and eat only soup and salad, but there will be some divine-looking dessert destined to demolish my good intentions — I just *know*.

There are activities planned for children all day long, and for the teenagers in the evenings as well. About the only time we see the boys is at mealtimes. It is *marvelous*. We've had plenty of togetherness for these two months. We're glad we're traveling economy class because we've met so many interesting people from other countries. We've made friends with quite a few from Japan and the Philippines. About 90 percent of the Americans in our part of the ship are missionary families, with whom we have lots in common. The missionary kids and our boys have been sharing experiences and having a wonderful time.

We will have all day Wednesday in Honolulu, and our old Berkeley school friends, Larry and Lois Somers, will meet us at the ship. We're looking forward to spending the day with them. We arrive in San Francisco at 8:00 a.m. on June 5. We can't wait to see everyone! It will be two-and-a-half years, almost to the very day, since we left on this adventure.

After Returning Home

December of 1967, March of 1989, and October of 2001
Davis, California

[This is what I wrote in a 1967 Christmas letter after we returned home from Africa]:

"We came home this past June 5, 1967 — almost exactly two-and-a-half years from the day we left for the Peace Corps in Malawi, Africa. We're back again in Davis in the same home, the boys happily back in American schools, Will teaching at the University, Jane stumbling and grumbling through housework (spoiled, just plain spoiled). Ever-faithful Sparky is ecstatically happy to have us back, having 'doggedly' waited through two-and-a-half years, three different families with an assorted fifteen children, in our house. His neurotic itch has subsided, in spite of the fact that we were compelled to fulfill our Malawi promise to get a German shepherd and two kittens to replace those left behind."

At least we didn't promise a monkey, which really would have had poor Sparky itching and scratching into eternity.

What I didn't say in my Christmas letter was how changed we all were by the whole experience — Will and I, especially. Our lives have taken a different course from that in which we had been quite happily "meandering" before our Peace Corps Africa experience. For more than thirty years now, I've been trying to put it into words. I still can't.

Perhaps it's that we are no longer meandering. There is a big world out there that we hadn't been truly seeing and feeling before, especially the world of the have-nots. We have hurled ourselves into human rights work, both at home and in Central America (it's closer to travel to than Africa), spending two to three months every year in Guatemala.

I fully realize that I am married to a man who is hellbent on *saving the world.* A daunting challenge, I'd say. However, an important lesson the Peace Corps teaches is: If you can make a difference in the life of just one person, you have done a job. This is such a hopeful (and more manageable) thought that it has become almost like a mantra for me.

In Africa, it seemed to me that all aspects of life were especially close at hand: birth, death, sadness, joy, strangeness, fear, laughter, disease, love — and it all led to some deeper part of me that I hadn't known was there before. Wanting to share our experiences in Africa and the Peace Corps has given me the mission and drive to write this book, and perhaps to encourage others to be open to opportunities for new life experiences.

They say that "Africa gets into your blood," and certainly we found that to be true. There is no one answer as to "why." It just does. After talking and dreaming for years about going back to Malawi, our whole family managed to do that in 1989. When Will's mother died in 1987, leaving us some money, we decided that since her own trip to Malawi had been so meaningful to her, it would be fitting that we put some of her money towards the family trip. So after twenty-two years, our family went back. Our two Bravinder "daughters," Jennie and Sarah, were with us, Sarah especially wanting to see where she had been born. Don, who had worked his way back to Malawi at age nineteen, was the only one who had returned. It was an incredible experience for all of us.

On that trip in 1989, in addition to seeing much of the countryside and visiting our Malawian friends, a lot of our time was spent searching for our friends, Mas, Phillip, and Friday, who had worked for us. We showed their photos all around, but to no avail. Will and I stayed on for another month after all the family left to return home and miraculously located one of Mas's sisters, Ellen Balakasi. Through an interpreter, Ellen said she would walk us to Mas's village to see him! Her teenage son, Austin, who spoke some English, would accompany us. We arranged the day and met very early that morning in Zomba.

Ellen worked in town and said she hadn't seen her brother in a very long time, but said it was "not a long walk." Because it was "not a long walk," I'd worn sandals. There were only footpaths to the village, and after walking *four* hours (in the rain and wearing those stupid sandals, which filled with wet sand and gave me huge blisters), we finally came to Balakasi village. Looking forward to seeing our much-loved Mas and taking him photos and gifts had given me the stamina to overlook the pain of my blisters.

First we met many Balakasi relatives, who greeted Ellen warmly, but who looked at us strangely. Thinking this was because no white people ever go there (kids were scared of us, especially of my blue eyes), we were not prepared for the awful news — that Mas had *died* only two months before. Ellen obviously had not even known and was quite stricken. We were all speechless with disbelief. However, with no roads, phones, radios, or electricity, it was understandable that she had not heard. No wonder the strange looks when we said we'd come to visit Mas. Ellen and I both cried.

Needless to say, the four-hour hike back was horrible for all of us — the "hike from hell." The rain did not let up, and we slipped and slid in the mud all the way. Even carrying umbrellas, we were soaked. By this time my bleeding blisters were the size of quarters, and the wet bandages would not stay on. I couldn't stop crying about Mas, and we had to try to hurry because it was nearly dark. Ellen and I held hands all the way. Her only words in English were, "Don't cry" — through her own tears.

Never to be erased from my memory and heart were these hours. Here we were — two women from entirely different worlds, not even able to converse, holding hands and bonded in our tears, mutual grief, and humanness.

Looking back, I think that this story epitomizes all that our African Peace Corps experience was about: that mutual love and compassion can overcome cultural barriers, no matter how strong these may be.

Postscript

February 2002

All four of our sons have an abiding love for Africa.

Don, being the eldest, was especially influenced by our time in Malawi. He was fourteen when we came home, and by nineteen he had taken off on a two-year trip to work his way back to Malawi. On that trip he became interested in tropical agriculture and ecology, and in June of 2000 received his Ph.D. in Agroecology from the University of California at Davis. Don and his wife, Elsa (Bressler), have been living in Vancouver, British Columbia. Don has recently accepted a post-doctoral position at The Rodale Organic Crop Research Institute in Pennsylvania.

Mike's interest is in health, physical fitness, and training. He is a certified physical trainer. In 1989, when we all went back to Malawi, Mike, an avid cyclist and runner, rarely rode in the van with us, preferring to bicycle ahead and meet us at our destination. He lives in Marin County, California.

Scott and his wife, Tracy (Enghusen), have two children who have often said to us, "Tell us an African snake story from Malawi!" Three years ago, for Dustin's tenth birthday, we gave him a Kenyan sand boa which he periodically loses in their house, much to the dismay of his older sister, Chelsea. Scott, whom I always used to accuse of wanting to "run the show" at birthday parties, is actually doing just that — "running the show" — he manages movie theaters. They live in Paradise, in Northern California.

Rick, whose love of drumming I thought would wear off, is also doing "just that." He is a professional drummer, making a living teaching and playing drums in Sacramento, California. He and his vocalist/songwriter wife, another Tracy (Walton), are members of a popular band named *Mumbo Gumbo*. An important part of their full schedule of "gigs" is performing fundraisers for worthy causes. One annual favorite, "Dance for Human Rights in Central America," is for our Sanctuary group's work. Rick and Tracy's little daughter, Emma Elizabeth, has always heard drumbeats and music all day long.

Our whole family is very supportive of Will's and my work in human rights in Central America.

Through Malawi "bush radio," we finally located the mailing addresses of Friday and Phillip, the other two of the three men who had worked for us. Unfortunately we did not get to see them, but we did correspond with them. As related in the previous chapter, Mas died in 1989. Recently we received a letter from Friday's wife, telling us that Friday had died. He was probably in his early fifties. The average life expectancy in Malawi is tragically short, having been estimated at thirty-six years of age in the year 2000. Ten years ago it was forty-seven.

In 1989 we found Maluwa, Will's former tennis partner and good friend, who had become Sports Director for Malawi. All ten of us surprised him in his office in Blantyre. It was a grand reunion. However, he had been ill and looked thin. He soon ended up in the hospital and we were afraid it was AIDS, which is rampant in the heterosexual community. During the two months we were there, he went downhill rapidly. We visited him many times in the hospital and found out that he did, indeed, have AIDS. He died only two weeks after we left to come back to the U.S. We feel so fortunate to have had some time with him just before he died.

Will and I returned to Malawi again in 1994 as United Nations election observers for the first democratic election *ever* in Malawi, and stayed on for another two months. Among the many Malawians we visited at that time were Maluwa's wife, Eunice, and their two children, who seemed to be in good health. Unfortunately, we learned this past year that Eunice died in 1997.

As for the election, our former neighbor, President Hastings Kamuzu Banda, then in his nineties, actually *ran* for election for the first time. He lost, in spite of having proclaimed himself President For Life in 1965. It was a fair and well-run election and exciting for us to have been invited to be observers.

An unforgettable experience was observing vote-counting by candle and flashlight late into the night in a dark schoolroom in a small village without electricity. Will and I were each assigned to different counting posts. Where I was sent, my face was the only white one. The Malawians expressed their gratitude to us over and over again. But, truth be known, *we* were the grateful ones — for the opportunity to be there and to be a part of it.

We went back to Malawi again in July and August of 2000 with a group of twenty-six former Peace Corps Volunteers. Malawi truly still feels like a second home to us. A new project to which many of us are now dedicated is the Malawi Children's Village. Located in Mangochi in southern Malawi, it is a village-based orphan care program. Orphan care is a sad new need in all of Africa. There are more than 500,000 orphans in Malawi right now, mainly because of AIDS.

The Malawi Children's Village began with the recognition that it would be impossible to build and administer enough traditional orphanages for all the orphans in Malawi. The concept of community-based orphan care was developed and organized principally by two of our former 1960s Peace Corps Health Volunteers, Kevin Denny, who is a child psychiatrist, and Mike Hill, a social worker/therapist. Together with a dedicated and innovative Malawian, Chakunja Sibale, they created the Malawi Children's Village, in which orphans are placed with families in villages in the Mangochi district. Chakunja has had many years of experience as a clinical officer in public health, specializing in maternal and child care.

Before going to the village chiefs, the District Chief was first approached with the idea of placing orphans with families in the thirty-six villages in the district. The idea was enthusiastically received. To support the orphans, a network of seventy-two young Malawian volunteers was set up, two from each village being appointed by their headman. These village volunteers are trained at the Malawi Children's Village center in health care, AIDS education, and general supportive care for orphans. Among the professional trainers for the volunteers are Dr. Tom Nighswander and his nurse/wife, Ruth, who travel from Alaska to work each summer during their vacation — two more of "our" 1960s Health Volunteers — making us feel very proud to be a part of the Peace Corps family.

In the year 2002, Malawi Children's Village is providing care for more than three thousand orphans in the thirty-six villages in a twenty-mile area surrounding Mangochi. Almost all the funding support currently comes from returned Peace Corps Volunteers and friends in the United States. Wholly administered by Malawians and headed by Chakunja Sibale and his wife, Faith, it is very much in the spirit of the Peace Corps philosophy.

The long-term interest and commitment to the people in the countries in which they served is just one example of the powerful effect that the Peace Corps experience has had on many Peace Corps Volunteers. The Malawi Children's Village is an inspiring project that could be a model for all of Malawi, as well as for other African countries.

[For more information on Malawi Children's Village, e-mail: Kdenny0000@aol.com]

Acknowledgments

This book would never have seen the light of day had it not been for Pat Allen and Ted Sneed: Pat for saving all of my more than ninety letters, and Ted for putting them all on computer for me. What generous gifts these were!

My husband, Will, and our four sons were my rooting section. My dear friend and Sunset Court neighbor, Pat Allen, however, was my Head Cheerleader. Pat kept spurring me on and encouraging me to keep going. Soon becoming my co-editor, she has spent countless hours over the last few years proofreading and helping me edit the manuscript. Every page of this book has been back and forth across Sunset Court at least a hundred times. I could not have done this without her, or without the aiding, abetting, and support of her husband, Tom Allen.

Many thanks to graphic designer Robin Walton (sister of our daughter-in-law, Tracy Walton) for her cover design and map layouts.

Thanks to our neighbor Nancy Hardaker, the "Sunset Court Comma Cop," for her experienced eagle eyes and last-minute editing help.

Thanks also to the family of the late Phil Durand, our favorite Peace Corps Malawi cartoonist, for giving us permission to print some of his cartoons.

To our wonderful publisher, Jeanne Pietrzak of Graphic Gold, for her competence, enthusiasm, and patient guidance through the bewildering maze of putting a book together for the first time — a *million* thanks!

Acknowledgments would not be complete without mentioning our gratitude to the late Emil Mrak, who was Chancellor of the University of California at Davis in 1964, and Clark Kerr, who was President of the University of California at that time. These two men had the vision to grant Will a then-rare two-year leave from the University. Later Will's leave was extended even another six months at the request of the Peace Corps.

I especially want to emphasize how fortunate we still feel for the opportunity of being part of the Peace Corps. Having four children precluded our going as Volunteers (PCVs), so we will always be thankful for the staff position which allowed Will to serve and to drag all of us along. Be it Peace Corps Volunteer, staff-person, staff spouse or staff kid — I don't think anyone returns home the same person after living the Peace Corps experience. Certainly our lives were changed and enriched, and for this I am forever grateful.